MW01680136

# THE BARNES FOUNDATION HANDBOOK

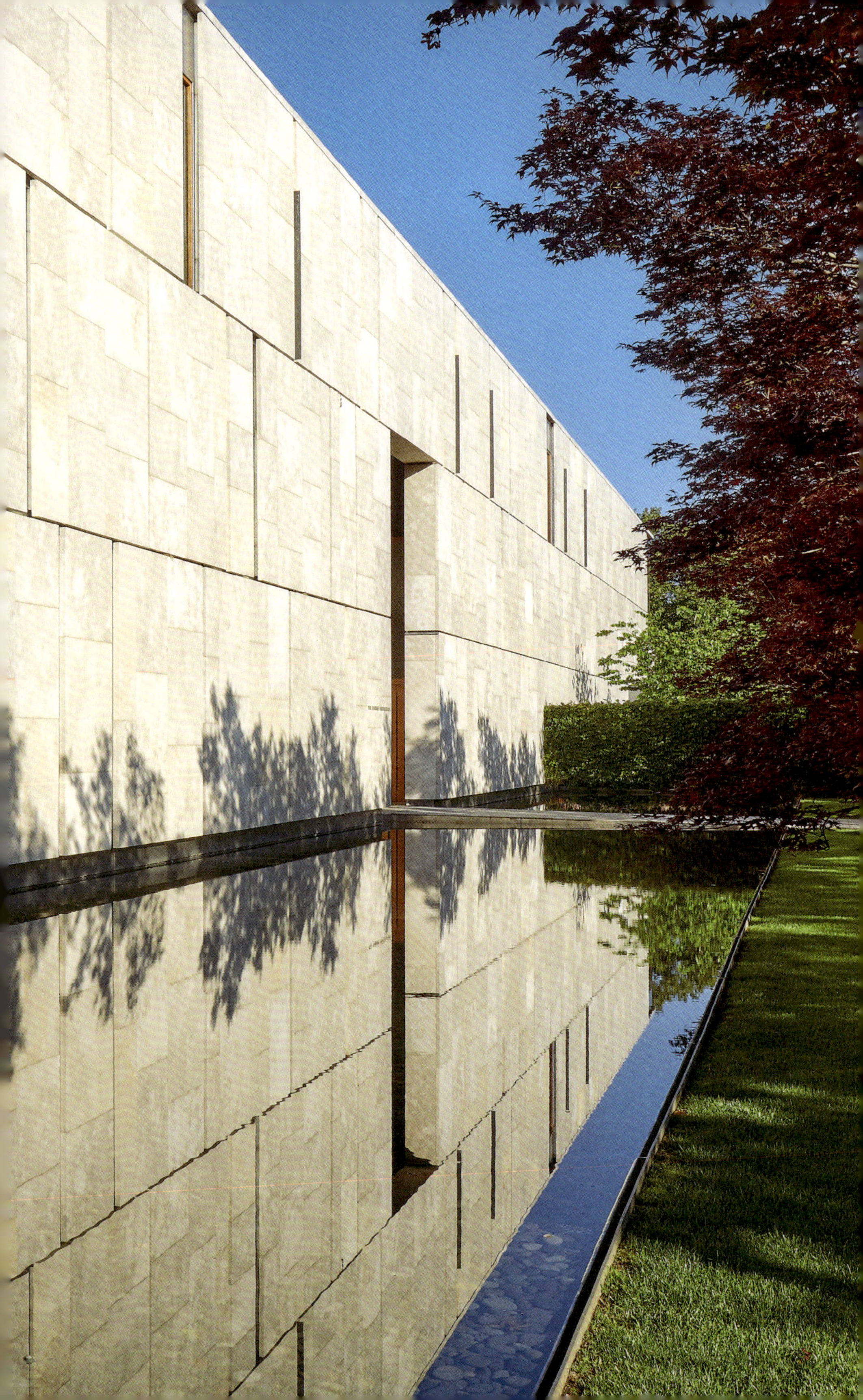

# THE BARNES FOUNDATION
# HANDBOOK

THE BARNES FOUNDATION
PHILADELPHIA

Published by
The Barnes Foundation
2025 Benjamin Franklin Parkway
Philadelphia, PA 19130
barnesfoundation.org

Director of Publications: David Updike
Curatorial coordination by Cindy Kang
Edited by Kelly Borgeson, Mary Cason, and Daniel Huppman
Designed by Olivia Verdugo with additional typesetting by Pauline Nyren
Printing and binding by Brilliant Graphics, Exton, PA



Library of Congress Control Number: 2021934087
ISBN: 978-1-7361252-0-5

Cover: Vincent van Gogh (Dutch, 1853–1890). Detail of *The Postman (Joseph-Étienne Roulin)*, 1889. Oil on canvas. The Barnes Foundation, Philadelphia. BF37

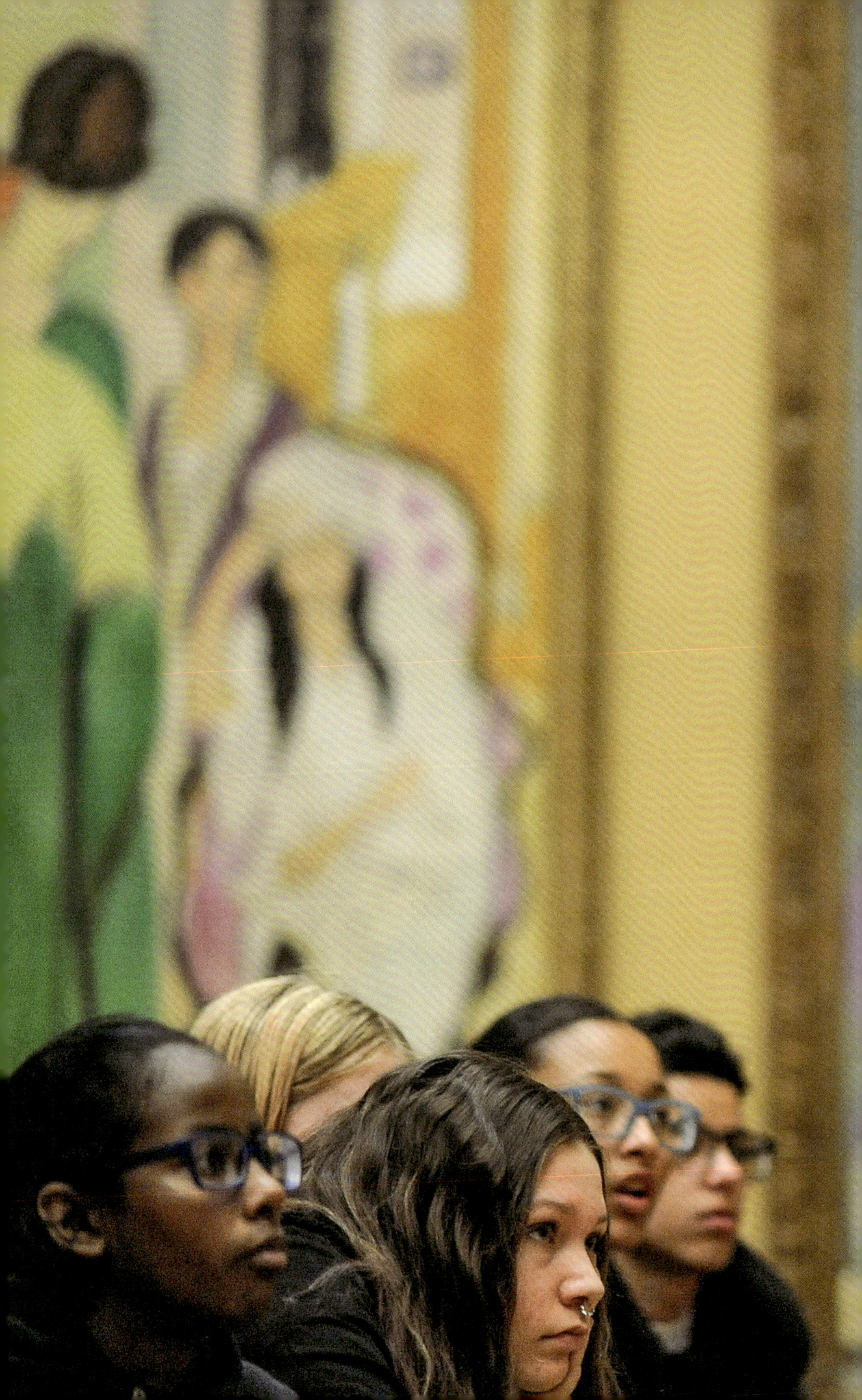

# WELCOME

We hope this handbook of the collection helps you get to know the Barnes Foundation and makes your visit more enjoyable. Dr. Albert C. Barnes founded our institution in 1922 to promote his belief that art had the power to transcend boundaries and transform lives. Since moving to the Benjamin Franklin Parkway in Philadelphia in 2012, we have been better able to serve his mission: bringing art education to the broadest possible public, especially those who historically have been excluded from that education. The unique displays in our collection galleries mix a wide variety of objects from all across the world—from paintings to door hinges and jewelry, dating from ancient times to the mid-twentieth century—to celebrate the boundless ways in which human creativity is expressed. The short essays and texts on individual works of art in this book share some of our history and the many stories contained within our collection. We hope they help you see the Barnes, and your world, in a new light.

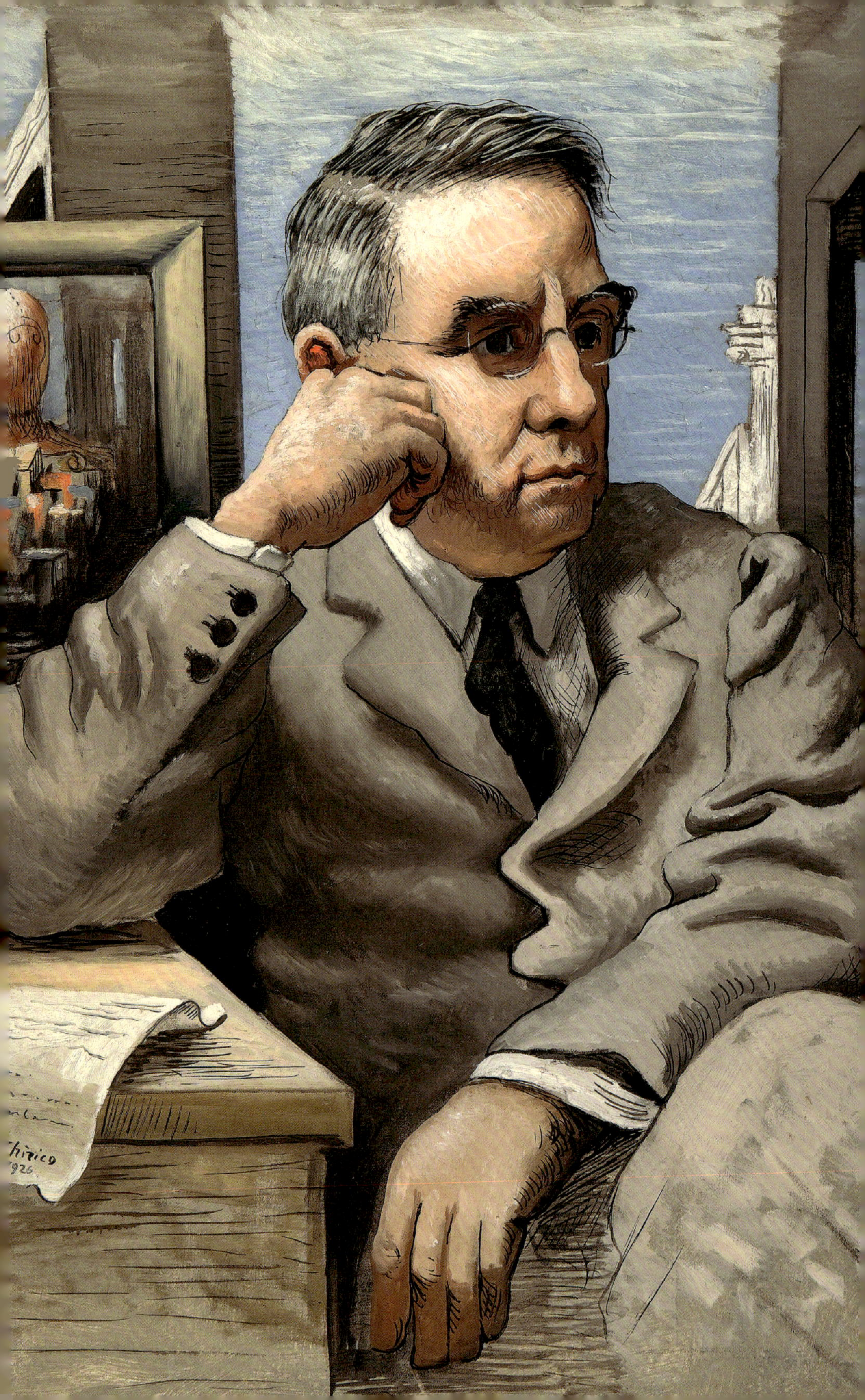

# ALBERT C. BARNES, HIS COLLECTION, AND HIS LEGACY

Born in a working-class neighborhood in Philadelphia on the eve of an economic depression, Albert C. Barnes (1872–1951) relished defying the odds. He became an enormously successful pharmaceutical entrepreneur who amassed one of the most important art collections of his time (fig. 1). Unlike any other art collector, however, he used his collection to lead a radical experiment in democratic education and social justice, a legacy that continues today in the work of the Barnes Foundation.

**FIG. 1:** Giorgio de Chirico (Italian, 1888–1978). *Dr. Albert C. Barnes* (detail), 1926. Oil on canvas. The Barnes Foundation, Philadelphia. BF805

As a child Albert Barnes was close to his mother, Lydia Schaffer Barnes (1846–1912), whom he later described as "marvelous... endowed with a keen, penetrating intelligence...but best of all she had poise and balance."[1] She was a devout Methodist with Pennsylvania German roots. At the Methodist camp meetings they attended together, Albert witnessed the spiritual traditions and practices of African American worshipers. In an era of widespread, enforced segregation, these early experiences ignited in him a love of human expression that would later take shape in his intertwined commitments to art and racial equality.

Dr. Barnes remembered drawing and painting as a child, though he was equally if not more enthusiastic about baseball and boxing as a teenager, the latter to defend himself against neighborhood bullies. Seemingly born with a combative spirit, he was also a precocious student, gaining admittance to Philadelphia's rigorous

Central High School at the age of thirteen. There he befriended William Glackens (1870–1938), whose drawings he admired and who played on the school's baseball team with him. Barnes excelled academically and was elected vice president of his senior class. After graduation in 1889, he enrolled directly in the University of Pennsylvania Medical School and tore through his studies with the same intellectual energy that would characterize all of his later pursuits. He was a doctor three years later, at the age of twenty.

Though he later told friends that he spent the next few years gambling, Dr. Barnes was gaining practical experience in the medical field, interning and volunteering in various hospitals, including the Philadelphia Polyclinic Hospital, the Mercy Hospital of Pittsburgh, and the State Hospital for the Insane in Warren, Pennsylvania. In the summer of 1893, he took his first trip to Europe and visited hospitals in London and Paris. He soon realized that medicine was not for him, and instead wanted more specialized training in physiological chemistry. Scraping money together through odd jobs, he went to study at the University of Berlin.

After his return to Philadelphia, Dr. Barnes was hired by the pharmaceutical firm H. K. Mulford and Company in 1897. The company sent him back to Germany in 1900 to study pharmacology at the Ruprecht Karl University in Heidelberg. There, the seeds of his entrepreneurial ambition started to germinate. He met and recruited a chemist and recent PhD graduate, Dr. Hermann Hille (1871–1962), to come back and work with him at Mulford. Barnes and Hille quickly hatched a plan to develop their own antiseptic drug, which they called Argyrol. It was a silver compound used in the prevention and treatment of eye infections, especially in infants. With this promising new medicine, the two scientists struck out on their own, forming the Barnes and Hille Company in West Philadelphia in 1902 to manufacture and market it.

Despite or because of their rapid success, the relationship between the partners soon deteriorated. After much hostile litigation, Barnes bought out Hille's share in the partnership and formed the A. C. Barnes Company in 1908. Trademarking Argyrol, he ensured his financial independence for the rest of his life.

Dr. Barnes's lawyer during this dispute was John G. Johnson (1841–1917), who had a significant collection of European paintings that he hung over every surface of his home (and later donated to the City of Philadelphia, which houses them in the Philadelphia Museum of Art). Dr. Barnes also admired the collection of modern French painting amassed by Johnson's client Henry O. Havemeyer (1847–1907) and his wife, Louisine Havemeyer (1855–1929), which they later donated to the Metropolitan Museum of Art, New York. These figures likely piqued his interest in forming his own major collection of art. Barnes had already started to buy art from local dealers after forming the Barnes and Hille Company, though his first purchases were unremarkable. In 1910, he reconnected with his high school friend Glackens, who had become a leading modern American artist, and bought a few works by him and his contemporaries.

Barnes's collection was truly launched when he sent Glackens to Paris in February 1912 with twenty thousand dollars to spend on modern art. The results were spectacular. With the help of fellow American artist Alfred H. Maurer (1868–1932), who was living in Paris, Glackens returned with canvases by Vincent van Gogh, Pablo Picasso, Pierre-Auguste Renoir, Paul Cézanne, Camille Pissarro, and Alfred Sisley. Dr. Barnes was delighted and made two trips to Paris himself that year, securing further significant works.

Dr. Barnes displayed his new acquisitions not only in his home in Merion, outside of Philadelphia, but also in the pharmaceutical factory of the A. C. Barnes Company, where they became an integral part of his employees' work life. Motivated by his own marginalized background to invest in the education and welfare of his workers—largely white women and Black men—Dr. Barnes arranged production so efficiently that they could complete their daily tasks in six hours, leaving two hours at the end of the day free. They organized to fill that time with seminars, where they read and discussed books on psychology, philosophy, and aesthetics by William James, John Dewey, and George Santayana, among others. Several hours each week were devoted to discussing race and "the social and economic handicaps under which the Negro suffers, their cause and their cure."[2] Dr. Barnes's growing art collection became a hands-on tool for applying the ideas and principles of direct observation and critical thinking in these classes, which were led by an employee, Mary Mullen (1875–1957).

It was John Dewey (1859–1952), with whom Dr. Barnes became close friends, who encouraged the collector to expand the factory seminars into an innovative educational institution. The curriculum would be underpinned by a sincere belief in education for working people as the key to democracy and social transformation. The Barnes Foundation, chartered in 1922, thus began not as a gallery—Dr. Barnes never intended to create a museum—but as an experiment in teaching and learning. It offered those with no prior knowledge of the subject a route to understanding and appreciating art as part of human experience.

As he developed his educational philosophy, Dr. Barnes continued to collect voraciously, with yearly buying trips to Europe interrupted only by war (fig. 2). After his initiation into modern art with Glackens, Barnes turned to art critic and collector Leo Stein (1872–1947) as his confidant, intellectual sparring partner, and source for important pictures. Leo and his sister, the author Gertrude Stein, were early advocates for contemporary European artists; the Steins'

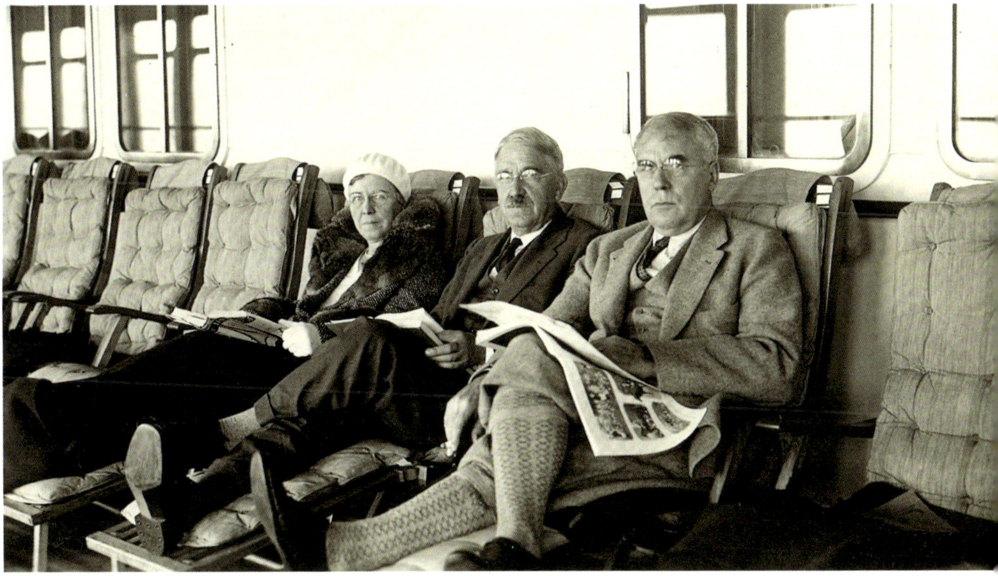

art-filled apartment in Paris became a hotbed for debating the scandalous and challenging work of Cézanne, Renoir, Picasso, and Henri Matisse, among others, in the early twentieth century. Several of these pictures would end up in Dr. Barnes's collection. By the time the Barnes Foundation opened its doors in 1925, Dr. Barnes had more than seven hundred works to fill the elegant new building in Merion, designed by French-born Philadelphia architect Paul Philippe Cret (1876–1945). The building was situated within an arboretum that would serve as the site of a horticulture program run by Dr. Barnes's wife, Laura Leggett Barnes (1875–1966). The daughter of a successful grocer from Brooklyn, she had married Albert in 1901. Her amateur interest in horticulture blossomed into a serious pursuit of expertise with the purchase of the land and opening of the Foundation. Laura Barnes brought nature into dialogue with art.

**FIG. 2:** Dr. Barnes (r), John Dewey, and Laura Barnes on the steamship *Europa*, 1930. Barnes Foundation Archives, Philadelphia

The new galleries were filled not only with modern European and American paintings, but also with a significant collection of African art. In the early 1920s, Barnes purchased more than a hundred works—masks, figural sculptures, utilitarian objects—from the Parisian dealer Paul Guillaume (1891–1934).[3] At the time, France had colonized much of western and central Africa, and the traffic of goods between continents reflected colonial exploitation. At Guillaume's gallery, Barnes met philosopher and educator Alain Locke (1885–1954) and soon became actively involved in the cultural and social justice movement that burgeoned into the Harlem Renaissance in the 1920s. With Locke and the National Urban League's Charles Spurgeon Johnson (1893–1956; fig. 3), Dr. Barnes came to see that the study of African art, as an important form of Black cultural expression, could serve as a tool for African American advancement. Dr. Barnes's African art collection was featured in *The New Negro* (1925), an anthology edited by Locke, and in the National Urban League's *Opportunity: A Journal of Negro Life*. Dr. Barnes also funded scholarships for African American artists, musicians, and writers recommended by Johnson, including Aaron Douglas (1899–1979) and Gwendolyn Bennett (1902–1981).

**FIG. 3:** Carl Van Vechten (American, 1880–1964). *Charles S. Johnson*, 1948. Photogravure. Smithsonian American Art Museum, Washington, DC

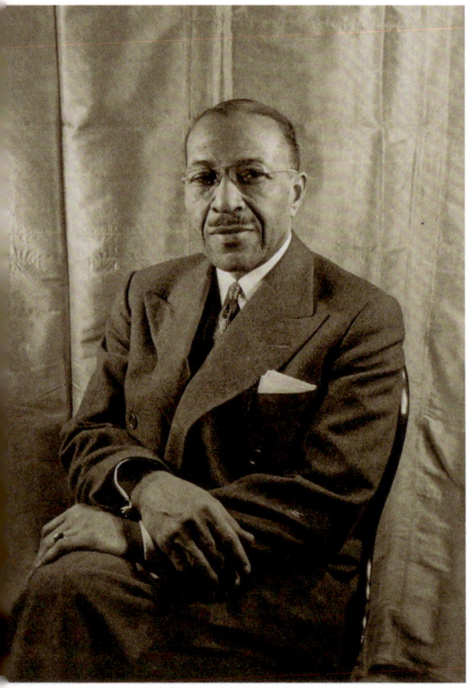

At the end of 1929, Dr. Barnes traveled to New Mexico, where Laura had been advised to take a rest cure due to respiratory issues. While Mrs. Barnes took in the therapeutic benefits of the air and landscape, Dr. Barnes began buying Pueblo and Navajo ceramics, jewelry, and textiles (fig. 4). As with previous new collecting interests, he acquired avidly and quickly built a narrow but deep collection of this material in the 1930s. He also contributed to the preservation of Native Southwest cultures by supporting the establishment and acquisitions of what would become the Museum of Indian Arts and Culture in Santa Fe.

By the mid-1930s, Dr. Barnes's collecting interests pivoted toward his own roots and home region. He began buying scores of Pennsylvania German objects—furniture, ceramics, and other utilitarian and decorative works. As he explained, "My interest in the Pennsylvania Dutch [German] comes naturally for my grandmother was one of them, and early in life I became acquainted with their furniture, their cooking, and their wonderful houses and gardens."[4] Dr. Barnes always staked his claim in the interests of everyday people, and the rustic, vernacular furniture he acquired was distinct from the high-style colonial American furniture favored by collectors such as Henry Francis du Pont. To house his growing collection, in 1940 Dr. Barnes bought a colonial-era farmhouse in rural Pennsylvania that he named Ker-Feal (fig. 5).[5] The installations of decorative arts there served as an extension of the galleries in Merion.

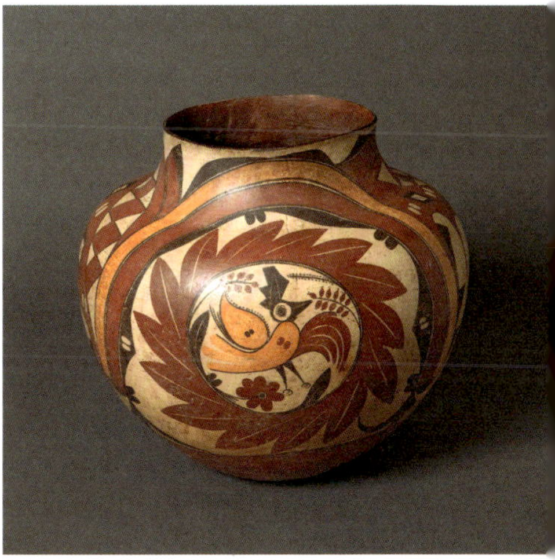

**FIG. 4:** Attributed to Acoma Mary (Mary Histia; Acoma Pueblo, 1881–1973). *Storage Jar*, c. 1900. Polychrome earthenware. The Barnes Foundation, Philadelphia. A383

Alongside Pennsylvania German art, Dr. Barnes began collecting hundreds of examples of European and American metalwork in the late 1930s. Hanging these hinges, locks, and other objects alongside modern European paintings, he emphasized the universal human impulse to create and innovate through aesthetic forms. In juxtaposing paintings by known artists with tools made by unrecorded artisans, Dr. Barnes sought to bridge the gap between fine and decorative arts. He furthermore sought to flatten time and distance, incorporating works of Asian art and Greco-Roman and Egyptian antiquities into his uniquely blended displays, which he called "ensembles." (This theme is explored in the essay that follows.)

Throughout his collecting career, Dr. Barnes steadfastly bought modern European art—181 Renoirs, 69 Cézannes, 59 Matisses, and 46 Picassos, as well as significant numbers of works by Chaïm Soutine, Amedeo Modigliani, Giorgio de Chirico, and Henri Rousseau sprinkled through with star canvases by Van Gogh, Georges Seurat, Edgar Degas, Claude Monet, and Édouard Manet. He became friendly with several of these artists: Matisse and De Chirico, as well as Renoir's son Jean (himself an artist and filmmaker), all visited him in Merion. Dr. Barnes commissioned Matisse to execute his mural *The Dance* (see page 134) during the artist's first visit in 1930. He also famously launched Soutine's career when, in the excitement of discovery, he bought more than fifty paintings in the early 1920s by the then relatively unknown artist. At the same time, he remained committed to contemporary American artists who also were or became friends, including Glackens, Charles Demuth, Maurice Prendergast, and Horace Pippin. The Barnes Foundation was, ultimately, in service to democratic education in the United States, and the inclusion of American artists was key to encouraging critical thinking in the American context.

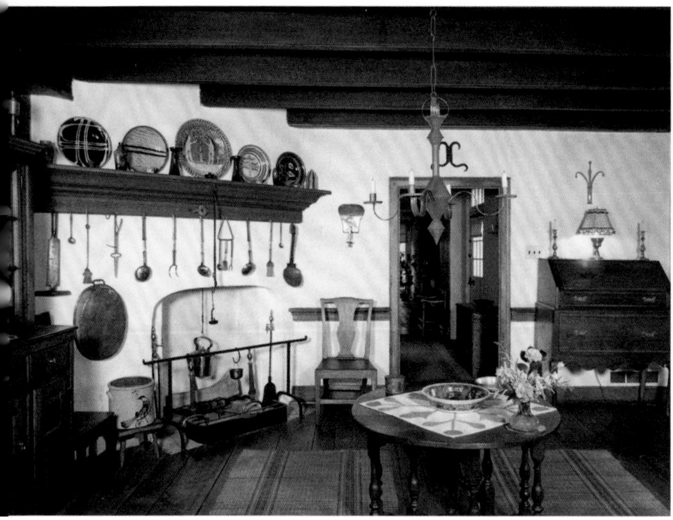

**FIG. 5:** Room 5 at Ker-Feal, 1952–53. Photograph by Angelo Pinto. Barnes Foundation Archives, Philadelphia

Dr. Barnes had sold his company in 1929, right before the stock market crash, to focus on the growth and mission of the Foundation. He collaborated with the francophone expatriate

Violette de Mazia (1896–1988), who had joined the staff in 1927, to publish books on his collection and the Barnes Foundation's educational philosophy throughout the 1930s (fig. 6). She would become the director of education and carried on the Foundation's classes and publications following Dr. Barnes's sudden death in an automobile accident in 1951.

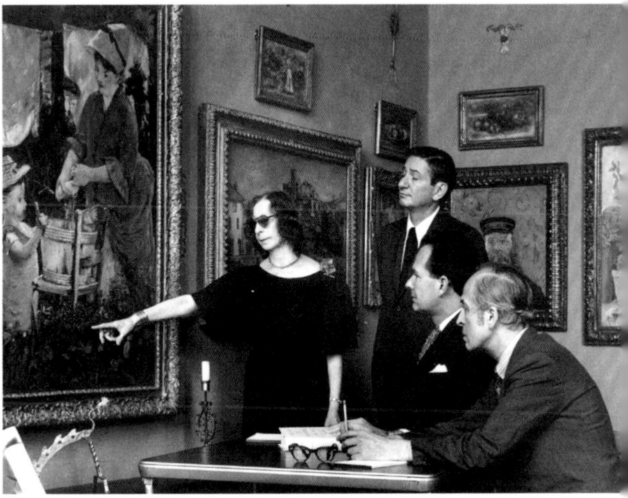

**FIG. 6:** Violette de Mazia with (l to r) Harry Sefarbi, Barton Church, and Angelo Pinto in Room 23 of the Cret Gallery, 1972. London Collection

When he died, Dr. Barnes had been in the process of establishing an educational partnership with Lincoln University, a historically Black university some fifty miles west of Philadelphia; Lincoln's board of trustees still nominates trustees to the Barnes Foundation, continuing this relationship that Dr. Barnes valued. To the end, Dr. Barnes was committed to art education for all in the service of social justice. His legacy lives on in the Barnes Foundation's classes, programs, exhibitions, and activities today.

**NOTES**

1. Dr. Albert C. Barnes to Alice Dewey, September 20, 1920, Albert C. Barnes correspondence, Barnes Foundation Archives.
2. Mary Mullen, "An Experiment in Adult Negro Education," *Opportunity: Journal of Negro Life* 4, no. 41 (May 1926): 161.
3. See Christa Clarke et al., *African Art in the Barnes Foundation: The Triumph of L'Art nègre and the Harlem Renaissance* (Philadelphia: Skira Rizzoli in association with the Barnes Foundation, 2015).
4. Dr. Albert C. Barnes to John J. Cabrey, November 29, 1950, Albert C. Barnes correspondence, Barnes Foundation Archive. Pennsylvania Dutch refers to German-speaking people who immigrated to the area in the eighteenth century. "Dutch" is a corruption of the term they used to refer to themselves, Deitsche.
5. Dr. Barnes named the estate after his dog Fidèle, whom he had found in the northern French province of Brittany; Ker-Feal means "Fidèle's House" in Breton.

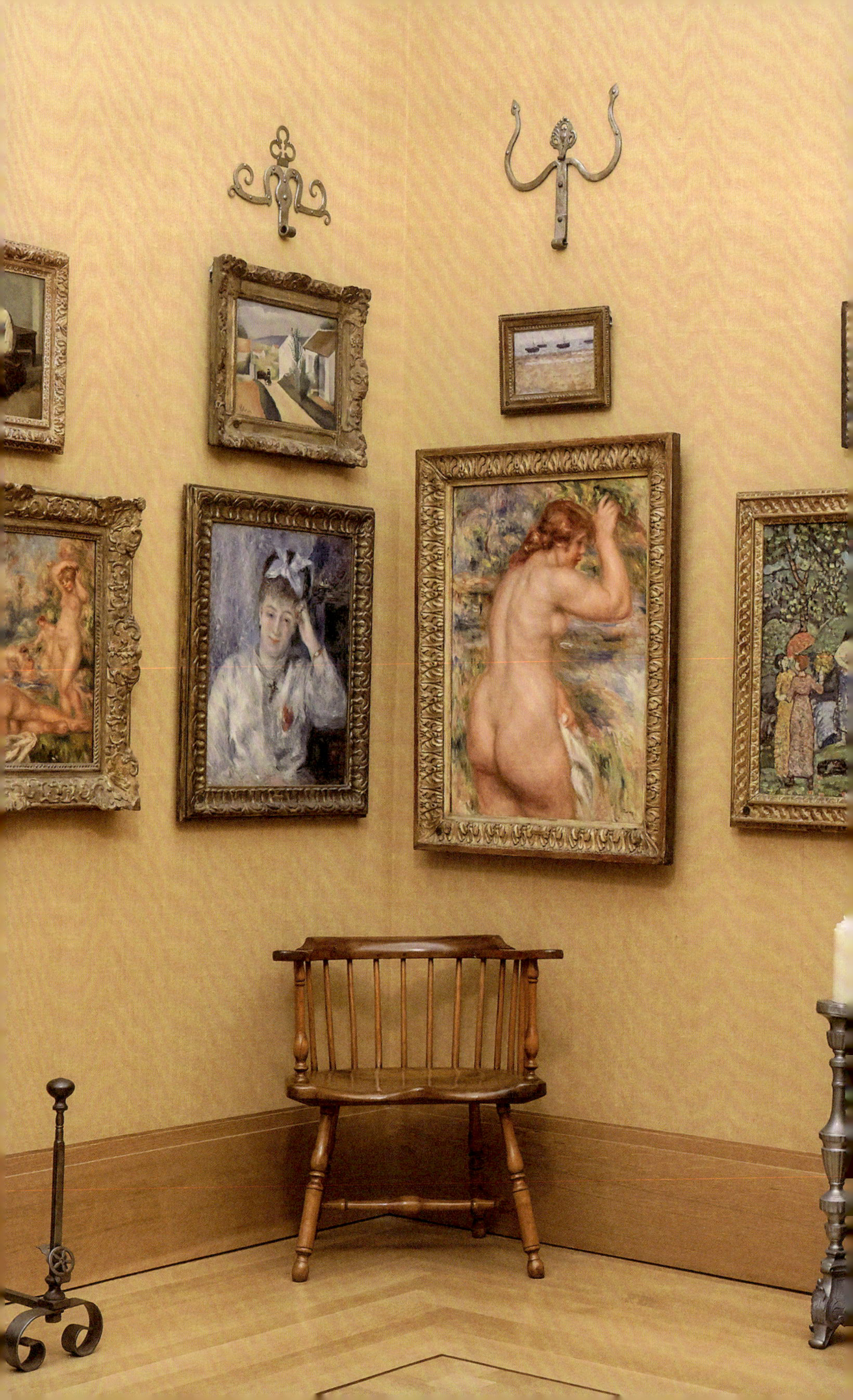

# THE BARNES METHOD: ADVENTURES IN PERCEPTION

**LEFT:** Room 6 (detail)

In 1912, Dr. Albert C. Barnes set out to build a collection of the best modern paintings he could acquire. However, as the collection grew so did his frustration in trying to make sense of these unconventional works. In response, he developed an analytical approach to art shaped by his commitment to education and informed by his background in science. Barnes came to believe that art is more than a diversion—it communicates essential human experiences that transcend time and geography. Meaningful encounters with works of art, he asserted, can change us, reshaping how we see and think about our world. He also believed that in order to fully appreciate a painting, the viewer needs to understand its visual language.

Dr. Barnes's approach, which he modeled on the scientific method, guided not only his acquisitions but also how he arranged and displayed his collection. One of the most striking elements of this approach is the way Dr. Barnes combined objects of different media and traditions in groups that he called "ensembles," which will be discussed in more detail below.

Dr. Barnes described his method as "objective" because it addresses a painting as a physical object created by another individual. In other words, it recognizes that the image a painting presents, regardless of how realistic or abstract, is the product of the artist's intent shaped by the artist's experience with an object or idea. When we see a painting of an apple by Paul Cézanne or

Pierre-Auguste Renoir, what we experience is not an apple per se but *Cézanne's apple* or *Renoir's apple*. These painted "apples" possess qualities distinct and independent of the real-world object, qualities selected and emphasized by the artists.

The Barnes Method is also objective in that, like the scientific method, it encourages the viewer to put aside personal preferences and concentrate instead on those aspects of a painting perceptible to most observers—specifically, color, light, line, and space. While complete objectivity may not be possible, awareness of our own likes and dislikes and how these biases influence our perceptions allows for more objective conclusions. Such cultivated objectivity, Dr. Barnes believed, would also allow people from various backgrounds and with different interests to meet on common ground.

The Barnes Method begins with close looking and critical thinking focused on the painting itself. As in scientific research, observations are made, evaluated, and refined. From these, inferences are drawn that are assessed against continued observation. Deductions are made, tested, and confirmed by others using the same process of evaluation. Finally, conclusions are drawn. However, as with the scientific method, those conclusions are always subject to reevaluation if new information is discovered or clarifying observations are made.

Dr. Barnes encouraged viewers to focus less on *what* is pictured, on a painting's subject, than on *how* it is pictured. This means close attention to the painting's visual elements: how the artist uses color, light, line, space, decorativeness, unity and variety, and so on. However, these formal qualities are not an end in themselves; they are only significant to the degree that their combined effect creates a unique visual experience. They are plastic, or malleable, and can be shaped and adapted to fit the artist's needs and interests. Like ingredients blending into a single flavor or notes forming a musical chord, a painting's visual elements should work together, each serving its own role while supporting the others to create a sense of unity and order.

Of all the visual elements, Dr. Barnes held color to be foremost. Every analysis, therefore, begins with a careful consideration of the artist's choice, arrangement, and application of colors, and of the interrelationships created between and among them. Colors can be transparent or opaque, bright or muted; they can be organized in clearly delineated compartments or with soft, porous edges; they can be pure or intermixed, smoothly blended or applied in obvious brushstrokes. The qualities of an artist's colors and the relationships created among them form a painting's visual vocabulary. Dr. Barnes believed that to be fully effective, color should do more than merely identify things; it should express all of a painting's perceived qualities, including texture, weight, volume, and luminosity. Color should enter into all aspects of a painting and be inseparable from them.

All of the other visual elements share color's plasticity. Line, for instance, presents limitless possibilities: it can be thick or thin, even or varied, continuous or broken, straight or curvilinear; it can interrelate with areas of color or be autonomous; it can be a drawn element, or it can be formed where different colors meet; it can be soft and feathery or hard and firm. It can even be as simple as an individual brushstroke.

The illusion of light in a painting can be a product of value or, better still, of color. Conventionally, artists expressed light and shadow in terms of values of light to dark. Modeled on a shape, the transition from light to dark creates the illusion of three dimensions. The creative artist, however, conveys light and shadow through color. For instance, colors such as yellow or pink can read as light while darker hues like blue or green read as shadow.

Intervals of light and shadow can also create visual rhythms that add variety and interest. Light can furthermore be directional, creating shadows that help locate objects in space or convey the distance between one thing and another. Rather than adhering to a single source, for example, it can appear where needed, highlighting the edge of an object, intensifying the color of another, or drawing our attention to a specific place in the picture. When used plastically, light helps illuminate the artist's expressive intent.

Space depends on color as well as light. Since the emergence of linear perspective in the mid-fifteenth century, artists have employed the relative size, shape, and position of objects, drawn to converge at a point on the horizon, to create a sense of receding space. As with many formulas, this technique can become mundane and commonplace, and artists working before and after linear perspective have found other creative ways to suggest spatial relationships, such as simply positioning objects one in front of the other. Space also means volume and mass. For a three-dimensional object to exist, it must have space to do so. The interrelationship of volumes to each other increases the effect of spatial depth even if no other means are used.

The intensity, value, purity, and clarity of colors can also affect how we understand spatial location. For instance, warm colors like yellow, orange, and red normally project, while cool colors such as green, blue, and violet usually recede. Pure, unmixed colors tend to be more prominent, while muted or mixed colors often fall away. Clearly defined objects usually read as nearer to the viewer, while blurred or less distinct things read as further away. And not every artist is interested in deep pictorial space. Works as diverse as Egyptian mosaics and the paintings of Henri Matisse feature shallow or flat areas of color. We live in a three-dimensional world, so we tend to take for granted how we navigate space or judge the distance between one thing and another. The distortion of space or volume in a painting shows us aspects of our natural world in ways we could never experience otherwise.

The Barnes Method makes clear that paintings show us familiar things in unexpected ways. As Dr. Barnes wrote, "The artist gives us satisfaction by seeing for us more clearly than we could see for ourselves, and showing us what an experience more sensitive and profound than our own has shown him." The artist's "interests compel him to grasp certain significant aspects of persons and things of the real world which our blindness and preoccupation with personal and practical concerns ordinarily hide from us."[1]

When Cézanne paints an apple, he is not showing us an apple as it looks in the natural world, but rather what he needs an apple to be in the context of a specific painting. For instance, in *Ginger Jar* (fig. 1), Cézanne's apple is not smooth, juicy, or enticing. Instead, it is angular and faceted, hard and heavy. It sits precariously near the lower right-hand corner of a table. Linear brushstrokes group to create distinct directional planes of yellow, red, orange, and green that accentuate its three dimensionality. A yellow patch suggests light on its forward surface, while a dark red patch to the right recedes as shadow. A black line that varies in weight—and, at one point, splinters—encircles and encroaches on the object. Placed at the corner of a tabletop that is itself broken into multidirectional sloping planes, the apple is visually destabilized as we anticipate it rolling off the edge. But Cézanne's apple is going nowhere because it is a painting, one that conveys the artist's interest in precariousness and tension.

**FIG. 1:** Paul Cézanne (French, 1839–1906). *Ginger Jar* (detail), c. 1895. Oil on canvas. BF23

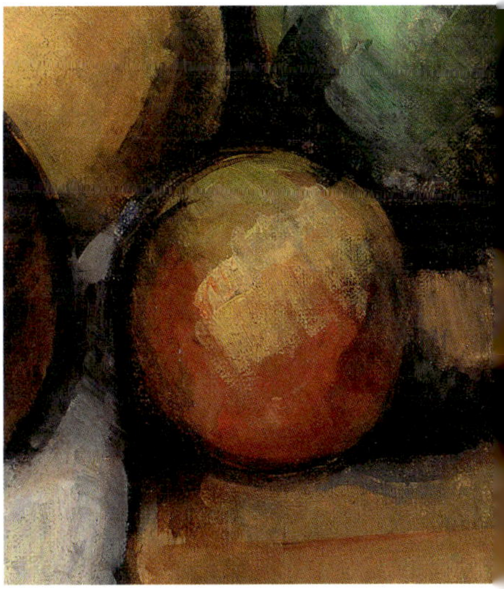

When Renoir paints an apple, such as in *Fruit and Bonbonnière* (fig. 2), his too is modeled in shades of red and orange with yellow highlights; it is solid, weighty, and three-dimensional. Yet, Renoir's color is rich and juicy. The surface of his apple is smoother, made of small, curving, feathered brush-strokes that softly blend and caress its surface, creating a rounded volume. Most of the apple's contour is blurred, and color seems to flow over its edges and merge with the surrounding space. Warm, glowing light appears to emanate from within. This luminosity permeates not only the apple but the whole picture, as color and light suffuse to create a gentle atmospheric effect. All the same, the apple as a unit remains solid, weighty, and clearly three-dimensional, nestled among other units, firmly situated within the picture. This expresses Renoir's interest in a set, warmly glowing, softly contoured, color-saturated volume.

**FIG. 2:** Pierre-Auguste Renoir (French, 1841–1919). *Fruit and Bonbonnière*, c. 1915–17 (detail). Oil on canvas. BF39

A viewer who begins to look at a painting this way comes closer to seeing it as the artist does—not as a representation of an object or idea, but in terms of the specific means used to create the image. This approach also allows the insightful viewer to discover the artist's voice and better understand the visual language of the work. In the case of the two paintings just discussed, Barnes assists our discovery by hanging them next to each other at a diagonal on the north wall of the Main Gallery—a wall composed entirely of works by Cézanne and Renoir, and the largest ensemble in the collection.

To the unassuming student or visitor, the arrangement of the Barnes Foundation's collection can be surprising, confusing, or outright frustrating. This was by design. Guided by the ideas of his close friend and colleague, the American philosopher and educator John Dewey, Dr. Barnes deliberately created a visual environment that would disrupt even the most seasoned gallerygoer's complacency. The ensembles are meant to provoke as well as instruct. By juxtaposing objects of dissimilar traditions, subjects, and media, Dr. Barnes drew attention to specific relationships between and among works in his collection. What at first may seem random or chaotic over time reveals itself to be deliberate, thoughtful, and complex. All aspects of the ensembles—the objects, paintings, frames, and their arrangement—is the work of the collector himself. The earliest archival photographs reveal that from the very beginning Dr. Barnes organized the collection in ensembles.

**FIG. 3:** Main Gallery, North Wall (detail)

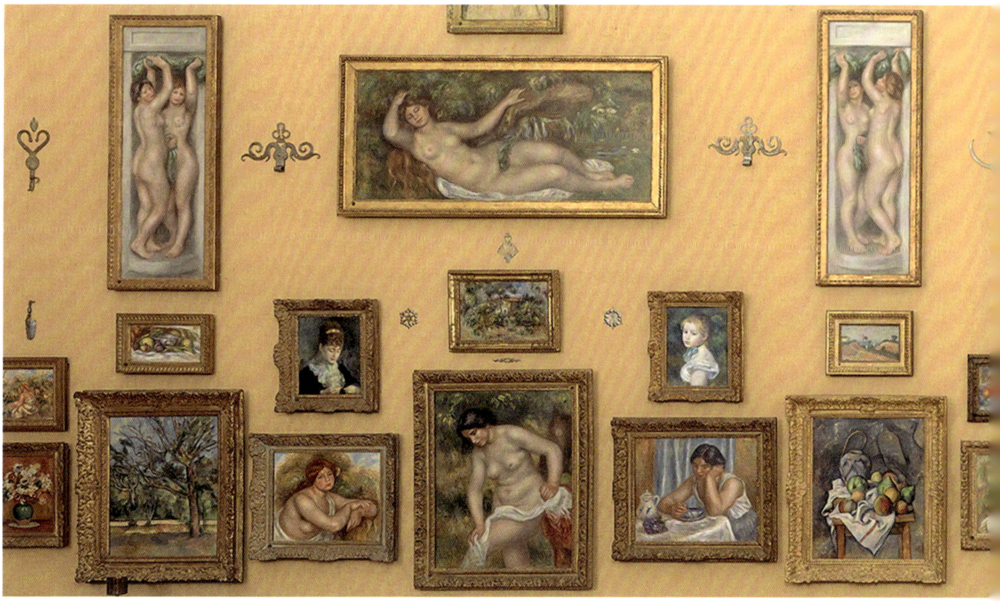

The ensembles serve many purposes. They allow viewers to easily compare and contrast works, revealing shared motifs or divergent qualities. The shape of a door hinge might echo the curve of a Renoir reclining nude nearby (fig. 3), or the lacy, decorative filigree of a lock face may call our attention to the swirling arabesques in an annunciation scene beneath it (fig. 4). A painting with shallow pictorial space hung next to one with deep receding space accentuates the spatial quality of each. The cool, mottled palette of a painted Pennsylvanian German chest may resonate with the colors in a painting hung above (fig. 5). The juxtapositions create visual connections between works and artists across periods and traditions, as an elongated figure by El Greco finds resonance with a standing figure by Cézanne. The ensembles also democratize the arts by breaking down the traditional hierarchy that raises painting and sculpture above the decorative arts. Dr. Barnes believed that anything invested with creative intent—whether it be a chest, chair, strap hinge, textile, or painting—embodies and expresses something of its maker's ingenuity.

**FIG. 4:** Room 4, North Wall (detail)

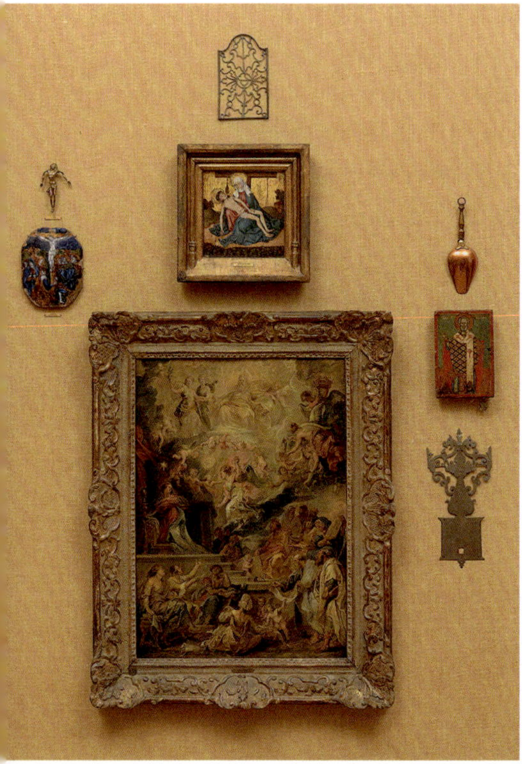

Above all, the ensembles throughout the Barnes Foundation make a forceful case for the modern art of the early twentieth century to be seen as an extension of the great traditions of painting that came before. Although recognized as such today, in Dr. Barnes's day this remained a point of fierce

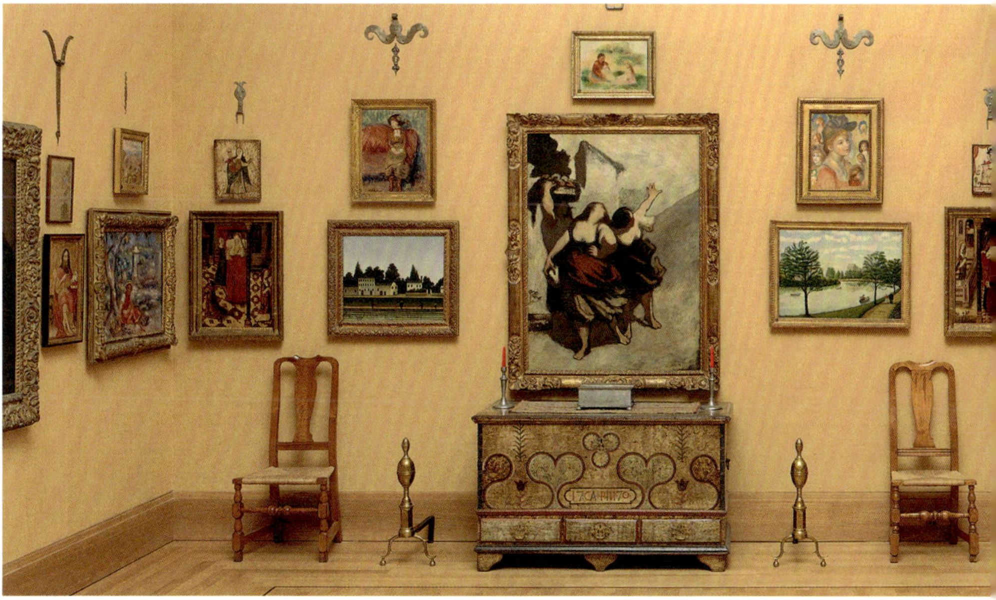

FIG. 5:
Room 14, West Wall (detail)

debate. Critics and the public alike saw the art of Matisse and Picasso as outside the trajectory of the great traditions of painting. Again and again in the ensembles, art from the past is juxtaposed with modern works in order to show their shared lineage.

The ensembles demonstrate that the Barnes Method is remarkably flexible and adaptable to any art form. It continues to be at the core of the Barnes–de Mazia Certificate Program, an immersive course of study exploring art's visual language through closer consideration of works in the Barnes collection. This knowledge is then carried out into the everyday world, providing an opportunity to experience familiar things through the eyes of the artist. This new way of seeing was, to Dr. Barnes, art's greatest gift.

**NOTES**

1. Dr. Albert C. Barnes, *The Art in Painting* (New York: Harcourt, Brace & World, 1925), 27.

# MAIN GALLERY

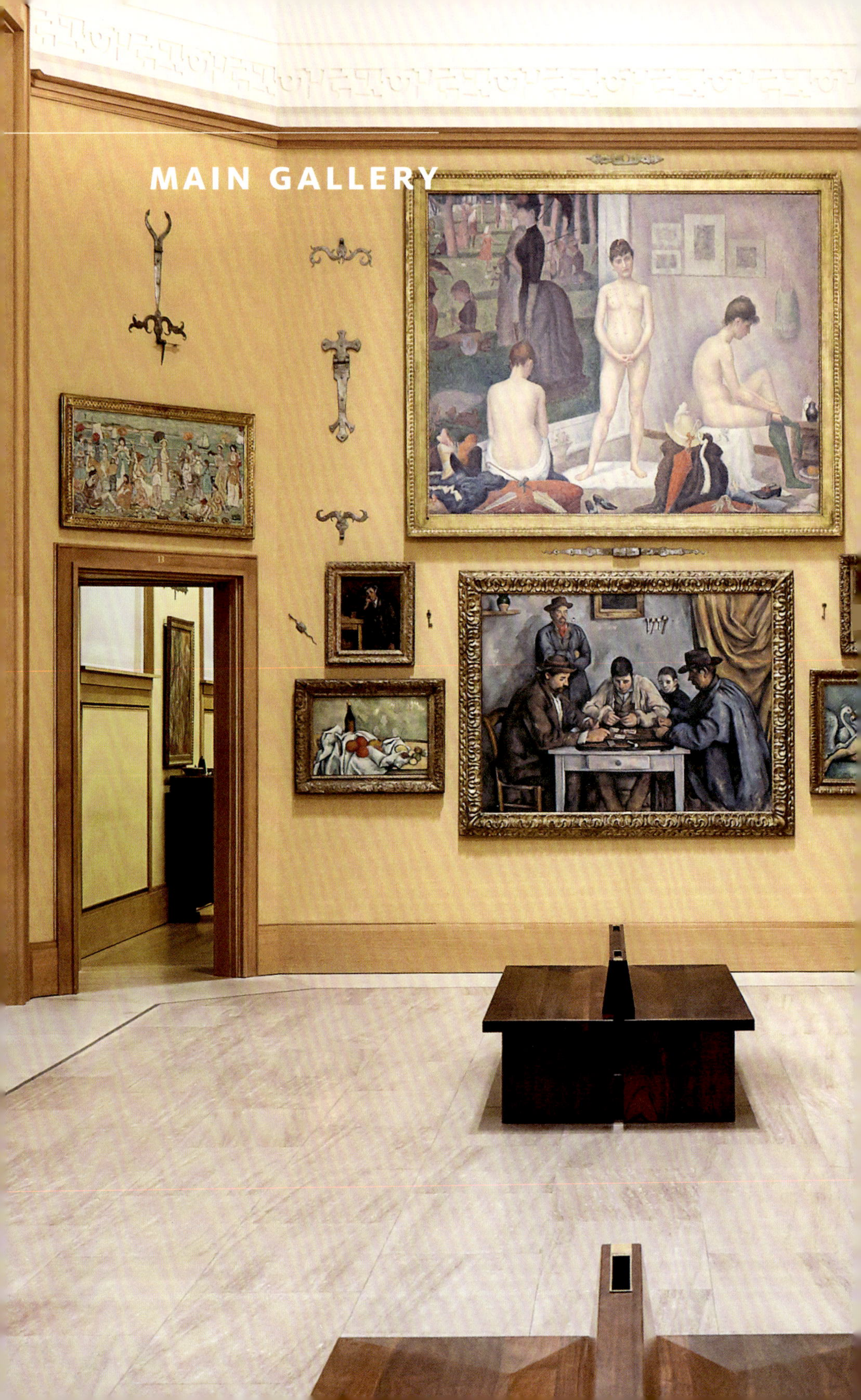

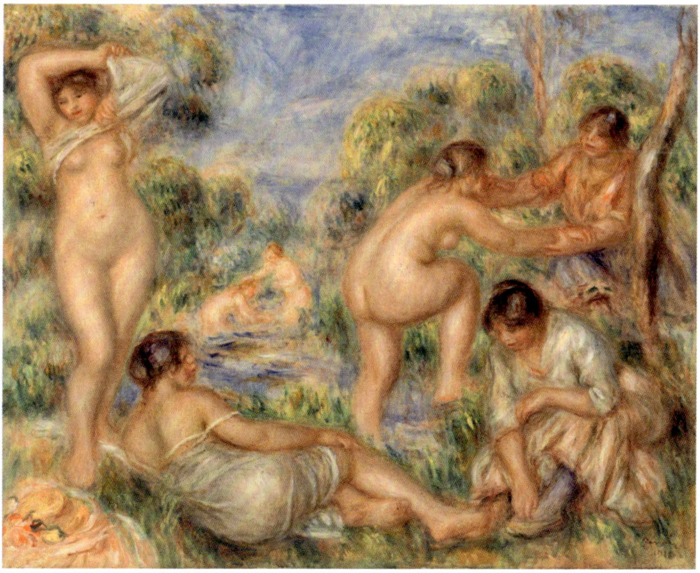

**PIERRE-AUGUSTE RENOIR (FRENCH, 1841–1919)**
***BATHING GROUP***
1916. Oil on canvas, 28 15⁄16 × 36 7⁄16 in. (73.5 × 92.5 cm). BF709

Toward the end of his life, while living in Cagnes-sur-Mer in the South of France, Renoir made many idyllic bathing scenes. Here, women pose as if in various stages of the process: from unlacing a first shoe on the right, to removing a last slip on the left. In this way—and many more—the entire composition interconnects. Even the receding landscape, with a bather leaving the water in the midground and two figures washing in the distance, ties in visually and thematically with the bathing process. Urban life is nowhere to be seen in this fantasy of female beauty.

When asked in a 1924 letter to name his favorite work by Renoir, Dr. Barnes landed firmly on this one, because "it represents the summation of [Renoir's] powers." He would have admired the compositional balance of the image: how cool green foliage frames the scene, for instance, or how the depiction of flesh throughout the canvas is flickering and sensual. He also understood Renoir's deep respect for tradition, seen here, for example, in his choice of colors, which was strongly influenced by French painters of the 1700s.

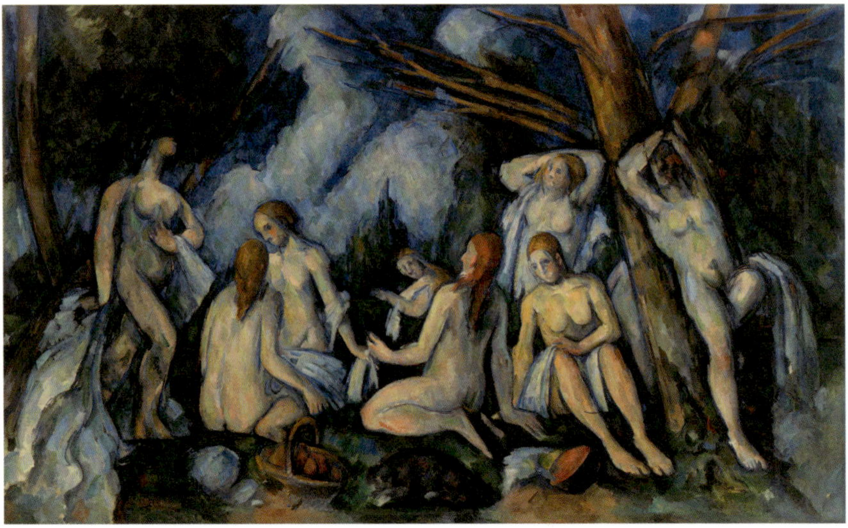

**PAUL CÉZANNE (FRENCH, 1839–1906)**
***THE LARGE BATHERS***
c. 1894–1906. Oil on canvas, 52⅛ × 86¼ in. (132.4 × 219.1 cm). BF934

In the last decade of his life, Cézanne produced three monumental bathing scenes featuring multiple figures in wooded settings. The largest and most resolved composition is in the Philadelphia Museum of Art; the National Gallery, London, owns another. This canvas, which Dr. Barnes acquired in 1933, was in many ways the most ambitious version. Beginning around 1894, Cézanne worked on it for roughly ten years. This labored process is evident in the canvas, whose built-up layers of paint create a dense, uneven surface.

It is unclear why Cézanne fixated on the theme of bathers. He was keen to find a place in the history of art—as a younger man he had written about wanting to "make of Impressionism something solid and durable like the art of museums"—which may have led him to tackle a subject that had interested European painters for centuries. But this does not wholly explain the figures, whose interrelationships and even gender are sometimes unclear. Though recent writers have explored *The Large Bathers* in relation to the artist's sexuality, for Dr. Barnes the formal qualities would have mattered most. The painting achieves a compositional balance comparable to that of the Renoir family portrait that hangs below it in the gallery (see page 31).

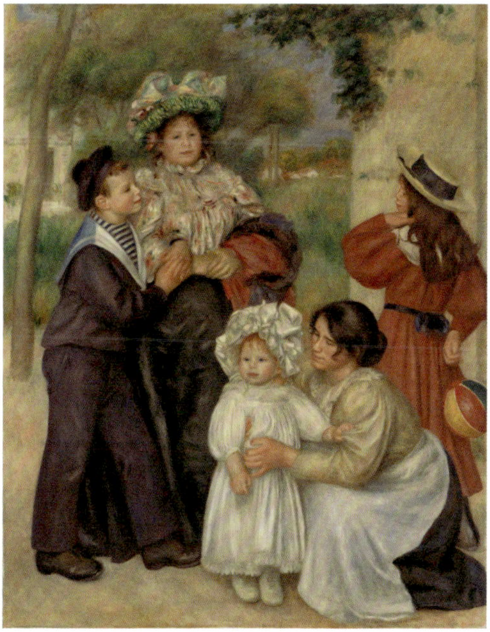

**PIERRE-AUGUSTE RENOIR (FRENCH, 1841–1919)**
***THE ARTIST'S FAMILY***
1896. Oil on canvas, 68 ⅛ × 54 in. (173 × 137.2 cm). BF819

In the largest portrait of his career, Renoir presents his family near their Parisian home, the Château des Brouillards in Montmartre. Renoir's wife, Aline, stands to the left, arm in arm with their eleven-year-old son Pierre, while his two-year-old brother Jean toddles in the foreground. Nursemaid and housekeeper Gabrielle Renard—who was also one of Renoir's favorite models—kneels to steady the child. The girl in a straw hat was likely a neighbor. The family's clothes reveal their newly acquired middle class status: Madame Renoir wears an elaborate hat; Pierre is dressed in a sailor suit. Renard stands out in her modest apron, but her presence suggests that she is integral to family life. Indeed, she was Aline's cousin.

The balanced composition would have appealed to Dr. Barnes, who appreciated Renoir's repeated use of color across a canvas, as well as his sensitivity to rhyming shapes (seen here, for instance, in the roundness of the faces). These qualities enhance the unified appearance of a group in which—through his distinctive painting style—the artist also seems present.

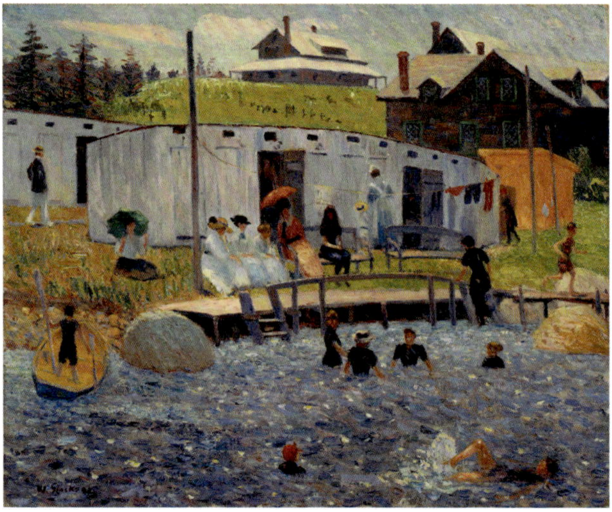

**WILLIAM JAMES GLACKENS (AMERICAN, 1870–1938)**
***THE BATHING HOUR, CHESTER, NOVA SCOTIA***
1910. Oil on canvas, 26 × 32 in. (66 × 81.3 cm). BF149

In this scene painted in Nova Scotia, Glackens captures the heat of summer. At the center of the composition, four women cool off in the water, as activity buzzes around them. A figure swims across the surface on his back, white paint describing the spray from his foot. A boy stands in a boat; another runs along the dock. Fashionably dressed women chat by the waterfront, and a nursemaid takes a child to the bathhouse.

Glackens, a close friend of Dr. Barnes, was entrusted in 1912 with buying the collector's first modern European paintings. Barnes purchased this work directly from Glackens two years later and would prove a constant patron in the decades to come. *The Bathing Hour* shows the influence of some of their favorite artists. Monet and Renoir had both created images of popular bathing spots, and the treatment of the water, with its lively purple and blue strokes, recalls many impressionist works.

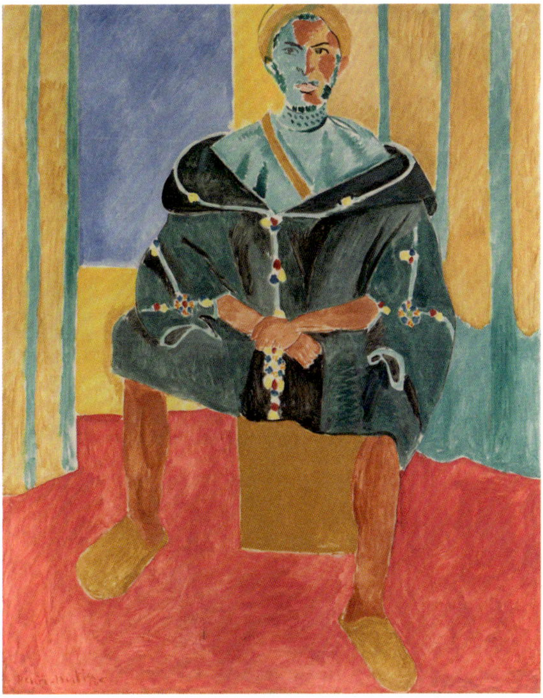

**HENRI MATISSE (FRENCH, 1869–1954)**
***SEATED RIFFIAN***
1912. Oil on canvas, 78⅞ × 63¼ in. (200.3 × 160.7 cm). BF264

After a visit to Algeria in 1906, Matisse took two extended trips to Morocco in 1912, the year in which the country became a French protectorate. His choice was not unusual. France's colonial interest in North Africa dated back to the 1830s, and countless European artists and writers had made the journey. Often these tourists were as eager to escape Christian morality as they were to experience new sights and sounds.

This work, like most from Matisse's second trip, features a single figure. While in Tangiers, the artist made several drawings and one other painting of the same man, but did not record his subject's name. The title tells us that he came from Rif, a rugged mountainous region that had resisted colonialization. In vibrant color, Matisse details the Riffian's clothing, which includes a rezza on his head and a djellaba across his shoulders. Legs spread wide, hands centered on the groin, the man's pose conveys virility. In later years, Matisse worried that this imposing canvas would detract from his mural *The Dance* (see page 134), which appears above. Dr. Barnes tried different locations for the painting but was ultimately undeterred.

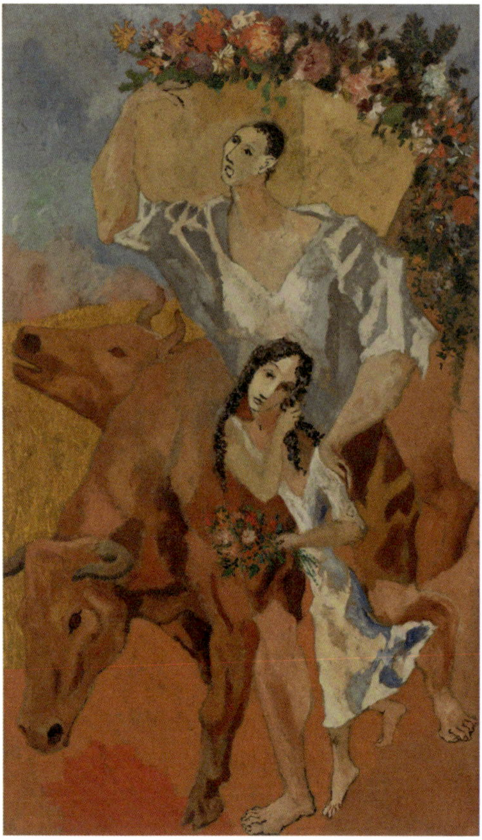

**PABLO PICASSO (SPANISH, 1881–1973)**

***COMPOSITION: THE PEASANTS***

1906. Oil on canvas, 87 × 51¾ in. (221 × 131.4 cm). BF140

Accompanied by his French girlfriend, the artist and model Fernande Olivier, Picasso spent the summer of 1906 in his native Spain. After a short stay in Barcelona, the couple moved on to Gósol, a remote village nestled in the Pyrenees. The arduous journey involved an eight-hour trek by mule, but the visit proved productive. Picasso worked freely in this new environment and enjoyed speaking Catalan with the local people. This is the most ambitious painting inspired by the trip. Picasso completed the work in Paris and at one stage even toyed with including the Eiffel Tower in the composition. His stylized, angular figures, abstracted from their richly colored background, seem to project out of the canvas.

Dr. Barnes claimed to have met Picasso in Paris in the 1910s, and even in the 1920s and 1930s, he preferred to buy the artist's youthful works. This painting hints at the cubism that Picasso would go on to develop but remains figurative, free of what Barnes would call "irrational abstractions."

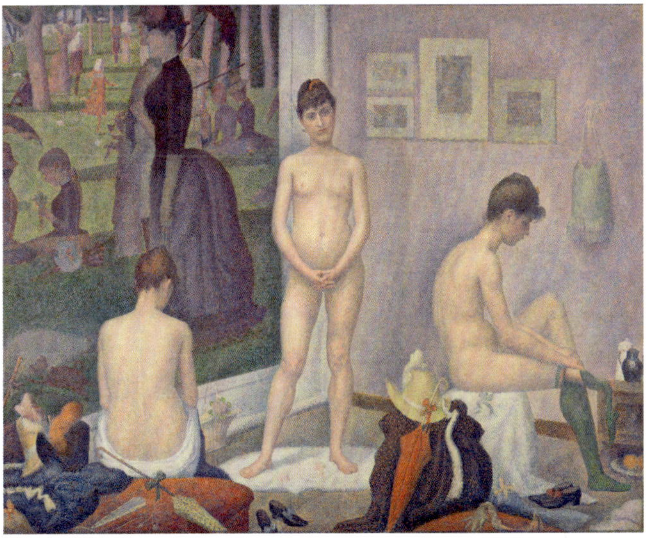

**GEORGES SEURAT (FRENCH, 1859–1891)**
***MODELS***
1886–88. Oil on canvas, 78 ¾ × 98 ⅜ in. (200 × 249.9 cm). BF811

Seurat's best-known work, *A Sunday on La Grande Jatte* (1884, Art Institute of Chicago), fills the left side of this studio scene. By including these fashionably clothed figures outside at a popular Parisian leisure spot, Seurat made it clear that his *Models* depicts contemporary women. The discarded clothes in the scene reflect current fashions, from dainty colored parasols to ribbon-tied shoes. On the wall, next to a small group of artworks, hangs a green item that viewers in the late 1800s would have recognized as a tournure. This padded out the back of a skirt, creating a silhouette like that of the main figure in *La Grande Jatte*. Its placement suggests that the central, unclothed figure could be the same woman who posed for the earlier painting.

If the components of the models' outfits are plainly visible, so too are the individual dots of paint that make up the picture. Seurat called this technique "pointillism," aligning it with scientific color theories of the day. For Dr. Barnes, the work's connection to tradition would have been key. While the women in the picture are of their time, the trio also references the Three Graces of ancient mythology, who were goddesses of beauty and elegance.

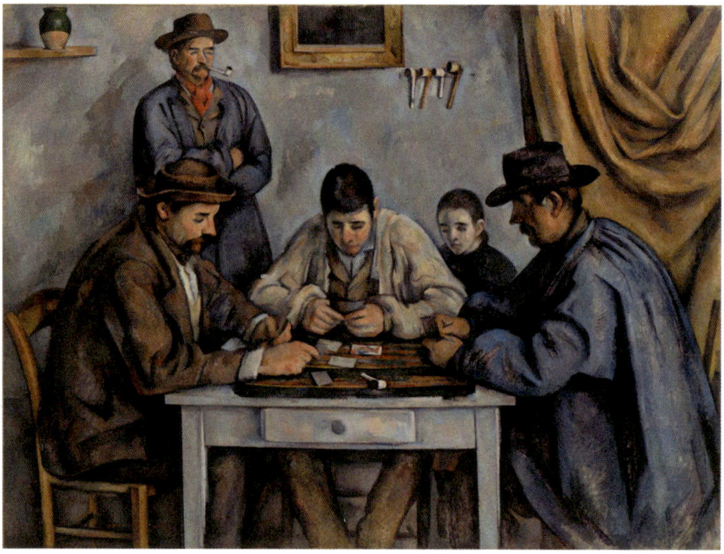

**PAUL CÉZANNE (FRENCH, 1839–1906)**
***THE CARD PLAYERS***
1890–92. Oil on canvas, 53¼ × 71⅝ in. (135.3 × 181.9 cm). BF564

Around a table, in a sparsely decorated interior, five figures stare at a game of cards. Their modest dress hints that these are workers from Cézanne's estate, who sometimes modeled for the artist to supplement their income. Léontine Paulet, who posed for the girl seated behind the players, recalled that she and her father, Paulin, earned five francs for this sitting. The staged scene—probably set in a farmhouse—suggests picturesque rural life during a period of dramatic industrialization.

Cézanne made at least five card player paintings in the 1890s, two of which share this composition. They were highly prized by early twentieth-century collectors, and Dr. Barnes spent five years trying to add one to his collection. When he bought this canvas in 1925 for $100,000, it was his most expensive purchase. This did not stop him and his collaborator, Violette de Mazia, from evaluating it critically. Cézanne's color in the painting, they argued, "lacks the effulgence, depth, solidity, and thoroughgoing organic activity found in his best work." But they praised his composition: "The processional effect of the static figures deployed across the canvas has the power and majesty of a range of mountain peaks."

## ROOM 2

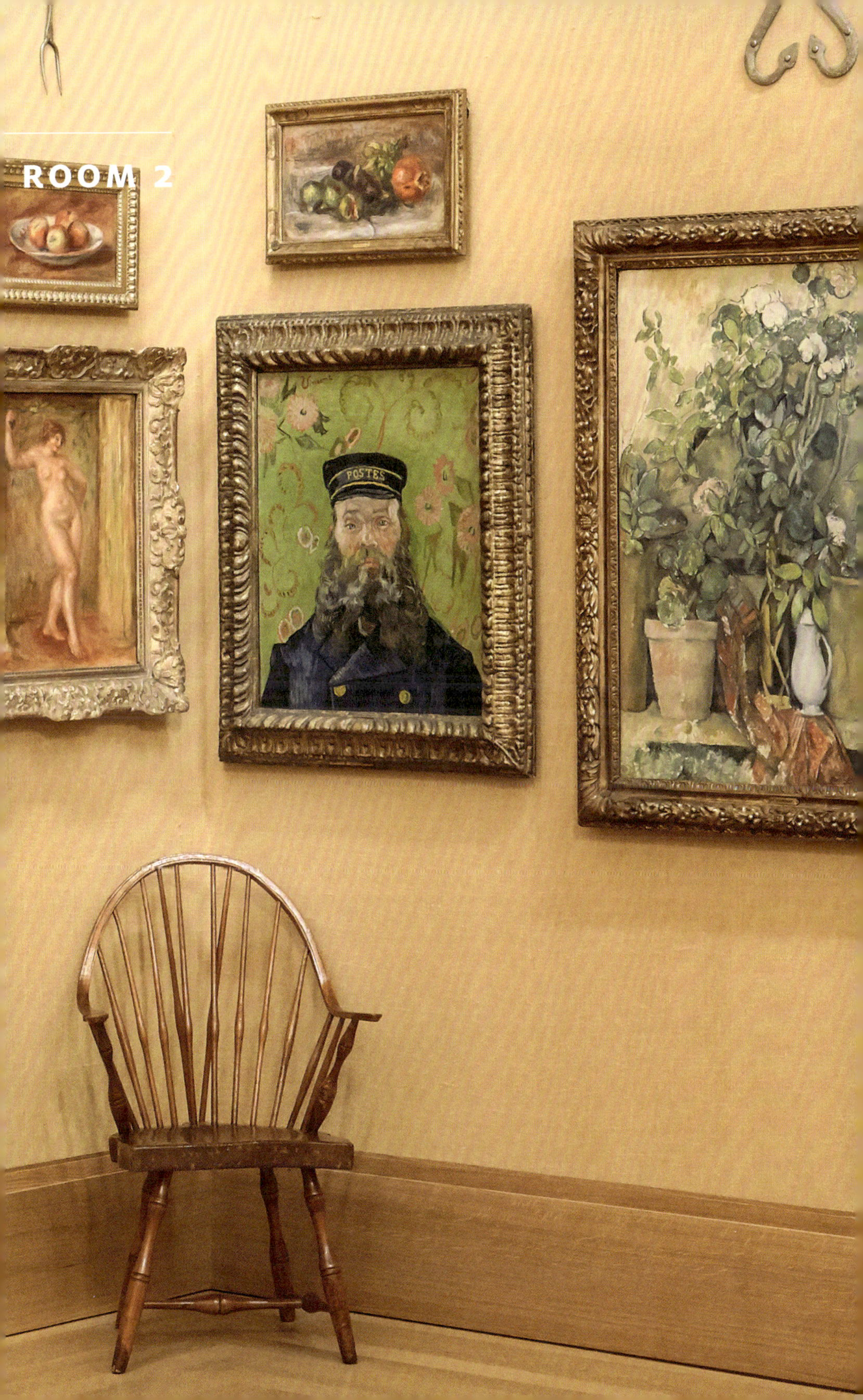

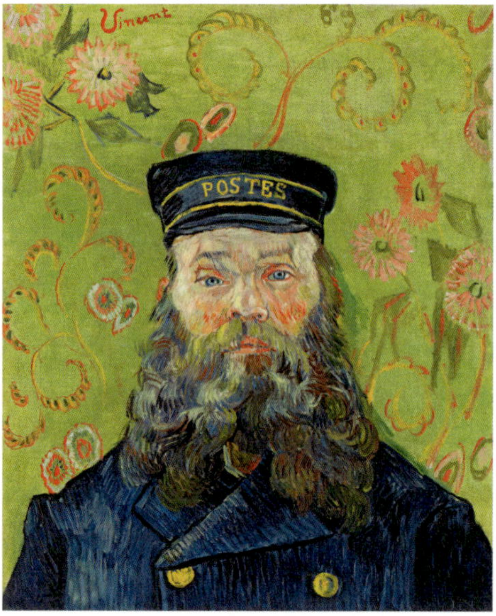

**VINCENT VAN GOGH (DUTCH, 1853–1890)**
***THE POSTMAN (JOSEPH-ÉTIENNE ROULIN)***
1889. Oil on canvas, 25⅞ × 21¾ in. (65.7 × 55.2 cm). BF37

Recently arrived in Arles, in the South of France, Van Gogh lived above a café near the train station. The local postman, Joseph-Étienne Roulin, was likely one of the regulars. The two became friends, and Roulin sat for several of Van Gogh's paintings. Here, he appears in uniform, suggesting pride in his occupation. Like many working people at the time, Roulin was a socialist who saw dignity in public service. His clothing also indicates Van Gogh's commitment to portraying a world beyond wealth and privilege. The elaborate background enhances the grandeur of the figure, who looks directly at the viewer from the center of the composition.

This painting, one of the first acquired by Dr. Barnes, was selected by his friend William Glackens, who bought it on his behalf in Paris in 1912. Van Gogh's distinctive use of color and pattern would have appealed to the collector. In Roulin's beard, unblended strokes of green, black, purple, and red create a convincing sense of texture. Although three versions of the portrait exist, this is the only canvas the artist signed, suggesting that it was the one gifted to Roulin.

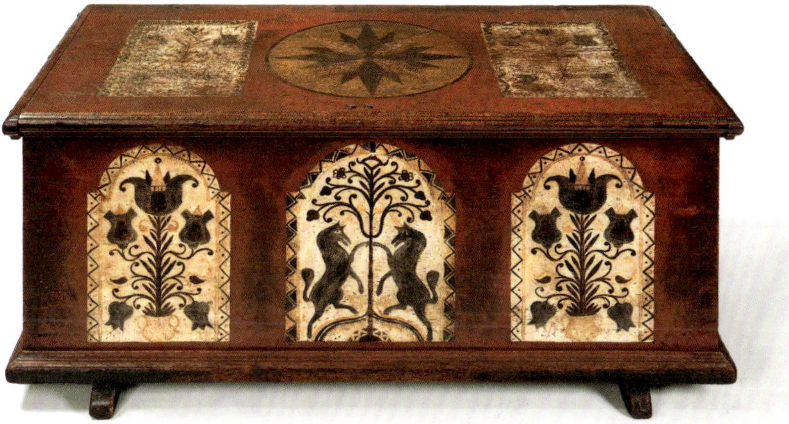

***CHEST*** **(AMERICAN, PENNSYLVANIA GERMAN)**
Unidentified maker. 18th century. Painted pine, 22¼ × 50½ × 23 in. (56.5 × 128.3 × 58.4 cm). 01.02.09

Berks County, located about sixty miles outside of Philadelphia, was settled by German and German-speaking Swiss immigrants in the eighteenth century. The area became known for its Pennsylvania German furniture. This black unicorn chest is an example of a design developed in Bern Township (ostensibly named for the Swiss city) featuring two rampant unicorns facing each other.

Pennsylvania German furniture was usually painted, in keeping with Swiss and German traditions. The architectural arches on this chest's front were created with paint, mimicking the look of wood molding. The sawtooth border around the arches, also painted, simulates wood inlay. These intricate designs required significant planning before execution, given the quick drying time of the materials involved.

The unicorn motif was likely borrowed from the British coat of arms and the Pennsylvania state coat of arms, which was adopted in 1778 and features two rearing horses. The unicorn, in traditional German culture, was a symbol of purity.

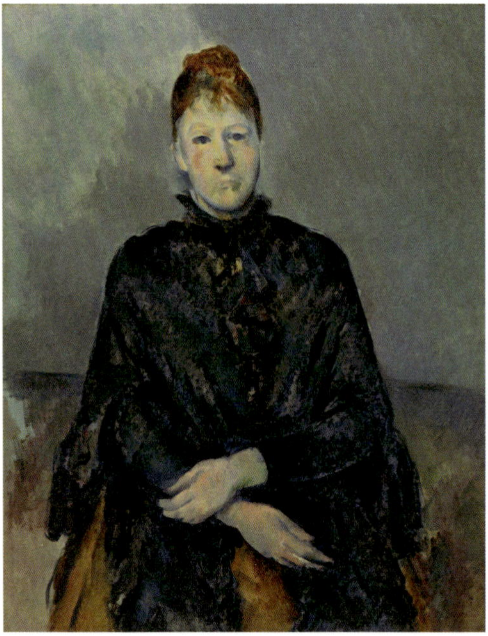

**PAUL CÉZANNE (FRENCH, 1839–1906)**
***MADAME CÉZANNE***
1888–90. Oil on canvas, 36½ × 28¾ in. (92.7 × 73 cm). BF710

As her partner's most long-suffering model—over the course of their relationship she posed for more than forty portraits—Madame Cézanne's look of resignation is perhaps unsurprising. Marie-Hortense Fiquet had met Cézanne almost twenty years before this work was made and was the mother of their teenage son, but the couple had only married in 1886. For many years, the artist had kept her existence a secret, afraid that his wealthy father would disapprove of the relationship.

Fiquet was from a modest background and had made a living by posing for artists before her relationship with Cézanne began in 1869. By the end of the 1880s—when she sat for this work—the couple were newly wealthy. But Dr. Barnes—like most early twentieth-century art lovers—was far more interested in the formal qualities of this work than in the life of the artist or his model. Bold color contrasts animate her face and hands, and her black clothing has matching undertones of red and green.

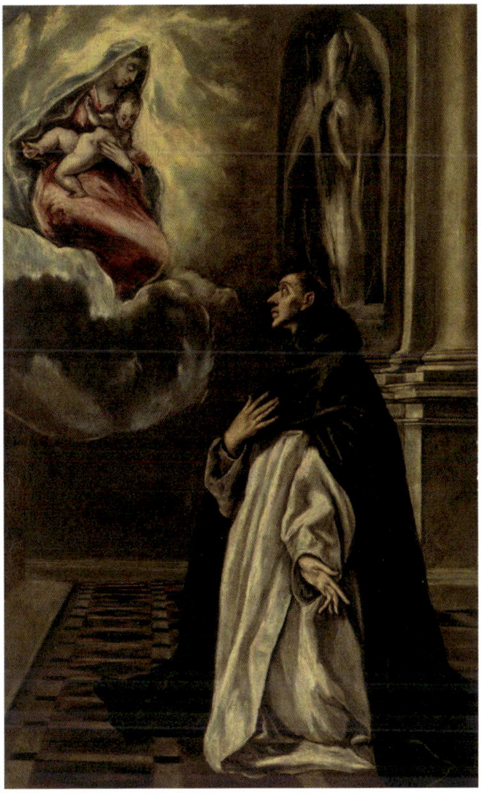

**EL GRECO (DOMENIKOS THEOTOKOPOULOS) (GREEK, ACTIVE IN SPAIN, 1541–1614)**

***APPARITION OF THE VIRGIN AND CHILD TO SAINT HYACINTH***

c. 1605–10. Oil on canvas, 62⅜ × 38⅞ in. (158.4 × 98.7 cm). BF876

When Dr. Barnes purchased this work in 1930, El Greco was newly popular with American collectors, having previously suffered years of critical neglect. Barnes saw stylistic similarities between El Greco and Cézanne—for instance, in their dramatic use of light and shade and angular treatment of figures—which is probably why he placed the painting in proximity to works by the French painter.

As an atheist, Barnes would have been less interested in its subject matter, but he created an altar-like ensemble with the work. Hyacinth was a Dominican priest born in Poland in 1185 who owed his sainthood to a miraculous vision of the Virgin Mary and the Infant Christ. He was canonized by Pope Clement VIII in 1594, which for El Greco's contemporaries was a relatively recent event. Kneeling, his hand to his chest, Hyacinth looks in awe at the holy figures. A dynamic shaft of light bears down from heaven, creating a sense of depth as it falls on the architecture and fabric, accentuating the bright white of Hyacinth's clerical robe.

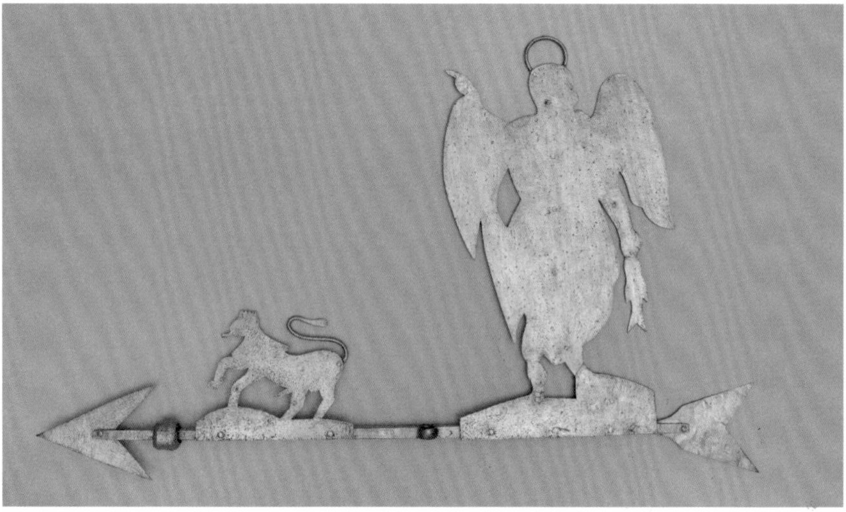

***WEATHER VANE*** **(FRENCH)**
Unidentified maker. Probably 18th century. Iron, 28 × 45¾ × 1¾ in. (71.1 × 116.2 × 4.4 cm). 01.02.31

The biblical book of Tobit tells how a disguised archangel Raphael, in his role as a guardian for travelers, accompanied the young Tobias and his dog to Media (in present-day Iran). The purpose of the journey was to collect money left by Tobias's father, who was now blind and unable to travel himself. On his return from Media, Tobias stopped to wash in a river, where he was attacked by a large fish. Raphael urged Tobias to capture the fish and make a medicine with its internal organs. Once home, Tobias used this to restore his father's sight, which prompted the archangel to reveal his identity.

This roughly worked weathervane was likely made by a regional craftsman to place atop a church steeple. Its iconography—including Raphael's prominent wings and halo, and the large fish in his hand—would have been familiar to churchgoing viewers in rural France in the 1700s.

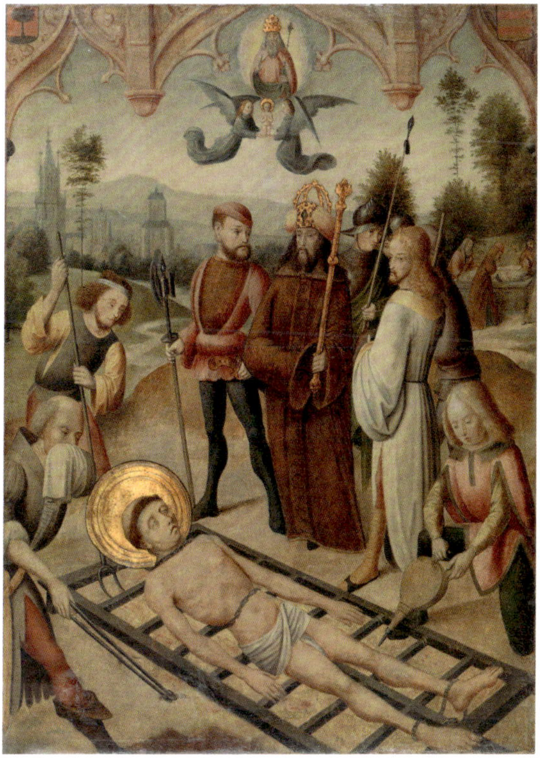

**MASTER OF THE SAINT URSULA LEGEND (GERMAN, ACTIVE 1480–1520)**

***MARTYRDOM OF SAINT LAWRENCE***

c. 1485/90–1510. Oil on canvas, 46 × 34 in. (116.8 × 86.4 cm). BF265

Once a decoration for a parish church in Cologne, Germany, this painting shows three distinct episodes from the martyrdom of Saint Lawrence (d. 258). In the foreground, the saint's frail body is chained to the gridiron on which he will burn to death. The emperor Decius—who wears a crown and holds a scepter—looks on; he has demanded the punishment because Lawrence served as an archdeacon in Rome at a time when Christianity was outlawed in the Roman Empire. Lawrence closes his eyes while the emperor's henchmen stoke and fan the flames. To the right, distant from the scene of torture, the saint's body is wrapped in a burial shroud and set upon a sarcophagus. At the top of the canvas, two hovering angels offer his innocent soul—in the form of a baby—up to God, whose regal attire indicates ultimate power.

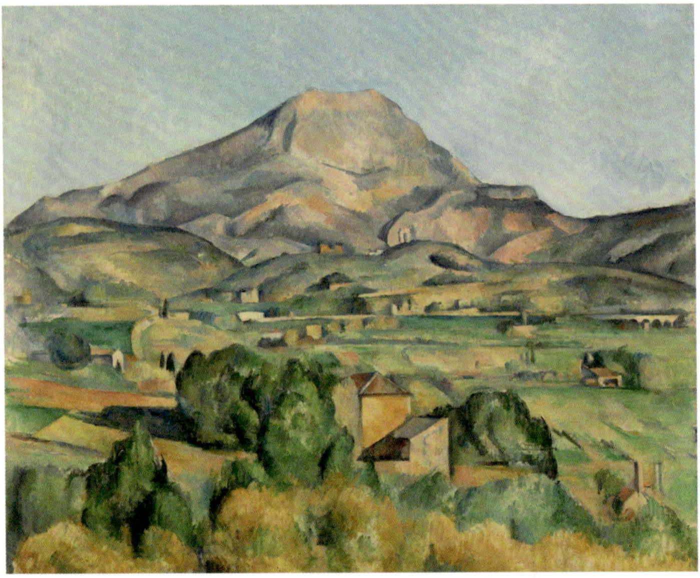

**PAUL CÉZANNE (FRENCH, 1839–1906)**
***MONT SAINTE-VICTOIRE***
1892–95. Oil on canvas, 28¾ × 36¼ in. (73 × 92 cm). BF13

Mont Sainte-Victoire, located in the South of France near the city of Aix-en-Provence, was well-known in local lore and possessed a great deal of symbolic resonance in the Provence region. Cézanne would have had a clear view of the mountain from his family's home at the Jas de Bouffan, and later from his studio on the Chemin des Lauves. Likely done close to his sister's property at Montbriand, this painting features the broad, geometric, vertical brushstrokes characteristic of Cézanne's work, especially noticeable in the yellow and green foliage he builds up at the bottom edge. Along the ridge of the mountain, he left faint traces of the raw canvas exposed. Mont Sainte-Victoire became a focal point for Cézanne, and he produced nearly ninety works of the subject. In this series of depictions, the artist not only experimented with his brushwork but also subtly recorded the impact of modern life on Aix-en-Provence, as with the faint indication of the Arc River Valley railway viaduct that appears in the midground at the canvas's right.

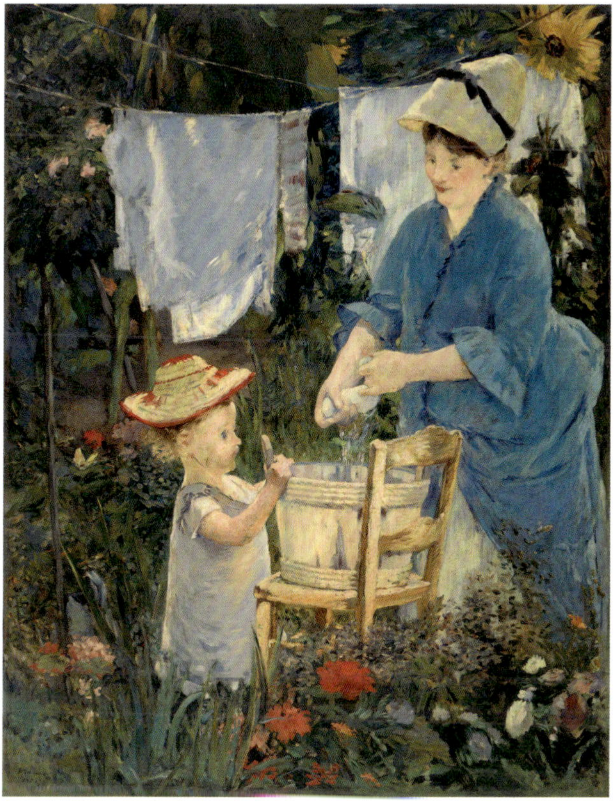

**ÉDOUARD MANET (FRENCH, 1832–1883)**

***LAUNDRY***

1875. Oil on canvas, 57¼ × 45¼ in. (145.4 × 114.9 cm). BF957

In this idyllic domestic scene, Manet depicts a woman washing clothes, accompanied by a small child. With their bodies central to the composition—and a foreground filled with flowers—an everyday task becomes a source of wonder. Dazzling rays of sunlight animate the drying laundry beyond. Although the journalist Antonin Proust recalled Manet referring to the woman as "Jeanne Lorgon," an 1883 inventory of the artist's studio identifies the figures as "le modèle Alice Legouvé et sa fille" (the model Alice Legouvé and her daughter). Legouvé was part of Manet's circle and posed for several of the artist's paintings. In his letters, Manet also refers to Legouvé posing for him in 1875.

Rejected by the jury of the Paris Salon (the state art exhibition), *Laundry* was featured in Manet's 1876 studio exhibition of his recent work. That year, the critic Stéphane Mallarmé wrote at length about the painting in his famous article "The Impressionists and Édouard Manet."

## ROOM 3

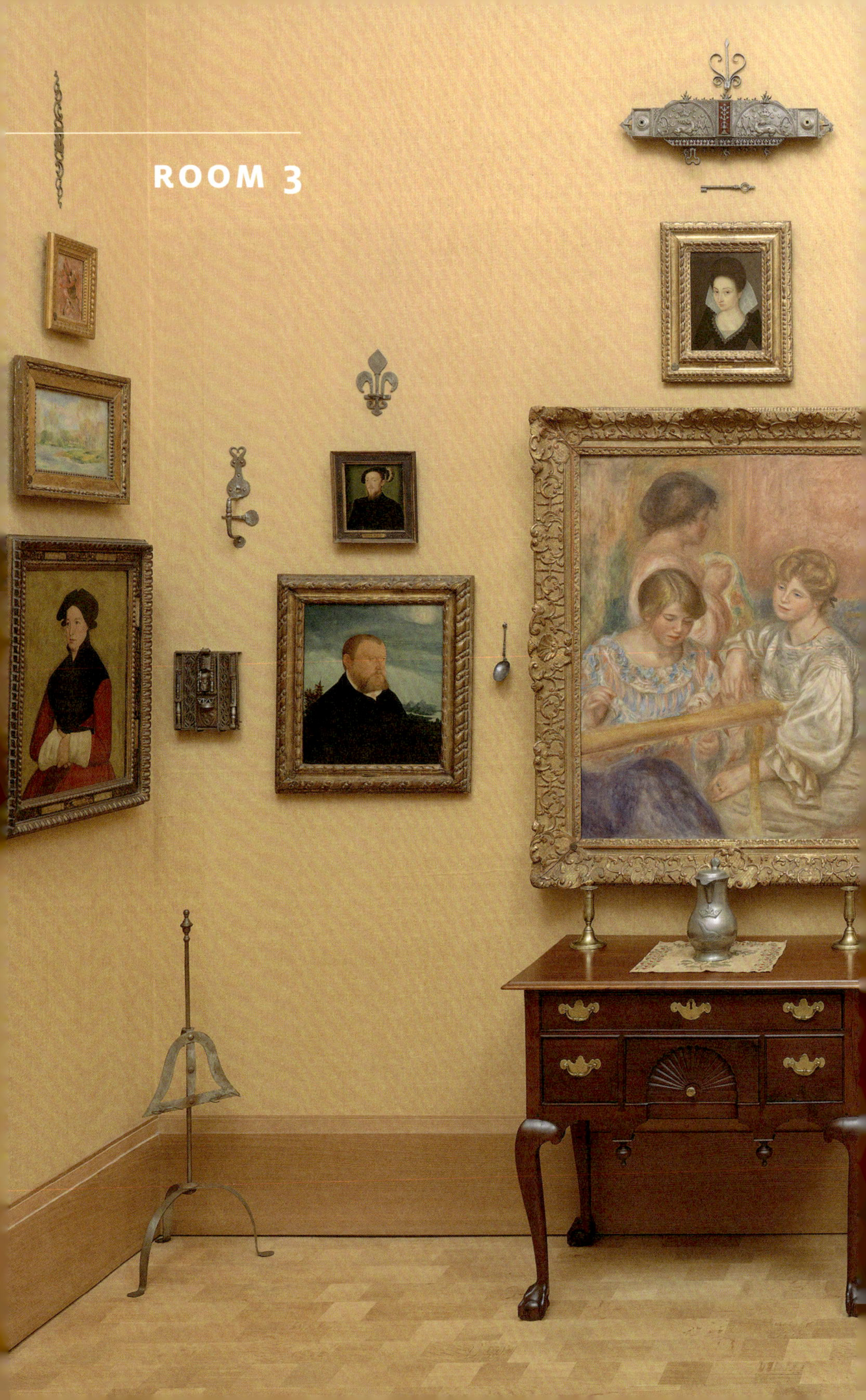

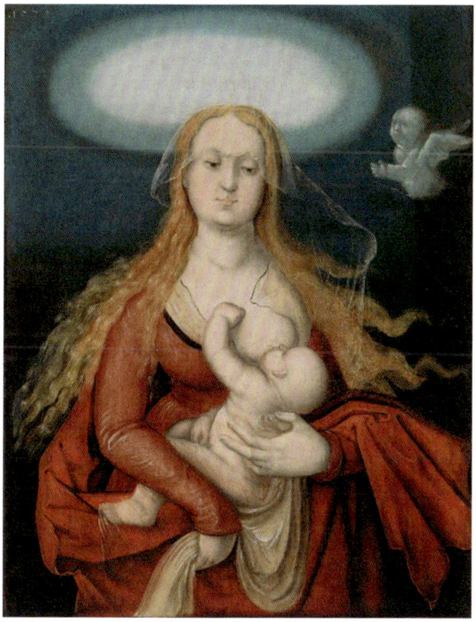

**HANS BALDUNG GRIEN (HANS BALDUNG) (GERMAN, 1484/85–1545)**
***MADONNA AND CHILD***
1539. Oil and tempera on panel, 13 9⁄16 × 10 3⁄4 in. (34.4 × 27.3 cm). BF316

Baldung was a German painter and printmaker who studied under Albrecht Dürer before distinguishing himself as an important and successful artist in his time. The small size of this painting indicates that it was hung in a household as an aid for private prayer. The picture presents the Virgin Mary as both mother and Queen of Heaven. She is shown feeding the Infant Christ from her breast (a common depiction known as Maria Lactans), while her royal role is evoked by the large halo over her head and the nearly translucent cherub to her right. The halo illuminates Mary's thin veil, which blows in some invisible wind with the golden strands of her hair, adding to the image's ethereal feel. The Barnes painting is a replica of one of Baldung's early works, identical except that his other Madonna wears an elaborate crown.

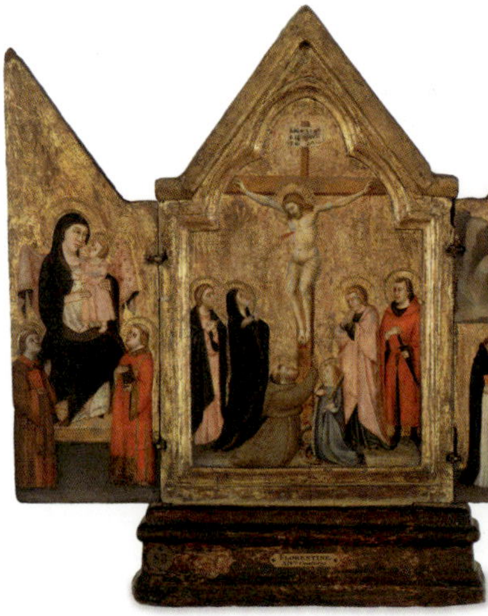

**MASTER OF THE SAN QUIRICO CRUCIFIX (ITALIAN, ACTIVE SECOND QUARTER OF THE 14TH CENTURY)**
***TRIPTYCH***
c. 1320s. Tempera and gold leaf on panel, 17 × 17½ in. (43.2 × 44.5 cm). BF83

In the central panel of this triptych with folding wings, the dead Christ hangs from the Cross, accompanied by a communion of saints: the Virgin Mary, in a blue starry robe, gazes and gestures toward him; the young John the Evangelist wrings his hands in grief; Saints Francis and Margaret kneel at the foot of the Cross; and two unidentified saints stand to Christ's left. The triptych's left wing is occupied by a Madonna and Child with two deacons holding books; the right shows Saints Dominic and Anthony Abbot in conversation, and the giant Saint Christopher carrying the Christ Child across a river.

The various figures would have offered focal points for prayer, most likely for individual use in an intimate setting. A friar may have used the triptych in his cell or on a private altar, a context that emphasized the connection between Christ's body and blood and the consecrated bread and wine of the Mass. Alternatively, the striking position of Margaret—the patron saint of childbirth—may indicate that a young or expecting mother used the triptych in her bedchamber, taking comfort in the sacred drama that unfolded as she opened and closed its wings.

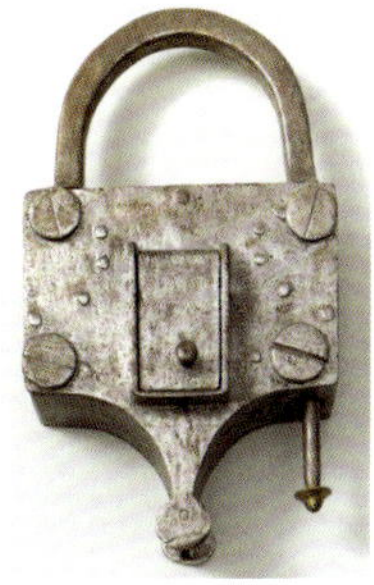

***CONFESSIONAL CAGE*** **(FRENCH)**

Unidentified maker. 17th or 18th century. Iron, 22 3⁄16 × 11 7⁄8 × 5 7⁄8 in. (56.4 × 30.2 × 14.9 cm). 01.03.32

***PADLOCK*** **(EUROPEAN)**

Unidentified maker. 18th century. Iron, 9 × 5 1⁄8 × 2 5⁄8 in. (22.9 × 13 × 6.7 cm). 01.03.31

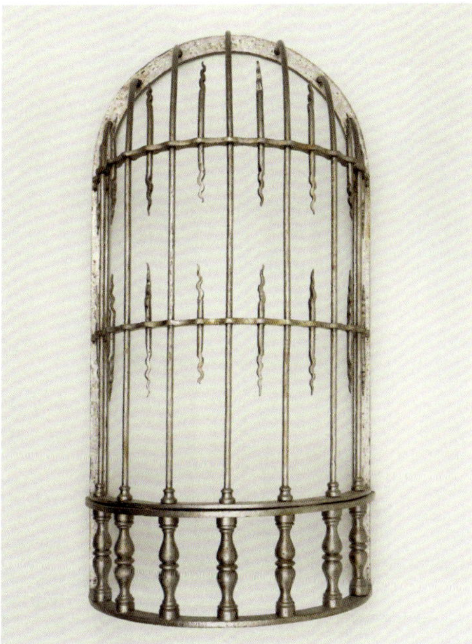

This semicircular, domed confessional cage was made for use in a Roman Catholic church, where it would have separated the priest and the kneeling penitent. Most screens were flat, but confessionals took many forms, and this cage may have been shaped to accommodate hands folded in prayer.

The decoration of the confessional cage consists of corkscrew ornaments interspersed with bars, and turned spindles at the bottom. Dr. Barnes displayed this object below a roughly contemporaneous padlock, whose sinuous pendant ornament echoes the spindles in the confessional. For Barnes, the juxtaposition of these unrelated items encouraged visual analysis. Indeed, he valued the "useful arts" as equal to the "fine arts," and celebrated the educational potential of finding visual and conceptual relations between them.

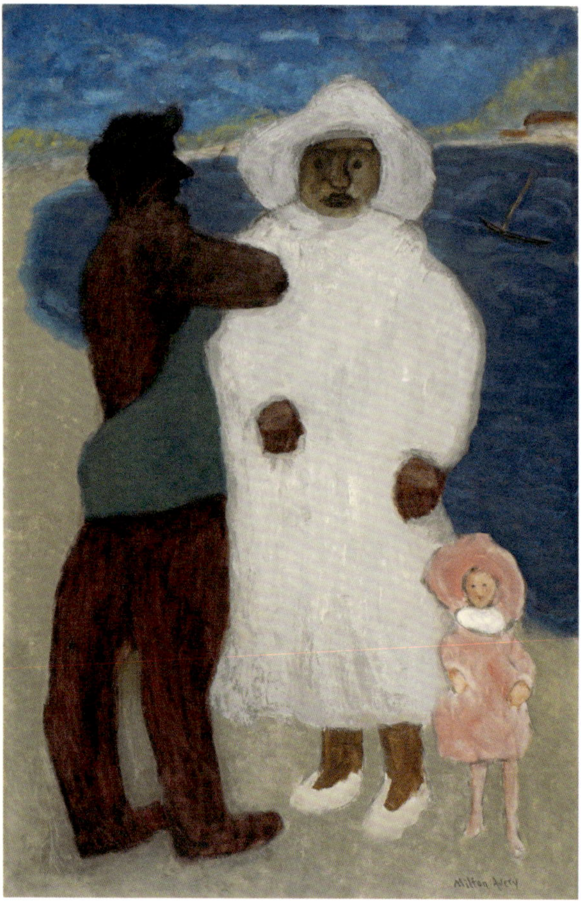

**MILTON AVERY (AMERICAN, 1885–1965)**
***THE NURSEMAID***
1934. Oil on canvas, 48 × 32 in. (121.9 × 81.3 cm). BF961

Avery, who lived in New York City, frequently visited Coney Island and spent summers by the ocean in Gloucester, Massachusetts. He captured his experiences in paintings such as this one, of three figures on a beach. The woman in white is probably "the nursemaid," as a child stands next to her, but the title does not identify the athletic bather in their company.

The work reflects the racism of the Jim Crow era. With limited job opportunities, many African American women made a living raising the children of white families. Public beaches were usually segregated, and only Black employees would have been present at beaches reserved for whites. Dr. Barnes purchased this work in 1935 after spying it in the back room of a New York gallery. The dealer had not displayed it, apparently doubting the painting's commercial value.

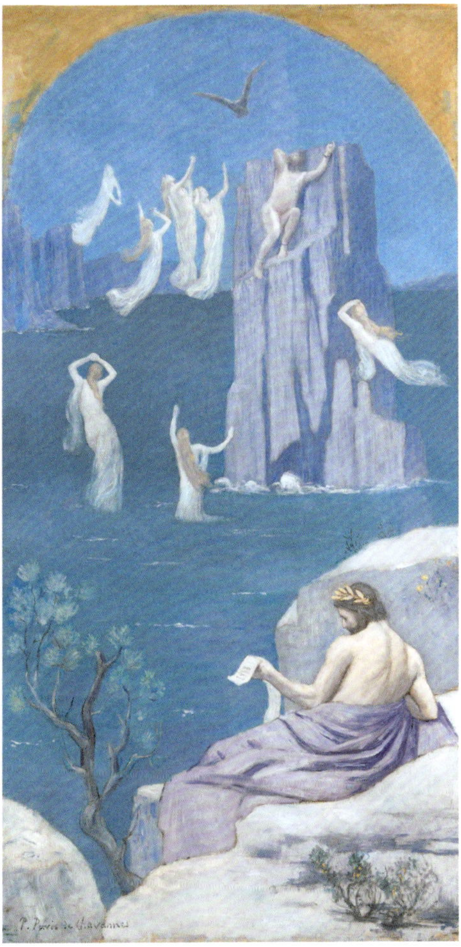

**PIERRE PUVIS DE CHAVANNES (FRENCH, 1824–1898)**

***DRAMATIC POETRY (AESCHYLUS)***

c. 1896. Oil on canvas, 48 7/8 × 24 7/8 in. (124.1 × 63.2 cm). BF100

A keen believer in artistic traditions, Dr. Barnes would have understood how Puvis de Chavannes had reinvigorated mural painting in the late 1800s, and how he had influenced younger artists such as Seurat and Picasso. In Paris, Puvis's murals decorated some of the city's most significant buildings, though this particular work is a scaled-down section of his only site-specific American painting, a monumental scheme in the Boston Public Library.

Seated in the foreground, script in hand, the ancient Greek dramatist Aeschylus reads his tragedy *Prometheus Bound*. Beyond, rendered in subtle shades of blue and gray, is its bloody climax. As punishment for stealing fire from the gods, Prometheus stands chained to a rock, shrinking from the hovering eagle that pecks daily at his liver. Around him, wailing in despair, sirens lament his fate. The scene was one of a series of nine panels that, in the context of the library, indicate the various spheres of human knowledge. The purpose of these smaller versions is unclear; perhaps they served to remind the artist, who was reluctant to travel in his later years, of murals that he would never see in context.

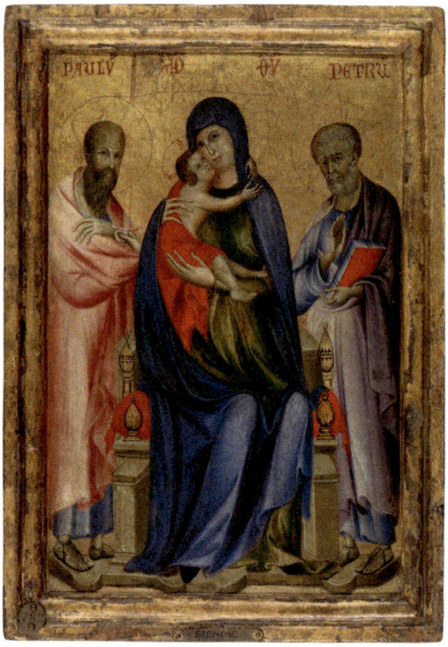

***VIRGIN AND CHILD WITH SAINTS PETER AND PAUL* (ITALIAN)**
Unidentified artist. Late 13th century. Tempera with gold leaf on panel, 11 13/16 × 8 3/8 in. (30 × 21.3 cm). BF782

The Virgin and Child sit enthroned between Saints Paul and Peter in this small panel painting, made in northern or central Italy. Paul holds a raised sword; Peter holds a book and extends his right hand in a gesture of blessing or invitation. Inscriptions at the top name each figure, with Paul and Peter (the patron saints of Rome) in Latin and "Mother of God" in abbreviated Greek. The Virgin cradles the Christ Child, their faces touching. This pose is related to Byzantine icon types with Greek names—Eleousa or Glykophilousa—that emphasize the Virgin's tenderness and loving-kindness, respectively. The figures are elegantly attenuated, and the vestments, book, and throne cushion are painted in vibrant jewel tones that enhance the image's sacred aura.

This panel originally formed the left side of a hinged diptych. The right panel (now in a private collection) shows Christ on the Cross flanked by the grieving Virgin and Saint John the Evangelist, with two distraught angels above them. The juxtaposition of Christ's infancy and death, both in the company of his mother, would have presented a poignant devotional platform for private prayer.

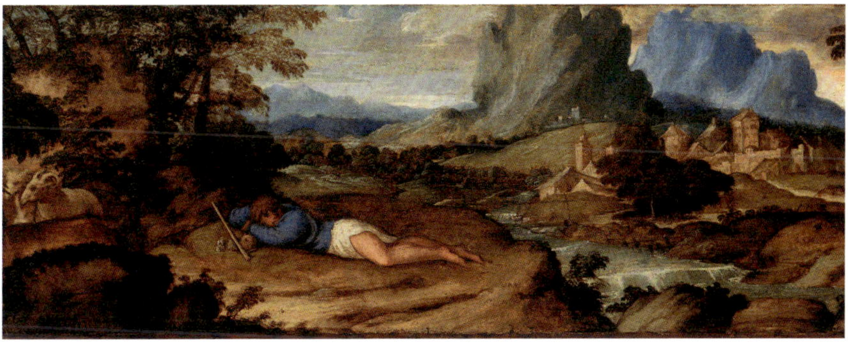

**ATTRIBUTED TO TITIAN (TIZIANO VECELLIO) (ITALIAN, C. 1488–1576)**
***SLEEPING SHEPHERD* (DETAIL)**
c. 1500–1510. Oil on panel, 10 ⅞ × 50 ¼ in. (27.6 × 127.6 cm). BF977

The shepherd at the center of this painting appears to be asleep on a rocky outcrop surrounded by trees, but a closer look reveals that he is raising his head as if he has seen the viewer. The artist may have intended this young man to represent the mythological figure of Endymion, who was placed in eternal slumber by Zeus at the request of the goddess of the moon, Selene, so that she might admire him. Attributed to the Venetian painter Titian, this work was probably made for an aristocratic household and designed to be placed over a door or on a decorated piece of furniture. The wide horizontal format allowed the artist ample room to depict a lush landscape with a city in the middle distance and mountains beyond. Pastoral poetry, which celebrated the beauty of nature and humankind's place in it, originated with the ancient Greek Theocritus and saw a resurgence in sixteenth-century Venice. Pastoral landscapes such as this painting emerged out of this literary genre, reflecting the principle *ut picture poesis* ("as is poetry so is painting)" and illustrating idyllic scenes of gods and goddesses, mythical creatures, and mortal shepherds that replicated their poetic counterparts.

# ROOM 4

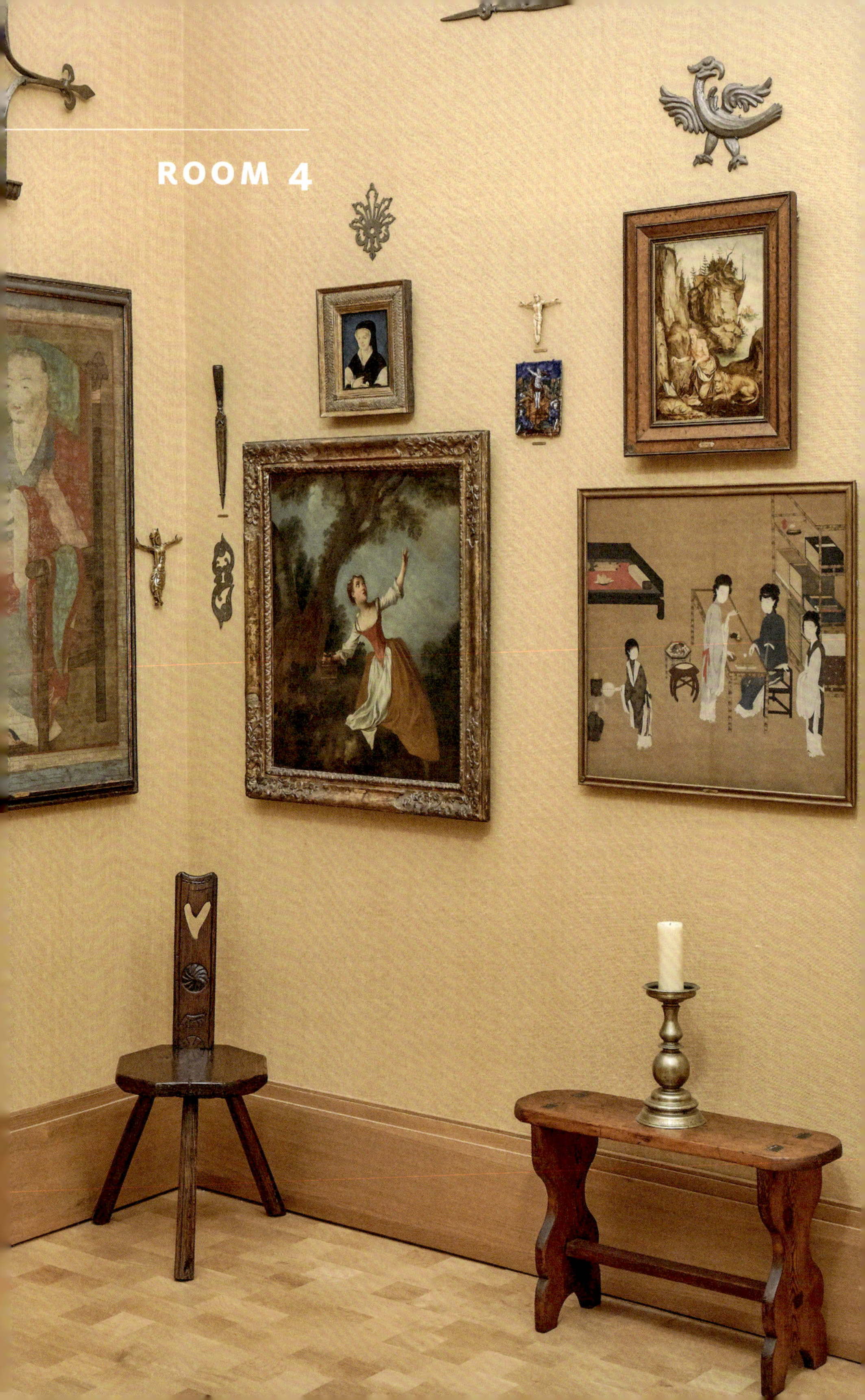

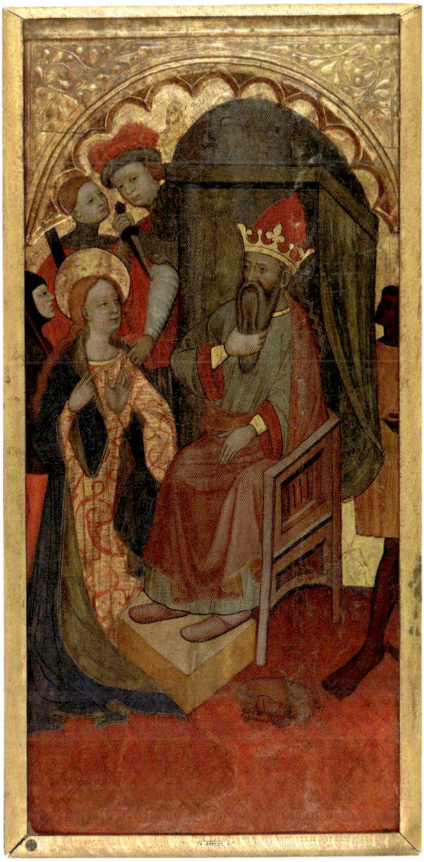

**NICOLÁS SOLANA (SPANISH, ACTIVE 1401–41)**
***SAINT KATHERINE OF ALEXANDRIA BEFORE THE ROMAN EMPEROR***
Early 15th century. Tempera and gold on panel, 53¼ × 25¼ in. (135.3 × 64.1 cm). BF872

The martyrdom of Saint Katherine of Alexandria by the Roman emperor Maxentius (r. 306–312 CE) is here depicted in the vivid colors and elegant lines of the International Gothic style. According to Christian tradition, the scholarly and beautiful Katherine, daughter of the Roman governor of Alexandria, Egypt, converted to Christianity around the turn of the fourth century, and died the year before the emperor Constantine legalized Christianity.

Richly dressed in gilt brocade, Saint Katherine smiles gently and addresses the enthroned Maxentius, who pulls his beard in frustration. She has refused to participate in pagan worship, rejected his advances, and converted thousands of his subjects to Christianity. The snarling dog in the corner refers to the emperor's command to kill Christians and throw their bodies to the dogs. Maxentius's dark-skinned assistant on the right probably evokes the Muslim inhabitants of Spain who, like the ancient Roman pagans, were seen as enemies of Christianity. As the emperor's other assistants, one of whom clutches a dagger, prepare to dispatch Katherine, her gold halo indicates that her martyrdom will be rewarded with eternal life in heaven. This panel would have originally been installed within an enormous, multitiered altarpiece in the sanctuary of a Spanish church.

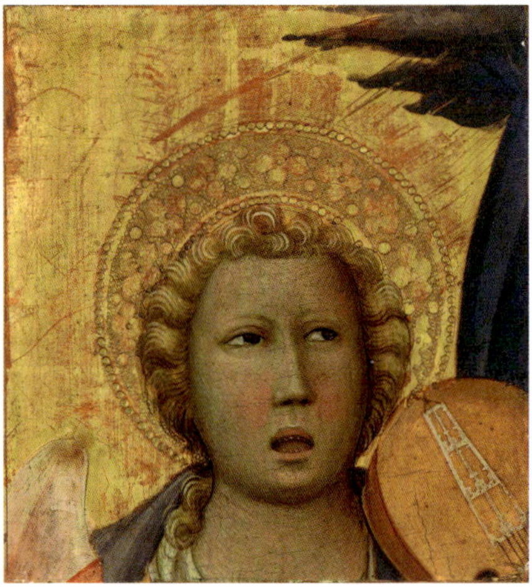

**GHERARDO STARNINA (ITALIAN, 1355–1412)**
***HEAD OF AN ANGEL***
c. 1404–7. Tempera and gold on panel, 6 ¾ × 6 ½ in. (17.1 × 16.5 cm). BF1003

This small image of a music-making angel was painted by a prominent artist from Florence who had also worked in Spain. The angel has curly blond hair, one visible pink wing, and a halo with a floral design stamped onto the gold background. He is shown singing and playing a vielle (a musical instrument similar to a modern violin). The painting's abstracted elegance, bright colors, and sumptuous effects are hallmarks of the International Gothic style, popular across Europe at the time.

Starnina's angel looks to his left, toward traces of blue clouds and a mandorla, an almond-shaped body halo that usually enveloped an image of the Virgin Mary as Queen of Heaven. These elements signal that the angel is a fragment of a larger assemblage: a polyptych altarpiece commissioned by Cardinal Angelo Acciaiuoli (1349–1408) for his newly built Chapel of the Virgin Mary within the Certosa del Galluzzo, just outside of Florence, where he was later buried. The Certosa was one of the most powerful monasteries in Europe. Today, fragments of Starnina's altarpiece are found in multiple collections in Europe and America

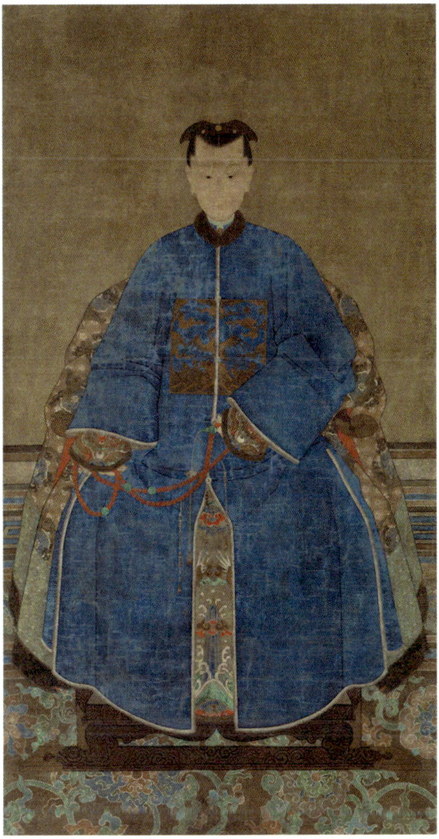

***PORTRAIT OF A WOMAN* (CHINESE)**
Unidentified artist. 17th–18th century. Chinese black ink and heavily applied pigments on silk, 62⅝ × 33¼ in. (159.1 × 84.5 cm). BF80

In Qing dynasty China, court officials followed a strict code of attire, and married women dressed according to their husbands' rank. This noblewoman's robelike garment is trimmed with fur for the winter season. The embroidered badge on her surcoat indicates rank through animal imagery. The bird identifies her husband as a civil official rather than a military one; the bird looks up to the sun, symbolizing the emperor.

The Qing dynasty (1644–1911) was established by the Manchus, an ethnic minority who came down from northern China to overthrow the Ming dynasty, ending the imperial rule of the Han Chinese. Manchu rulers used the arts to solidify their regime, continuing traditional court portraiture but introducing Manchu customs of dress. Note the three earrings worn on each ear, a Manchu style of adornment distinct from the single pair worn by most Chinese women.

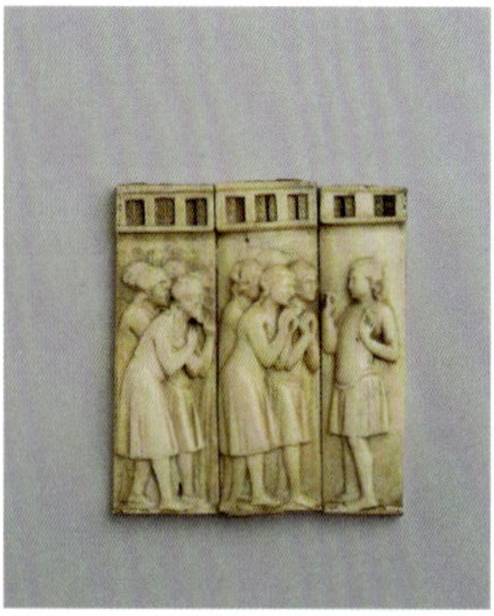 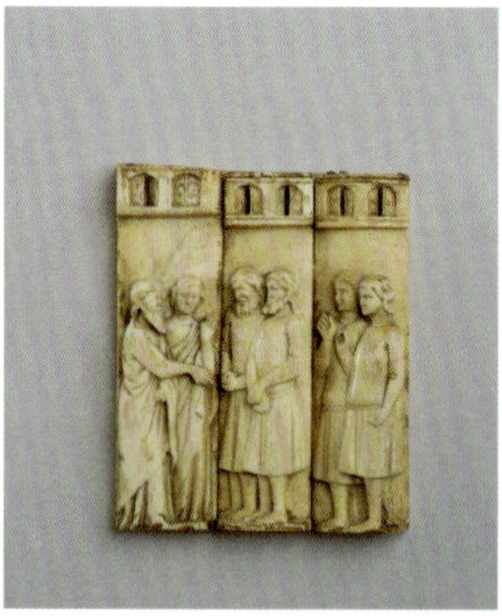

**WORKSHOP OF BALDASSARE EMBRIACHI (ITALIAN, 1385–1409)**
***CASKET FRAGMENTS***
c. 1400. Bone with traces of gilding; fragment 1 (left): 3⅞ × 3⅞ × ½ in. (9.8 × 9.8 × 1.3 cm); fragment 2 (right): 4⅛ × 3⅜ × ½ in. (10.5 × 8.6 × 1.3 cm). 01.04.61, 01.04.67

These objects are probably fragments of a bridal casket, carved around 1400 by the workshop of the Embriachi family. Each fragment consists of three long bones, probably from the legs of a hooved mammal, joined side by side. They depict groups of youths and bearded men, dressed in tunics and togas, who interact with each other in a shallow cityscape described by a row of windows at top, whose shutters are variably open and shut. The scenes may be episodes from the Greek legend of Jason and the Argonauts, which the Embriachi workshops portrayed with some frequency. Classical and contemporary romances were standard subjects for late medieval bridal caskets, which were usually given as gifts to hold documents or jewels.

Baldassare Embriachi founded his family's bone- and ivory-carving workshops in Florence, most likely in the 1370s. They produced many carvings with marquetry, including altarpieces, small-scale devotional tabernacles, and rectangular and polygonal caskets. Baldassare's participation in Florence's famed literary circles may account for these objects' diverse content—sacred and secular, modern and ancient. Around 1395, political and financial circumstances caused the Embriachi family to move with their workshops to Venice, where the two Barnes carvings were most likely produced.

# ROOM 5

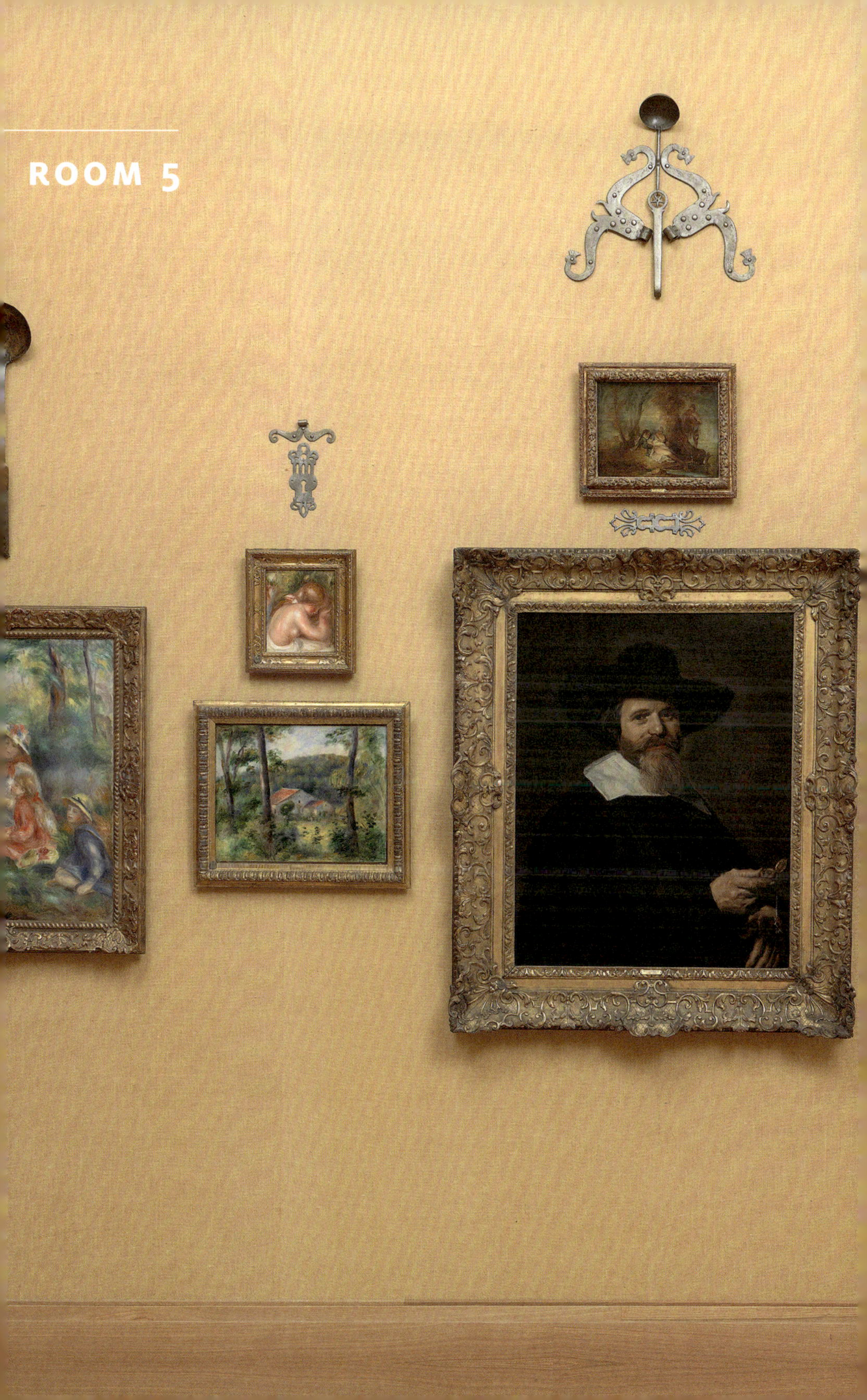

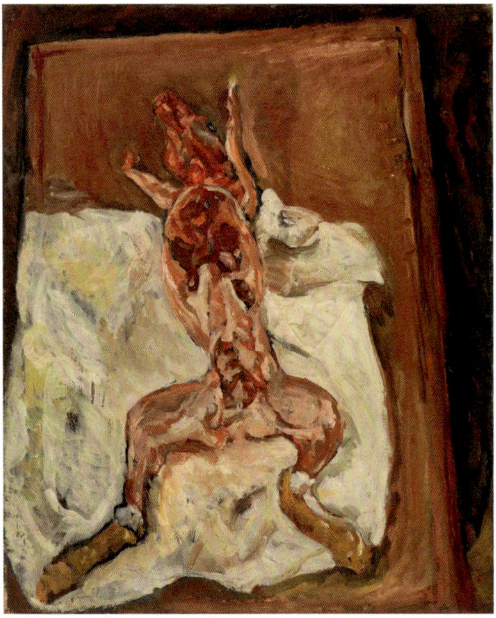

**CHAÏM SOUTINE (RUSSIAN, ACTIVE IN FRANCE, 1893–1943)**
***FLAYED RABBIT***
c. 1921. Oil on canvas, 28 ¾ × 23 ⅝ in. (73 × 60 cm). BF333

Soutine painted this skinned rabbit from a real carcass. Tawny, soft fur still covers the animal's hind paws, heightening the grisliness of the bloodied, exposed flesh. The lurid reds and pinks of the raw meat stand out against the white cloth, made grimy with yellows and browns. Although the rabbit is lying on a table, the overhead view gives the impression that it is hanging. The subject relates to European paintings of kitchen still lifes or hunters' trophies of dead game. In seventeenth-century Dutch and eighteenth-century French painting, these works often featured dead rabbits hung by their hind legs.

Soutine's picture, however, adds an emotional element to the genre. His gruesome depiction of the butchered rabbit aimed to express human pain and suffering through the animal's, while also conveying the physical experience of painting. His energetic brushwork and thick impasto combine paint and flesh, beauty and brutality.

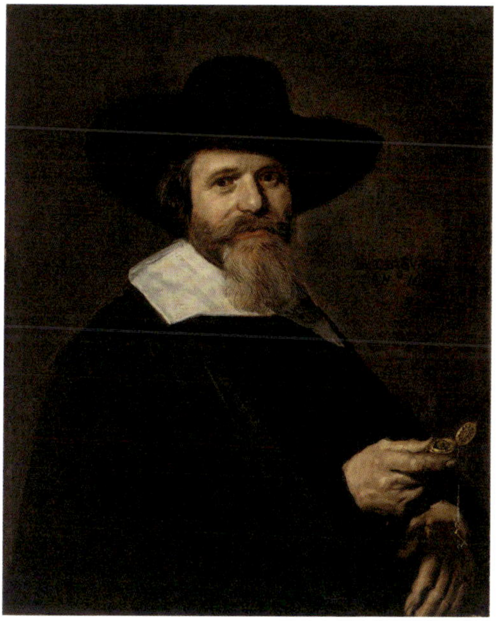

**FRANS HALS (DUTCH, C. 1581–1666)**
***PORTRAIT OF A MAN HOLDING A WATCH***
1643. Oil on canvas, 32½ × 26¼ in. (82.6 × 66.7 cm). BF262

The identity of this bearded man long eluded scholars. There are few identifying features, and his subdued clothing lacks the showy white cuffs that signified prosperity in the Dutch city of Haarlem, where the artist Frans Hals worked. Recent scholarship proposes the sitter is Mathijs Jansz Boeckels, a prominent Mennonite watchmaker in Haarlem. The dark and restrained wardrobe is one clue. Another is the timepiece. Hals used attributes sparingly in his portraits, so the inclusion of a golden watch in an otherwise simple portrait signifies its importance to the sitter.

An inscription to the right of the beard indicates that Mathijs was fifty-seven when the portrait was made. Hals painted Mathijs's wife, Maria Bastiaens van Hout, that same year. Though not yet identified, the husband-and-wife portraits were put up for auction together or sold as a pair until 1928, when Dr. Barnes purchased this work. The other portrait now belongs to the Nationalmuseum, Stockholm.

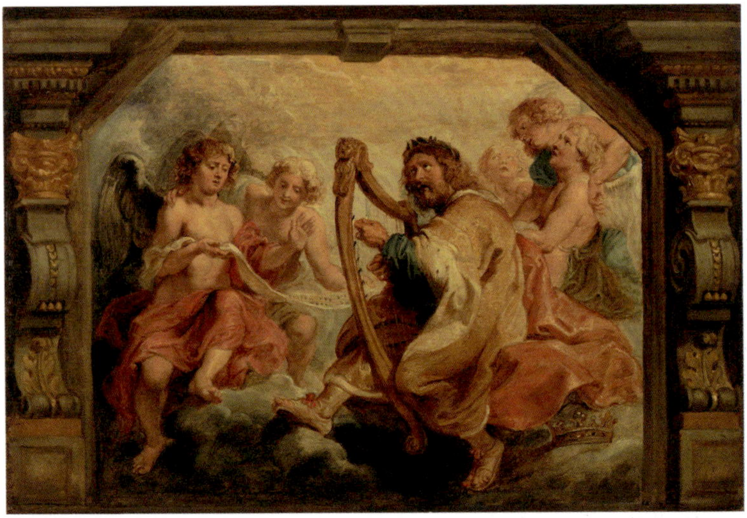

**PETER PAUL RUBENS (FLEMISH, 1577–1640)**
***KING DAVID PLAYING THE HARP***
c. 1627–28. Oil on panel, 17⅝ × 26 in. (44.8 × 66 cm). BF812

In the 1620s, Rubens designed a twenty-part tapestry series, *The Triumph of the Eucharist*, for Isabel Clara Eugenia (1566–1633), daughter of King Philip II of Spain and governor general of the Spanish Netherlands. Rubens, her court painter, created *modelli* (preparatory studies) for the tapestry weavers in Brussels to follow. This study captures David, the second king of Israel, playing his harp, performing the music of heaven in concert with five angels. Although the painting is quite small, the ornate architecture framing the figures creates a sense of monumentality.

Isabel ruled the Spanish Netherlands during a period of religious unrest. The elaborate commission aimed to strengthen and glorify the Roman Catholic Church; during important celebrations, the tapestries would be used to decorate the austere church of the Convent of the Descalzas Reales in Madrid, where the royal family attended mass. Tapestry was one of the most expensive art forms in the early seventeenth century, and the project's scope and size (the eleven main panels were nearly 16½ × 25 feet) represented an important act of patronage and piety by the ruler.

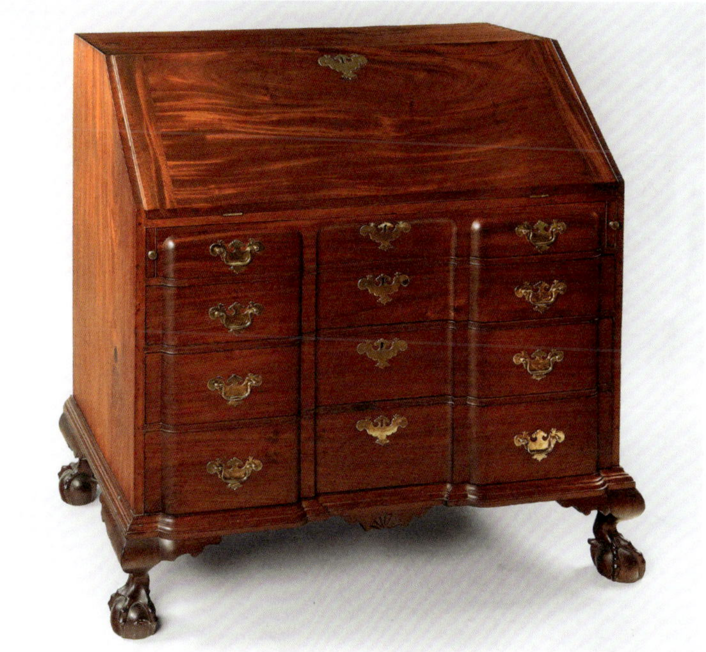

***BLOCKFRONT CHEST OF DRAWERS* (AMERICAN)**
Unidentified maker. 1760s. Mahogany, pine, and copper alloy; 44¾ × 41 × 21¼ in. (113.7 × 104.1 × 54 cm). 01.05.34

Albert Barnes was partial to Pennsylvania German furniture, but he collected fine examples of other American colonial pieces. This chest of drawers was probably made in Boston, where the slant front's swirled mahogany grain was fashionable. The hinged lid flips down to create a writing surface and reveal four pigeonholes (tiny compartments), several drawers, and a small door with an inlaid eagle medallion. The eagle motif was likely added in the early twentieth century to make the piece more desirable to collectors. The brass fittings and hinges, however, are original.

Below the hinged front are four wide drawers that curve in at the middle and curve out at both ends. Furniture with this type of blocking façade was popular in New England during the late eighteenth century and considered a sign of style and wealth. The cabriole legs and carved claw-and-ball feet add to the sense of luxury.

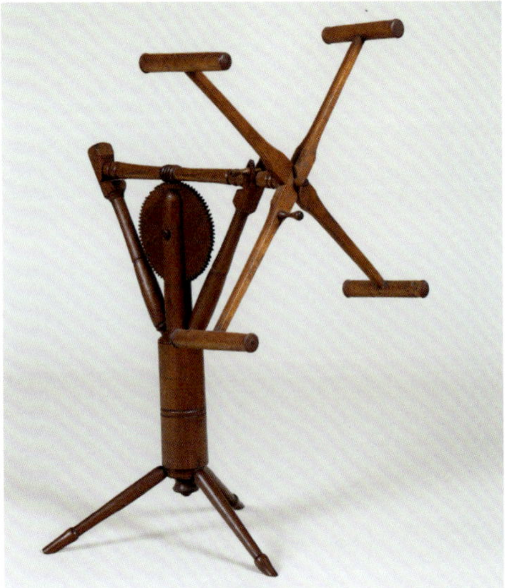

**YARN WINDER (AMERICAN)**
Unidentified maker. Late 18th–early 19th century. Ash and walnut, 49 × 23 × 20 in. (124.5 × 58.4 × 50.8 cm). 01.05.38

This windmill-style device was used for gathering and measuring lengths of yarn. The material would be draped around the ends of the four arms, which rotated on the horizontal shaft to form a loose coil called a skein. The "worm gear" in the middle of this shaft would spin the large, vertical clock reel on the stand. The reel had a set of gears that recorded each revolution of the arms with a loud "click." The person doing the winding knew the length of the yarn by counting the clicks.

Although the yarn winder was conceived as a functional object, Dr. Barnes also saw aesthetic value in its form. Its three turned legs, clock reel, and other vertical and horizontal components are balanced by a three-legged wooden candle stand displayed along the same wall. The device's humanlike appearance also relates to the ensemble's uppermost metalwork concoction: two hinges and a hasp arranged to resemble a person with arms thrown back in surprise. Likewise, the yarn winder establishes visual echoes—as well as conceptual connections with wood—with elements of the two paintings immediately above: the Christ in Gerard David's *Crucifixion* and the leaning trees in Cézanne's *Four Bathers*.

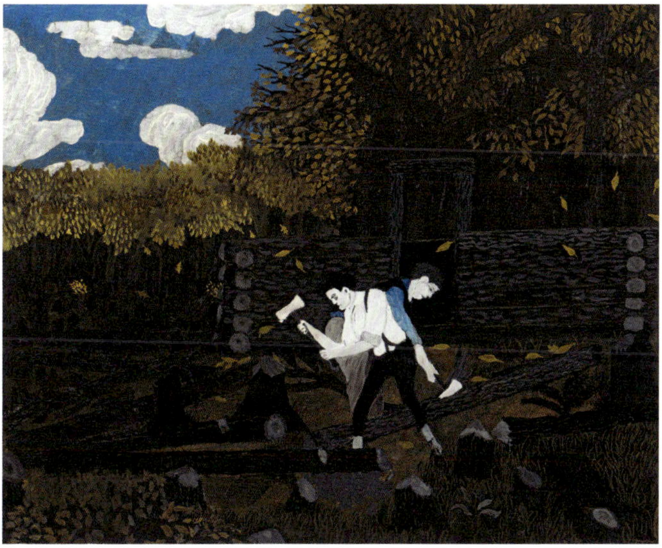

**HORACE PIPPIN (AMERICAN, 1888–1946)**
***ABRAHAM LINCOLN AND HIS FATHER BUILDING THEIR CABIN ON PIGEON CREEK***
c. 1934. Oil on fabric (later mounted to composition board), 16¼ × 20¼ in. (41.3 × 51.4 cm). BF978

When Abraham Lincoln was about seven years old, he moved with his family to a wooded land claim near Little Pigeon Creek in Indiana. This painting depicts young Lincoln in a white shirt helping his father clear the land and build the family's log cabin, partially constructed in the background. Lincoln appears to be an adolescent rather than a young boy in this picture; he comfortably wields an ax, a detail that may allude to the strength and skills he would develop growing up in this frontier town.

This picture is one of four by Pippin depicting moments in Lincoln's life. The series was part of a larger body of Depression-era arts and literature that portrayed Lincoln as a mythic figure in American history and in the collective imagination of African Americans. Dr. Barnes bought this work before Pippin's first solo exhibition in 1940 at the Robert Carlen Galleries in Philadelphia, where it was displayed as belonging to the Barnes Foundation. He subsequently invited Pippin to visit the institution, and the artist briefly enrolled in a class there.

# ROOM 6

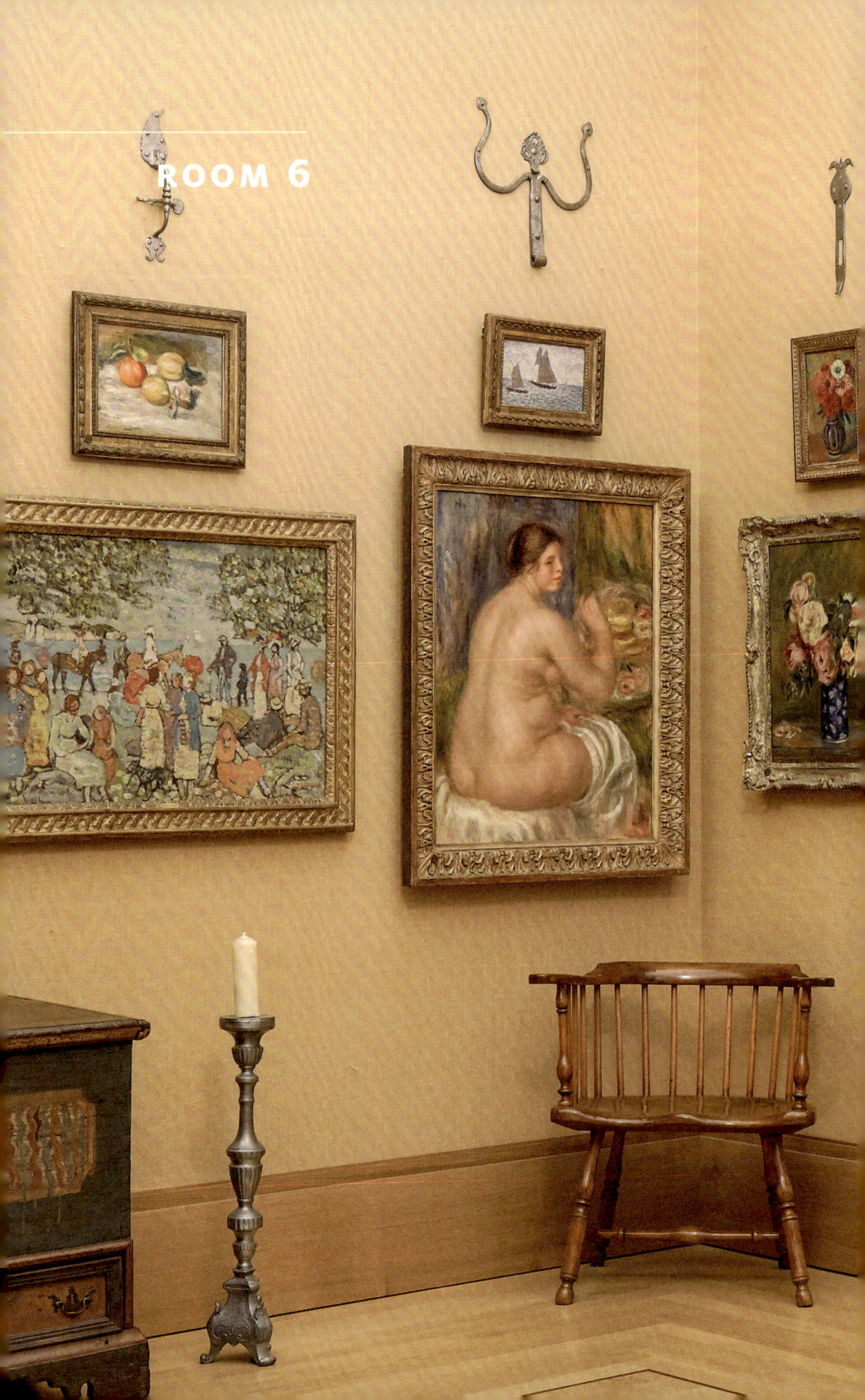

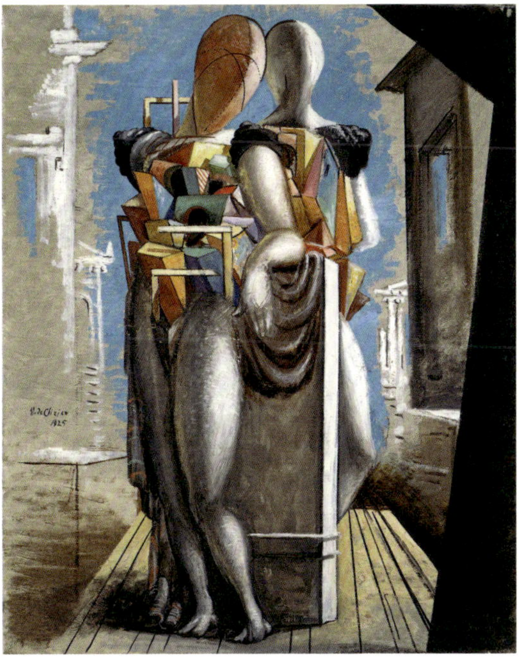

**GIORGIO DE CHIRICO (ITALIAN, 1888–1978)**
***SOPHOCLES AND EURIPIDES***
1925. Oil on canvas, 28 ⅞ × 23 ¾ in. (73.3 × 60.3 cm). BF575

The faceless mannequins against a stagelike backdrop represent the ancient Greek playwrights Sophocles and Euripides. De Chirico, who was Italian but born in Greece, often turned to ancient Greek myth and tragedy for inspiration; he painted several works on similar themes from World War I through the 1920s. By 1925, De Chirico had also started designing sets and costumes for ballet companies in Paris.

In contrast with earlier works, the mannequins here have a more fleshy, human quality—the front figure, for example, has a fully articulated arm and hand. The coloring of the limbs, however, evokes classical marble sculpture. Curiously, their torsos are made up of architectural structures and instruments, turning these rational forms into an irrational accumulation of ornament. De Chirico inspired many Surrealists, and he was briefly associated with the movement for his own mysterious, dreamlike images that combined disparate objects and symbols.

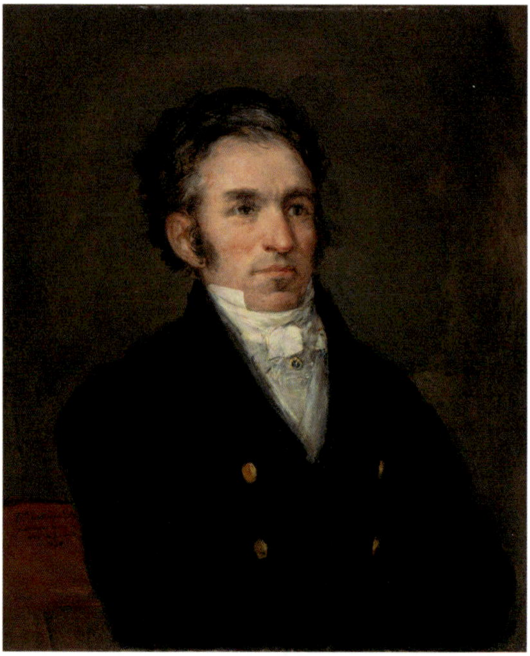

**FRANCISCO DE GOYA (SPANISH, 1746–1828)**
***PORTRAIT OF JACQUES GALOS***
1826. Oil on canvas, 21¾ × 18¼ in. (55.2 × 46.4 cm). BF5

Citing illness and his hope to find a cure, Goya left his home near Madrid for France in 1824. His motivation was also political; the Spanish monarchy had made life difficult for liberals. Settling in Bordeaux, where he continued his work as a painter and printmaker, the artist found himself part of a thriving expatriate community.

Jacques Galos, shown here in a starched collar and cravat, became one of Goya's friends. He won the artist's trust and, as director of the city's bank, took responsibility for arranging Goya's inheritance to his grandson Mariano. As was often the case in Goya's later years, during which his productivity slowed, the artist inscribed this painting with his age. The flushed cheeks and arresting gaze of the sitter show that, at eighty, the painter had lost none of his flair.

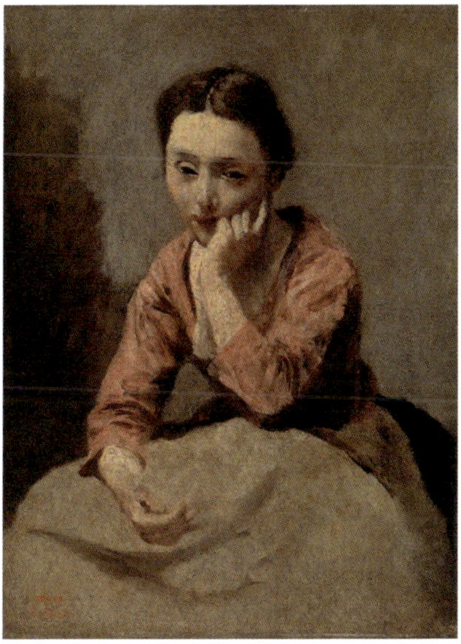

**JEAN-BAPTISTE-CAMILLE COROT (FRENCH, 1796–1875)**

***PENSIVE YOUNG WOMAN***

1855–60. Oil on panel (later mounted to plywood), 12½ × 9 5/16 in. (31.8 × 23.7 cm). BF822

This somber-colored portrait shows a young woman deep in thought. Comparable to other works by Corot done around this time, the background here features almost no detail and is painted instead in broad swaths of grayish brown. The young woman is depicted in muted tones of pink and brown. It is her eyes, lost in thought and dark against the faint blush of her cheeks, that mark the most intense color in the painting. The figure sits with her knees drawn up, her skirt creating a monumental abstracted form in the foreground. She rests one arm against her thigh; her fingers curl gently upward. The woman's other hand is held against her face, her chin against the palm of her hand, her index finger resting along her jaw. This pose was often used by artists to suggest the concept of melancholy, which was itself linked to the idea of artistic creativity, and it features regularly in Corot's later works. Renowned first as a landscape painter who worked outdoors, the artist turned in the last fifteen years of his life to melancholic portraits of women, such as this one, made in his Parisian studio.

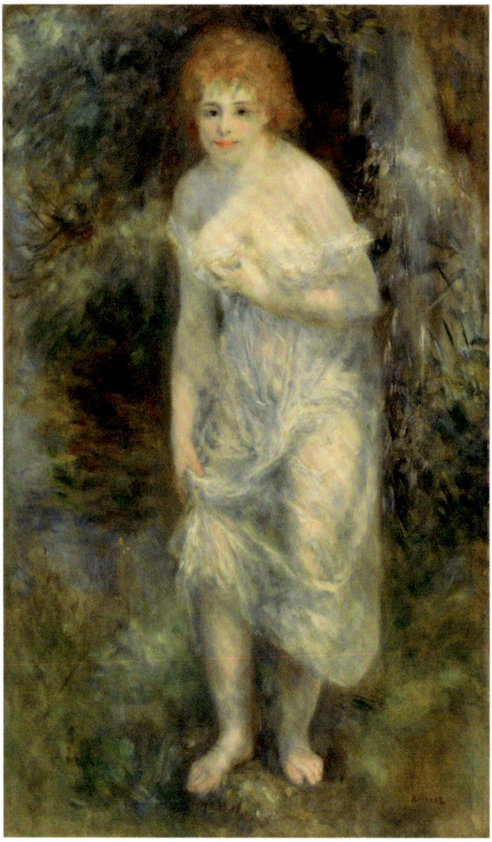

**PIERRE-AUGUSTE RENOIR (FRENCH, 1841–1919)**

***THE SOURCE***

1875. Oil on canvas, 51 9/16 × 30 ½ in. (131 × 77.5 cm). BF908

This light-drenched painting of a female bather would have shocked audiences in Renoir's time. Artists typically portrayed skin as smooth and even; here it is built up roughly and with multiple pastel shades. That the model clutches her undergarment to her damp body would also have caused a sensation. It suggests this is a modern woman who has just bathed in a stream, rather than a fictional nymph or goddess.

Although most viewers would not have known the model's identity—Renoir exhibited the painting with its current, generic title—Henriette Henriot was the woman who posed for the work. Henriot was one of the artist's favorite sitters and appears in several of his early paintings. This was a rare acquisition of an early Renoir on the part of Dr. Barnes, who generally preferred the artist's later work.

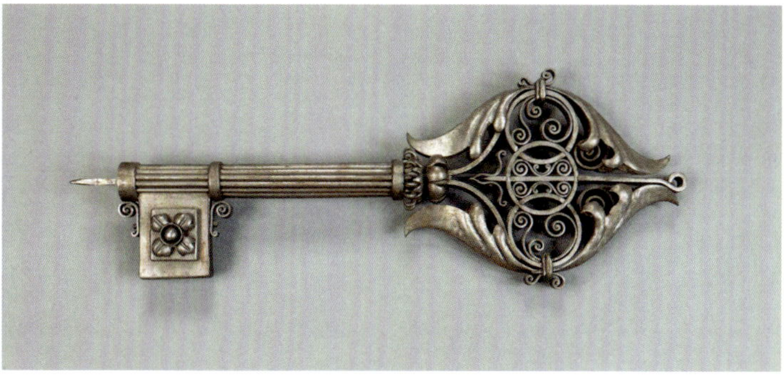

***SIGN FOR A LOCKSMITH*** **(FRENCH)**
Unidentified maker. 18th–early 19th century. Iron, 24⅛ × 8⅝ × 2⅝ in. (61.3 × 21.9 × 6.7 cm). 01.06.28

This monumental wrought-iron "key," measuring about two feet in length, was made as a sign for a locksmith's shop in France. The looped end of the stake extending from its head would have served to hang it vertically. Shaped signs have been in use since antiquity and proliferated through the 1700s, when their use was somewhat curbed by street numbering, introduced in France in 1720 and systematized under Napoleon from 1805.

The key's elaborate decoration advertised the metalworking skills of the shop owner. The junction of its head and fluted stem resembles a budding flower. Its head features three overlapping circles, inside of which tendrils curl into delicate spirals in a virtuoso display of metal forging. Areas of repoussé (low relief created by hammering the metal from the reverse) are seen in the four-petal flower adorning the bit and in the border around the head, where the metal is molded into sculptural shapes that surround the circles like leaves. The key's elegant design upholds Dr. Barnes's proclamation that "the motives, such as arabesques, patterns, etc., discernable in a picture have their analogue...in the iron work....We regard the creators of antique wrought iron just as authentic an artist as Titian, Renoir, or Cézanne."

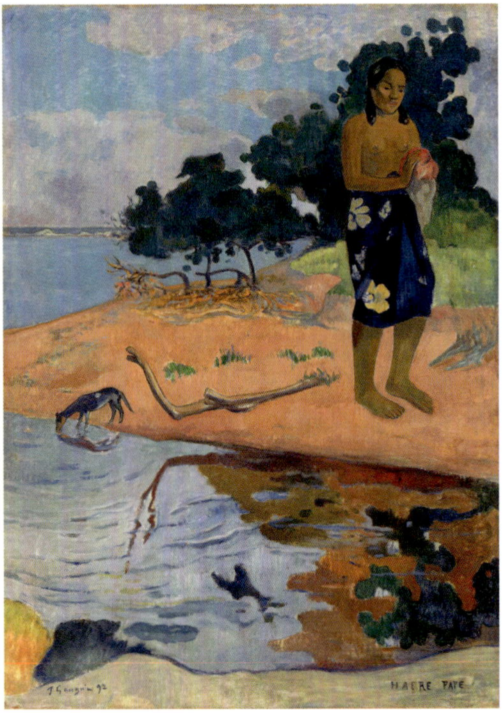

**PAUL GAUGUIN (FRENCH, 1848–1903)**

***HAERE PAPE***

1892. Oil on canvas, 36 × 26½ in. (91.4 × 67.3 cm). BF109

A young woman stands by the water, barefoot, wearing a Tahitian pareo around her waist. Gauguin did not paint from a live model here but, as was his practice, combined different elements for maximum visual impact. Her distinctive hand gesture, which appears in many of the artist's works, can be found on an ancient Javanese frieze of which Gauguin owned a photograph. Heightened colors and strong outlines further enhance his vision of Tahiti as an otherworldly place.

Dreaming of an escape from the Western world—and from the constraints of middle-class married life—Gauguin set sail for Tahiti in 1891. To his disappointment, he discovered that many Tahitians, through coercion or choice (Tahiti was then a French colony), had adopted European forms of dress and religion. Faithful to his colonialist fantasy, however, he created images in which eroticized Tahitian women appear in perfect harmony with the fecundity of nature. He attempted to give his works Tahitian titles, though many—including this one—are misspelled or approximated. "Haere pape," roughly translated, means "she goes down to the fresh water."

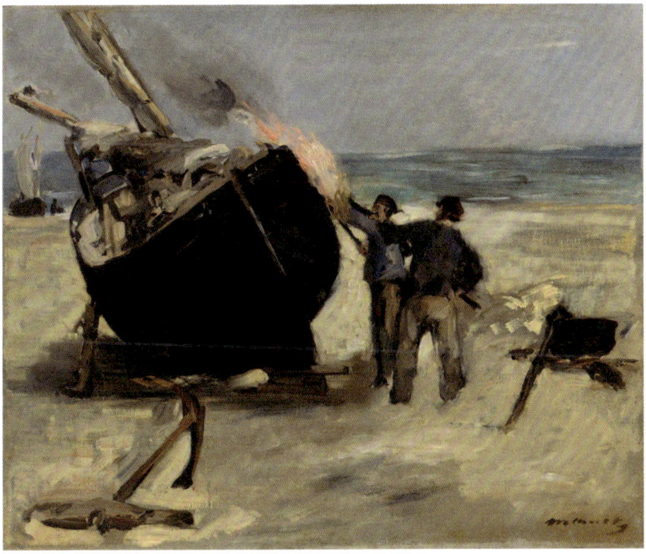

**ÉDOUARD MANET (FRENCH, 1832–1883)**
***TARRING THE BOAT***
July–August 1873. Oil on canvas, 19 11⁄16 × 24 1⁄8 in. (50 × 61.2 cm). BF166

During a family visit to the coastal village of Berck-sur-Mer, in northern France, Manet depicted local fishermen maintaining their boats. Smoke billows into the air as they apply flaming tar to make the vessel watertight. In other areas, this task would have taken place in a port; in the absence of one, the fishermen of Berck-sur-Mer beached their flat-bottomed vessels on the sand. Clearly captivated by the contrasts of rich blacks against the soft beige and blue of sand and sky, Manet rendered the scene with energetic brushwork. Many years later, when Dr. Barnes acquired the painting, he was probably attracted to its dynamic composition. However, he may also have known that it was admired beyond his immediate circle. The painting had been mentioned in critic Théodore Duret's 1902 monograph on Manet. In 1923 it was singled out by the respected art critic Waldemar-George in an article about the Barnes Foundation for the French-language newspaper *L'Ère nouvelle*.

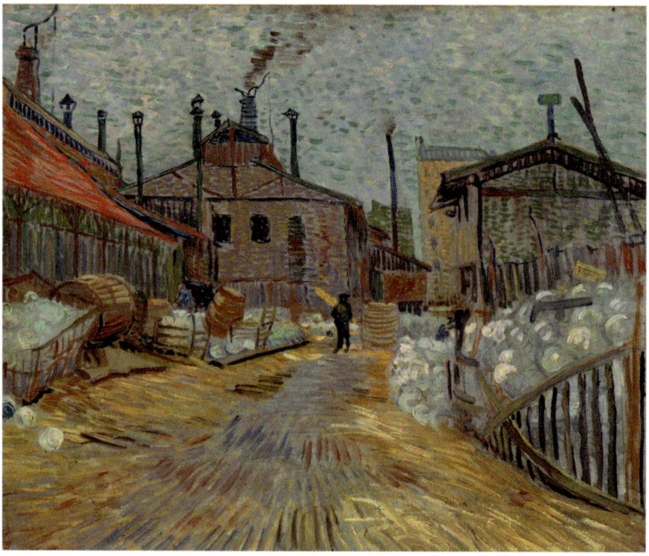

**VINCENT VAN GOGH (DUTCH, 1853–1890)**
***THE FACTORY***
July–September 1887. Oil on canvas, 18⅛ × 21⅞ in. (46 × 55.6 cm). BF303

Balls of glass, stacked beside the roadway, identify the building in this painting as a factory that made lantern globes for streetlights. It is the Verrierie du Pont du Clichy (Clichy Bridge Glass Factory), which was situated on the outskirts of Paris (in the district of Clichy) and employed around 130 people. The scene here is of the factory forecourt, filled with barrels and wicker baskets. A lone worker, walking away from the viewer, centers the busy composition.

The factory, which opened in 1866, also made soda bottles and glass ornaments. Dark smoke, billowing into the dappled blue sky, indicates the activity within its walls. Manufacturing had expanded rapidly in late nineteenth-century France, which made sights like this a novelty for adventurous artists. Van Gogh made several paintings of the industrial landscape, in Clichy and in neighboring Asnières, where his friend Émile Bernard had a studio.

# ROOM 7

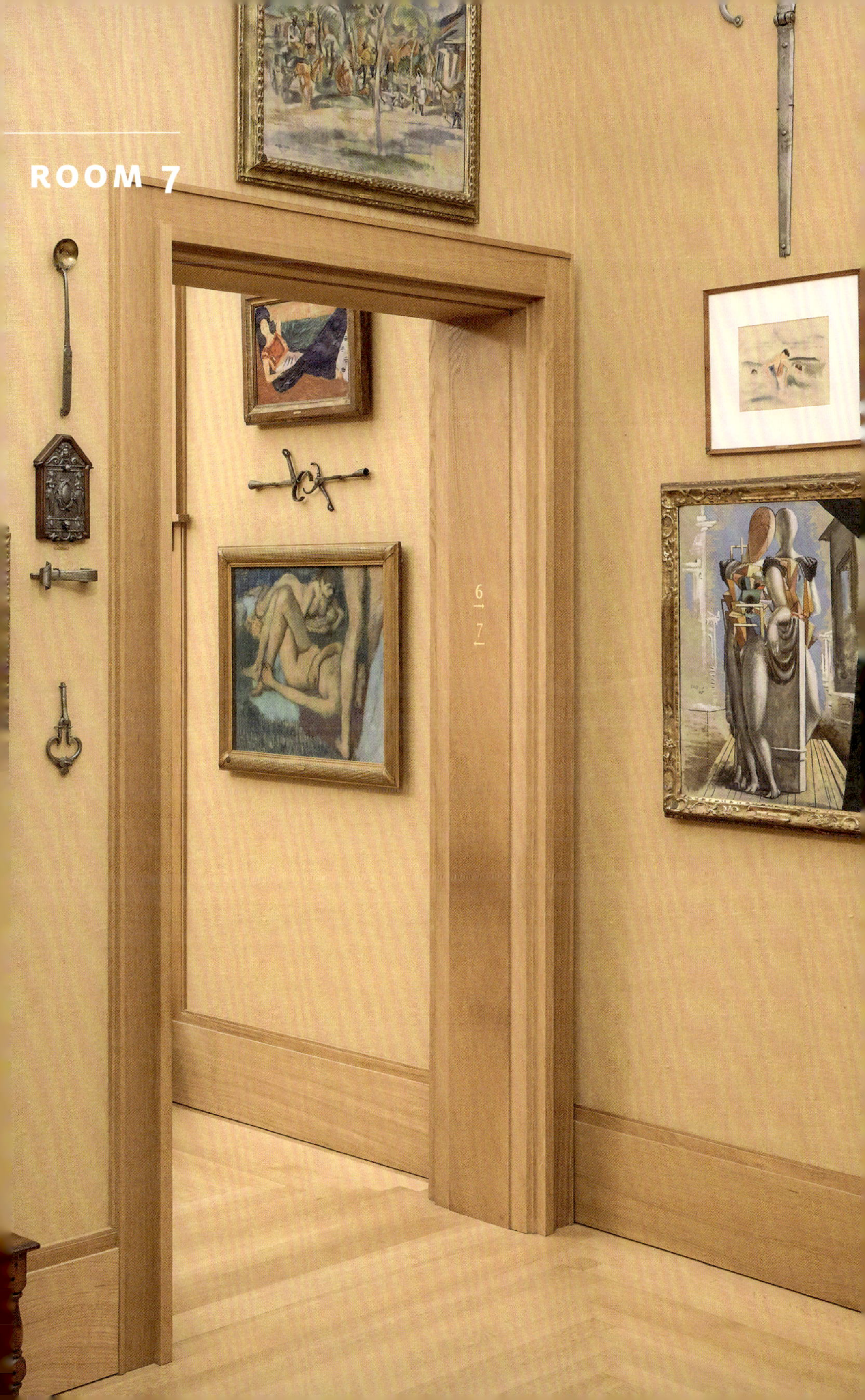

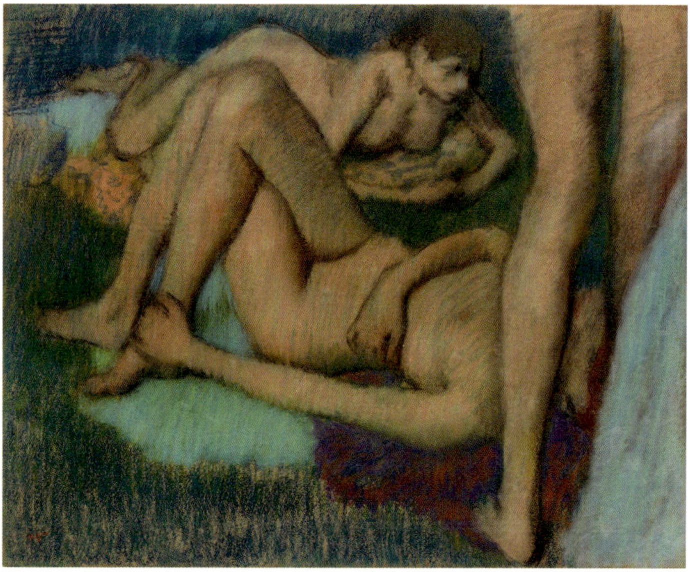

**EDGAR DEGAS (FRENCH, 1834–1917)**
***BATHERS***
1895–1900. Pastel with charcoal underdrawing on wove paper, 23¼ × 29 in. (59.1 × 73.7 cm). BF153

Throughout his career, Degas maintained an interest in the subject of female bathers, addressing the theme in paintings, drawings, pastels, prints, and sculpture. While his works from the 1870s and 1880s placed figures primarily in interiors—specifically bedrooms and brothels—pastels from the second half of the 1890s, like this one, tend to have more ambiguous settings.

The unusual placement of the figures heightens the strangeness of the scene. The legs of the standing woman obscure the face of the model stretched out at her feet, while the most visible of the group—lying on her stomach—is confined to the background. Degas's interest in photography, a medium that was advancing rapidly in the late nineteenth century, may have influenced his decision to create such a radical composition. His use of color here is equally bold: warm flesh tones contrast sharply with the surrounding blues and greens.

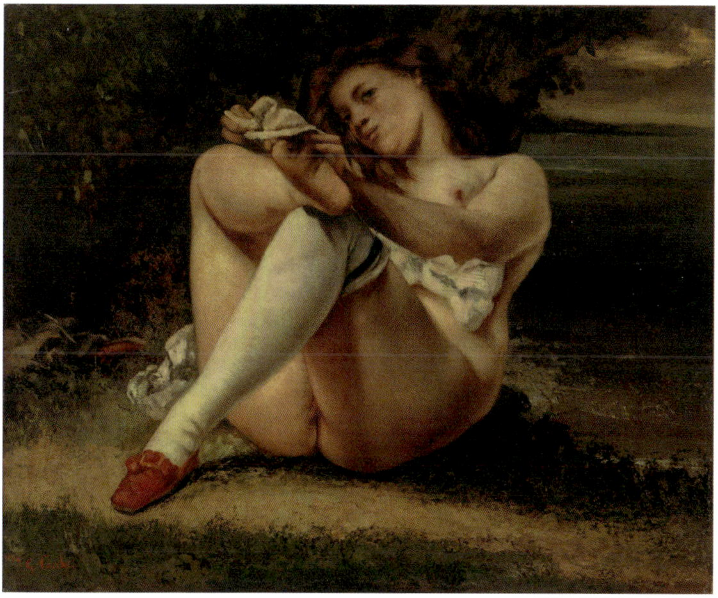

**GUSTAVE COURBET (FRENCH, 1819–1877)**
***WOMAN WITH WHITE STOCKINGS***
1864. Oil on canvas, $25\frac{9}{16} \times 31\frac{7}{8}$ in. (65 × 81 cm). BF810

*Woman with White Stockings* is one of several sexually explicit paintings that Courbet produced during the 1860s. The Turkish diplomat Khalil Bey owned two of them, and while the original owner of this work is unclear, it is likely that Courbet made it similarly as a private commission. The canvas was not exhibited publicly in the artist's lifetime.

The painting shows a half-dressed woman outdoors, wearing nothing but a red shoe and one long stocking. As her naked bottom rests on the dusty ground, her lifted leg reveals a flash of genitalia. The nude looks out directly, implicating the viewer in the encounter and adding to the painting's erotic charge. Some writers have argued that the model was Courbet's lover, Léontine Renaude, but this seems unlikely since Courbet ended his relationship with Renaude in 1862, two years before he completed the picture.

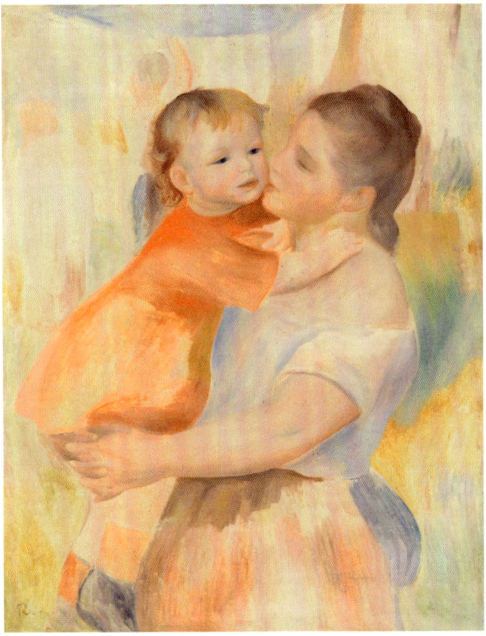

**PIERRE-AUGUSTE RENOIR (FRENCH, 1841–1919)**
***WASHERWOMAN AND CHILD***
1886. Oil on canvas, 32 × 25 9⁄16 in. (81.3 × 65 cm). BF219

The warm embrace of mother and child—she kisses the young boy's face and clasps him gently against her shoulder—and half-length view recall Renaissance images of the Madonna and Child. Here, however, Renoir has depicted his wife, Aline, and their child, Pierre. Renoir admired the fresco works of the Italian artist Raphael, and in this painting he endeavored to create a fresco-like surface by removing oil from the paint, resulting in a flattened, matte appearance. The child's eyes and the woman's arms reflect the hooded eyes and softly modeled flesh of figures by the nineteenth-century French artist Jean-Auguste-Dominique Ingres. A pastel by Renoir in the Cleveland Museum of Art depicts a similar topic, with a more fully finished background showing another female figure hanging laundry behind mother and child. The sketchy, nearly abstract background of the painted work suggests that Renoir may have left this painting unfinished.

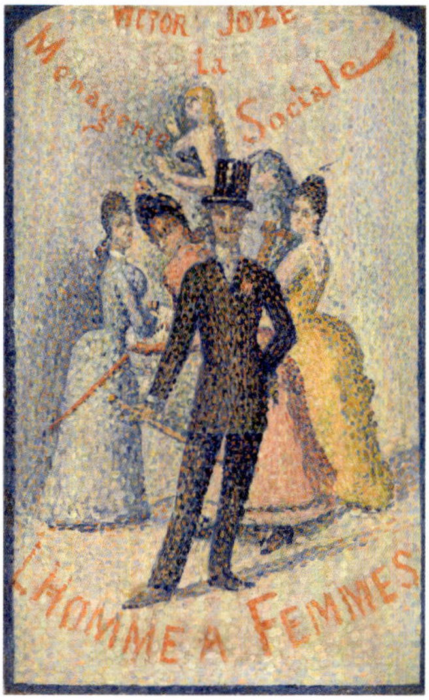


**GEORGES SEURAT (FRENCH, 1859–1891)**
***THE LADIES' MAN***
1890. Oil on panel, 9 13⁄16 × 6 5⁄16 in. (25 × 16 cm). BF1149

This small painting began as a cover design for *L'homme à femmes (The Ladies' Man)*, a novel by the Polish writer Victor Joze that took a satirical look at Parisian society in the late 1800s. Part of a series called "La ménagerie sociale" (which translates roughly as "Society Is a Circus"), the book tells the story of a writer and his scandalous relations with a number of women, including a prostitute, an actress, and a singer. In keeping with the book, Seurat made fun of his subjects, showing the central figure with a broad grin, top hat, and phallic cane. A troupe of admiring women steal glances at him, the figure in red straining to get a better view.

Though he made this painting first, Seurat went on to produce a similar but monochrome ink drawing, which served as the book's final cover. A black-and-white design would have been better suited to printing than this subtly colored picture.

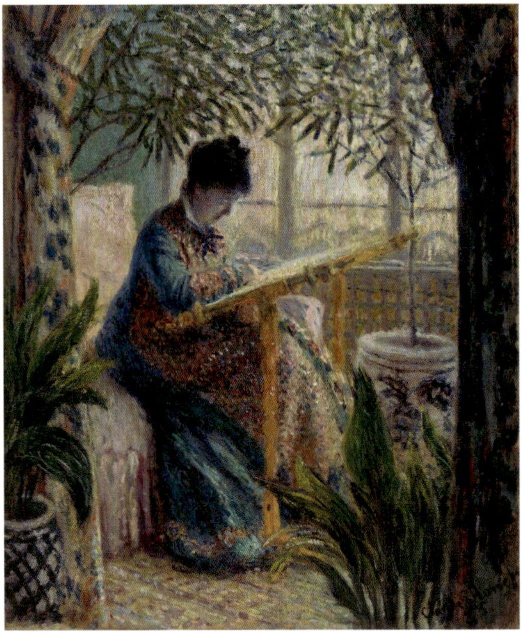

**CLAUDE MONET (FRENCH, 1840–1926)**
***MADAME MONET EMBROIDERING***
1875. Oil on canvas, 25¾ × 22 in. (65.4 × 55.9 cm). BF197

Illuminated by natural light flooding through the gauzy curtained window, Monet's wife, Camille, poses in their rented home in Argenteuil, a suburb of Paris. Verdant plants growing out of blue-and-white ceramic pots frame the tranquil scene. The intersecting grids of the window panes, wall, rug, and needlework stand create a sense of stability and structure.

Monet seldom painted figures in interiors, but here the artist may have hoped to update a time-honored theme. In the seventeenth century, painters in the Netherlands created many idyllic scenes of women engrossed in sewing and other domestic activities. He may also have been prompted by his friend Renoir, who frequently visited the Monets in Argenteuil and depicted Camille several times wearing this same ornately embroidered dress. Monet paints Camille set back through an archway of curtains, as if he is loath to disturb this quiet, intimate space.

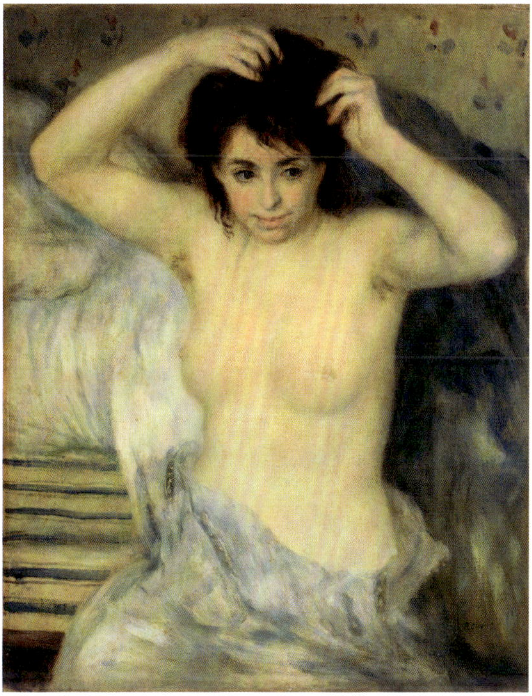

**PIERRE-AUGUSTE RENOIR (FRENCH, 1841–1919)**
***BEFORE THE BATH***
c. 1875. Oil on canvas, 32 5⁄16 × 26 3⁄16 in. (82 × 66.5 cm). BF9

Renoir depicts a young woman, partially undressed, arms raised above her head to undo her coiffure. She sits against a bed, whose striped sheet interjects a horizontal contrast to the diagonal arrangement of her arms. Above the woman, a strip of flowered wallpaper further encloses the intimate domestic space. The softly sculpted form evokes ancient Greek statuary. Possibly the model Henriette Henriot, the woman nevertheless remains an anonymous sign of feminine beauty.

A year after the impressionists' first exhibition, held in 1874 and organized outside of the strictures of the accepted exhibiting societies, the group again scandalized the Paris art world. The focus of critical ire this time was an auction organized by art dealer Paul Durand-Ruel at the Hôtel Drouot on March 23 and 24 and featuring works by the key impressionists, including Claude Monet, Berthe Morisot, and Renoir. *Before the Bath* was among the works auctioned. Despite its nod to classical beauty and composition, the painting was poorly received. Underneath the figure's arms, slight tufts of hair emerge—a shockingly everyday detail for viewers accustomed to sanitized nudity.

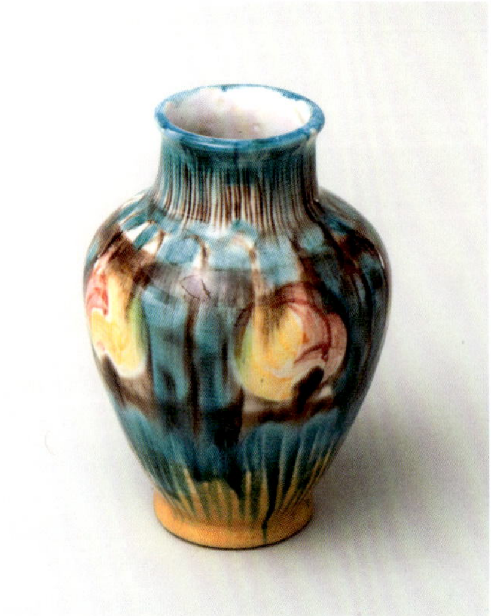

**JEAN RENOIR (FRENCH, 1894–1979)**
***VASE***
1919–22. Tin-glazed earthenware with polychrome decoration, 10⅛ × 7¼ in. (25.7 × 18.4 cm). 01.07.62

Jean Renoir, son of the artist Pierre-Auguste Renoir, made his name as a film director. Before forging a career in the movie business, however, he was a talented ceramicist. Working at Les Collettes, the Renoir family estate in the South of France, he created dozens of handmade earthenware pots. His father—who had begun his own career decorating ceramics—installed a kiln and encouraged Jean to use the clay from the surrounding fields.

Dr. Barnes bought forty-two of Jean's pieces, in two batches, between 1921 and 1922. Today, no other collection holds as many. The art dealer Paul Durand-Ruel, who sold them to Barnes, described them as "old country porcelains, quite rough." Given Barnes's later interest in Pennsylvania redware pottery, and his profound love of Pierre-Auguste Renoir's painting, it is easy to see why these ceramics appealed. They combine simple, solid form with layered, painterly glazes.

# ROOM 8

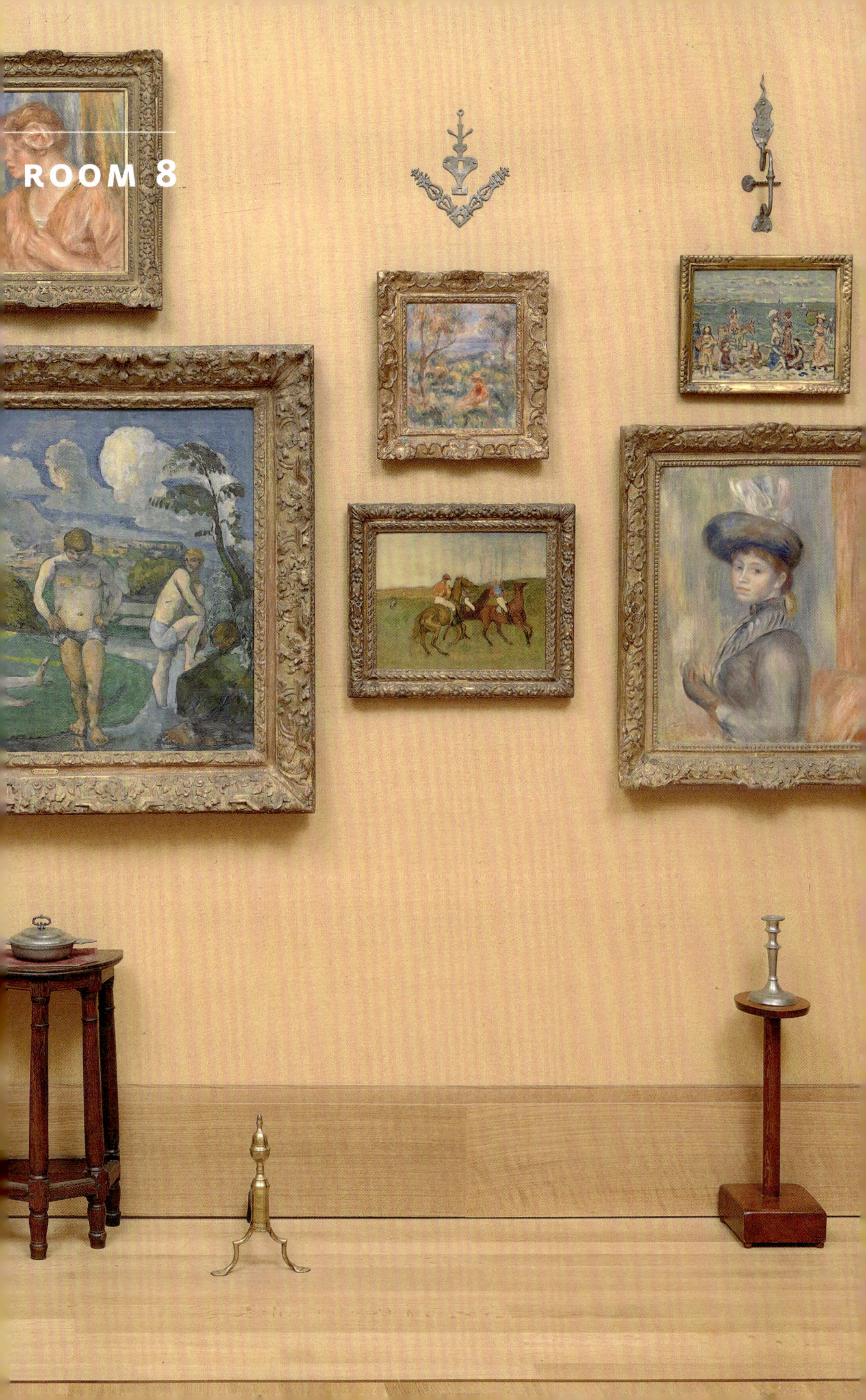

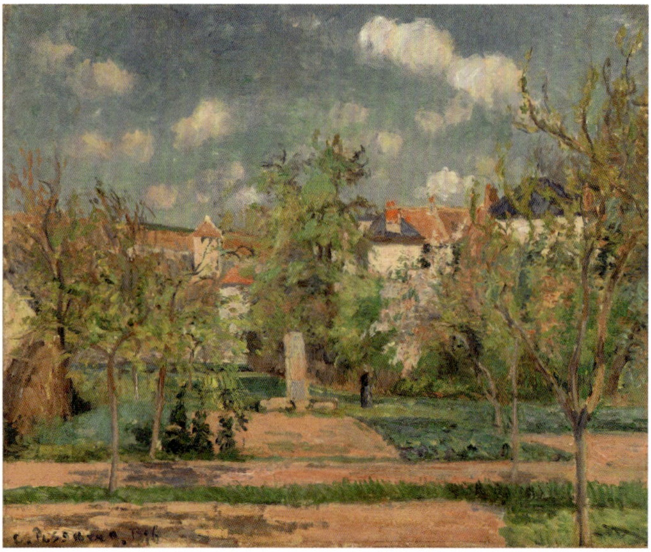

**CAMILLE PISSARRO (FRENCH, 1831–1903)**
***GARDEN IN FULL SUNLIGHT***
1876. Oil on canvas, 18 5⁄16 × 21 7⁄16 in. (46.5 × 54.4 cm). BF324

From 1866 to 1883, Pissarro lived in the provincial town of Pontoise, not far from Paris. Although Pontoise was characterized by extremes of wealth and poverty, Pissarro chose to use the location to create a variety of harmonized scenes in what was at this time a radical "impressionist" style of painting, characterized by loose, flickering brushwork. Here, surrounded by lush foliage, a solitary figure stands against a backdrop of buildings. Nature and modern life appear in unison, with the tamed garden complementing the neat new houses.

Pissarro's love of different light effects is particularly evident in his sun-dappled rendition of the earth in the foreground. Fluffy white clouds, created with loose, curved brushstrokes, punctuate the blue sky above.

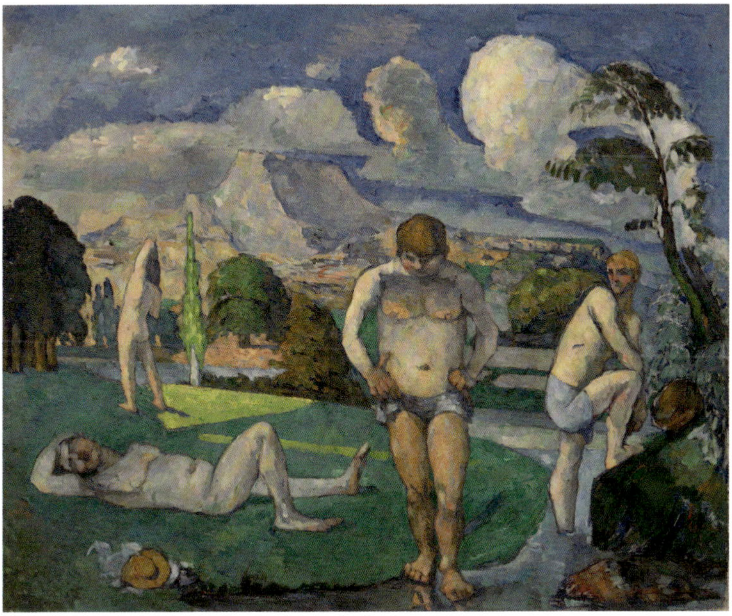

**PAUL CÉZANNE (FRENCH, 1839–1906)**
***BATHERS AT REST***
1876–77. Oil on canvas, 32 3/8 × 39 13/16 in. (82.2 × 101.2 cm). BF906

In this painting—shown in the Third Impressionist Exhibition in 1877—Cézanne depicts a group of bathers in a Provençal landscape. He would return to the theme toward the end of his life in works including *The Large Bathers* (see page 30). Against the backdrop of Mont Sainte-Victoire—one of the artist's favorite motifs—a group of men appear in various states of undress. Bathing in rivers and streams was common in the region, but it is unlikely that Cézanne painted the scene from life. He had taken every opportunity to paint outdoors on his many excursions with Camille Pissarro in the 1870s, but gradually lost interest in capturing atmospheric effects. Here the emphasis is on structure; even the clouds appear solid.

The picture confused critics at the time, and it has attracted different interpretations ever since. The ambiguous gender of the reclining figure, for instance, has prompted speculation about the artist's sexuality. Despite their proximity, the relationship between the figures in the painting is unclear, as each looks in a different direction.

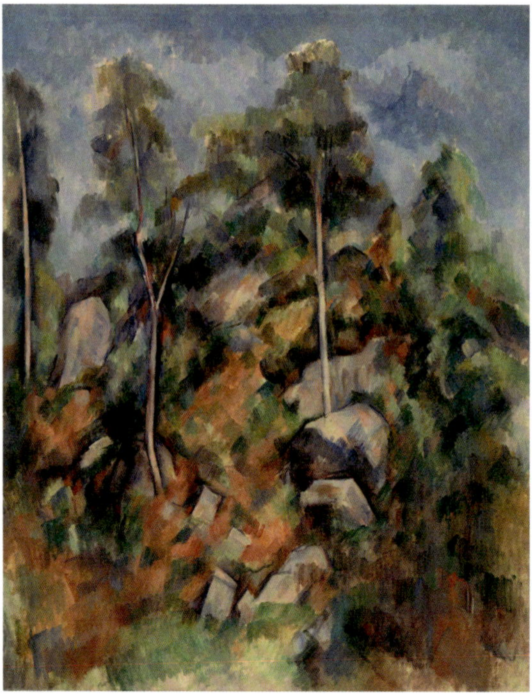

**PAUL CÉZANNE (FRENCH, 1839–1906)**

***ROCKS AND TREES***

c. 1904–5. Oil on canvas, 32 3/16 × 26 in. (81.8 × 66 cm). BF286

The vertical composition of this landscape emphasizes the steep rocky hill and tall pine trees. It may have been painted near the Château Noir, a neo-Gothic castle with views of Mont Sainte-Victoire in Provence, or within the forest of Fontainbleau, an area southeast of Paris. The painting bears comparison to two others in the Barnes collection, those of the rock quarry Bibémus located to the east of Aix-en-Provence—*Bibémus* and *Bibémus Quarry*—where Cézanne rented a *cabanon*, or small rustic shack, around 1895. The rock-strewn hillside in this painting is made up of short brushstrokes of green and orange, broken up by the gray, blue, and pink of the stone and its shadows. These "constructive brushstrokes," a style the artist had developed by the late 1870s, are layered and vary in direction to render the forms and structure of the objects and the space around them.

Cézanne's interest in geology is evident through his careful depiction of rocks and their surroundings in roughly thirty canvases. The landscape of Provence, where he spent much of his career, allowed for this exploration, as it was scattered with defunct quarries like Bibémus and overgrown with lush green pines, red earth, and rocky ridges.

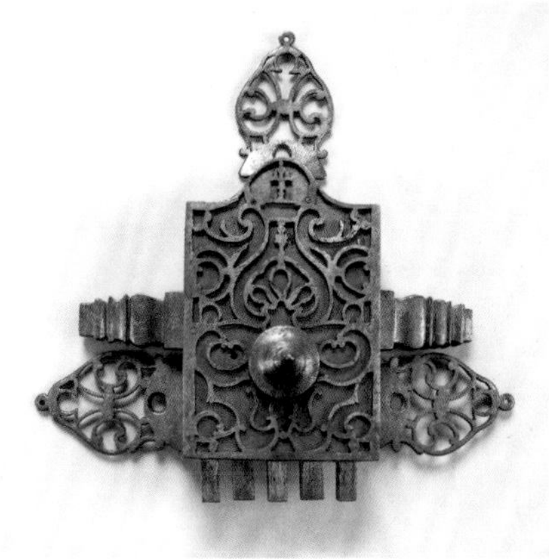

***LOCK* (FRENCH)**
Unidentified maker. c. 1700. Iron, 10⅝ × 11¼ × 3⅜ in. (27 × 28.6 × 8.6 cm). 01.08.46

An unknown locksmith may have made this mechanism—which serves no function beyond decoration—to meet the entry requirements of a locksmiths' guild. "Masterpiece locks" proved a maker's skill, and this intricate piece would have been challenging to produce.

There is no record of Dr. Barnes's thoughts on the lock, but as with many items in his metalwork collection, he chose to display it in a way that emphasizes symmetry. Shown at this angle, the arched top connects the lock, both visually and structurally, with elements of other works. The support bar that runs through the center also marries form with function. Had the piece been operational, the five bolts on its underside suggest that its position on a door would have been horizontal. Its vertical orientation here sets aside practical considerations in favor of presenting a balanced shape, echoing the form of the wider ensemble.

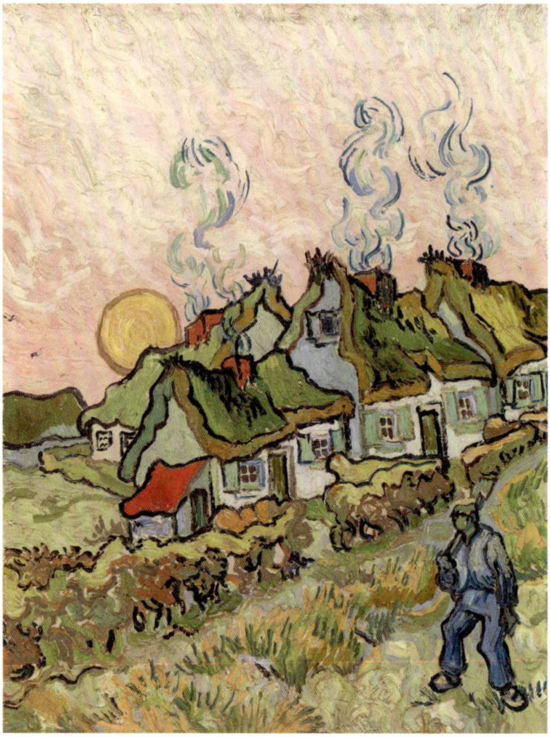

**VINCENT VAN GOGH (DUTCH, 1853–1890)**
***HOUSES AND FIGURE***
1890. Oil on canvas, 20½ × 15 15/16 in. (52 × 40.5 cm). BF136

During the last year of his life, Van Gogh was an asylum patient in Saint-Rémy, France. With limited access to the outdoors, he had to paint what he could see from the window or, as is the case here, picture in his mind. This work recalls his native Netherlands, with thatched cottages dotting the landscape. Van Gogh wrote to his mother and sister: "I continued painting, even when my illness was at its height…a memory of Brabant, hovels with moss-covered roofs and beech hedges on an autumn evening with a stormy sky, the sun setting amid ruddy clouds."

Van Gogh conveys a feverish memory of his younger days with his roiling brushwork, the undulating cottage rooftops, the line of hedges that seems to fall out of the frame, and the disproportionately large figure with his shovel. His description of the autumn sky as "ruddy" may indicate that his original pigment faded to pink over time. This work was formerly in the collection of Dr. Paul Gachet, who took care of the artist after he left the asylum.

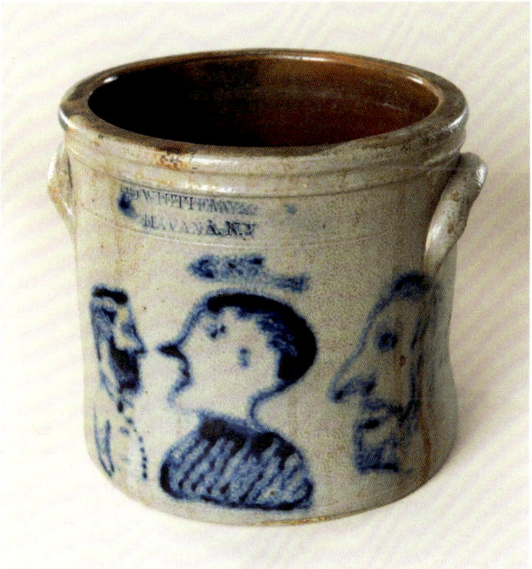

**WHITTEMORE POTTERY (AMERICAN, 1855–1893)**

***CROCK***

1868–75. Salt glazed stoneware, 7 × 8¾ × 8 in. (17.8 × 22.2 × 20.3 cm). 01.08.67

This crock was made in Havana, New York, around the end of the Civil War. A production stamp, noting the maker's name, appears above the central figure's head. Whittemore Pottery supplied stoneware to parts of New York and Pennsylvania, using clay from New Jersey and transporting finished goods by canal. Owned by the entrepreneur Albert O. Whitman, who even rebuilt the factory after a fire in 1862, the company operated for over thirty years.

Crocks were not luxury items. In the late nineteenth century, they were popular storage containers for common household goods. This one would be unremarkable without its decoration, which connects it to the Reconstruction era. In the center is Abraham Lincoln, whose image proliferated across all types of media following his assassination. He faces a bearded Ulysses S. Grant in a buttoned coat. On the right, Robert E. Lee opens his mouth as if to shout, perhaps in reaction to the war's outcome.

## ROOM 9

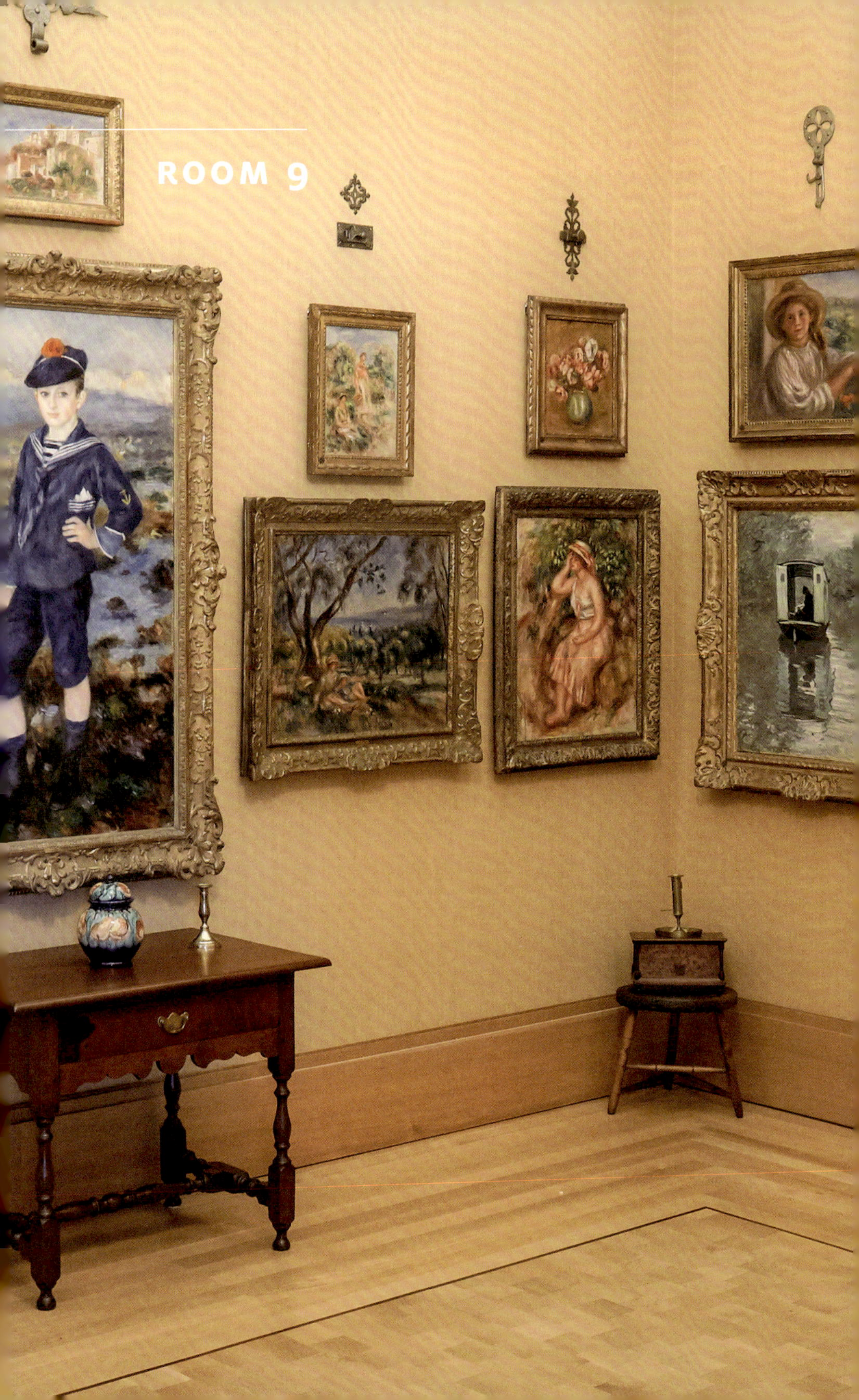

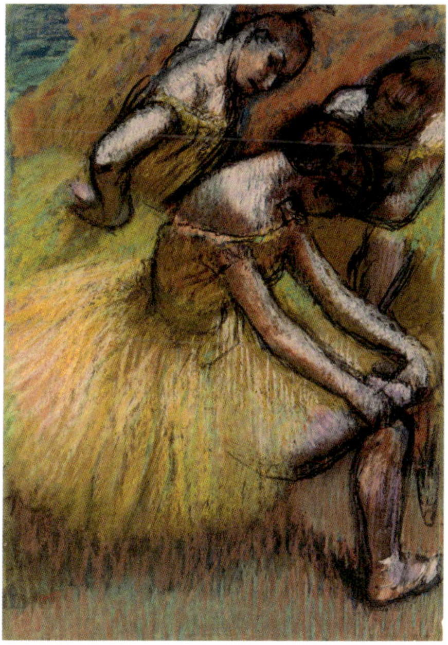

**EDGAR DEGAS (FRENCH, 1834–1917)**
***GROUP OF DANCERS***
c. 1900. Oil pastel on three pieces of paper pieced together and adhered overall to thin paperboard, 22 ¾ × 16 ⅛ in. (57.8 × 41 cm). BF121

Degas had a subscription to the Paris Opera, which gave him behind-the-scenes access. He relished depicting intimate moments offstage as much as the performances onstage. Here, he captures three ballerinas backstage during a performance, stretching and huddled together. Bright stage lighting falls on their bare arms and shoulders. Their torsos emerge from a mass of gauzy, electric-yellow tutus; their arms and legs form a scaffolding for the composition, descending diagonally across the picture plane.

Oil pastel, a preferred medium in Degas's later years, was ideal for describing the delicate fabric of tutus. In the foreground dancer, for example, the artist superimposed lines of yellow, pink, and green to convey light passing through the gossamer layers. Flamboyant colors dominate his late pastels. Here, the expanses of vivid yellow, orange, and blue-green flatten the composition, an effect reinforced by the artist's strong black outlines.

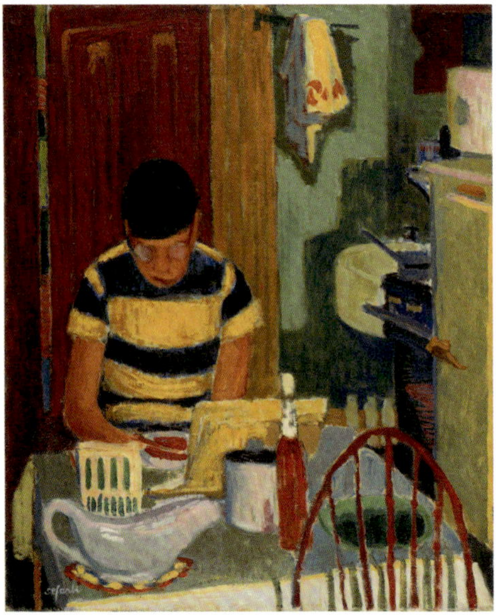

**HARRY SEFARBI (AMERICAN, 1917–2009)**
***INTERIOR: JIM***
1949. Oil on canvas, 24 × 20 in. (61 × 50.8 cm). BF2540

Sefarbi (who also painted under the name Harry Smith) was born in Chester, Pennsylvania, in 1917. A veteran of World War II, he first learned of the Barnes Foundation while enrolled at the Pennsylvania Academy of the Fine Arts (PAFA) in Philadelphia. He was a student at the Barnes from 1947 to 1949. In 1950, he traveled to Europe, spending three and half years in Paris studying art and teaching. Upon his return to the United States in 1953, Violette de Mazia, director of education at the Barnes, offered him a teaching position, which he held until 2008.

In the recollections of former staff members, Sefarbi is often remembered alongside Barton Church, another devoted student and later teacher, who began working at the Barnes in 1952. The works of both artists are some of the last that Dr. Barnes added to his collection. He purchased this painting by Sefarbi in 1950 after its exhibition at PAFA, noting "[it] struck me as one of the three or four in the show that is really a picture—i.e., it carries out an idea, accomplished by intelligent use of the plastic means that gives it an individuality."

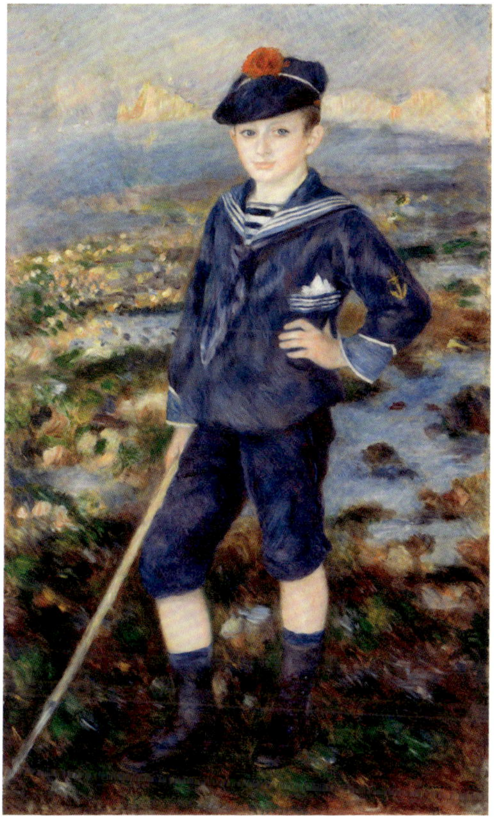

**PIERRE-AUGUSTE RENOIR (FRENCH, 1841–1919)**
***SAILOR BOY (PORTRAIT OF ROBERT NUNÈS)***
1883. Oil on canvas, 51 9/16 × 31½ in. (131 × 80 cm). BF325

Radiating the confidence of a young boy, ten-year-old Robert Nunès stands with his hand against hip and his knee jutting out. He looks directly at the viewer and holds a metal-tipped spear traditionally used to gather oysters. The boy's elaborate sailor costume, with a small embroidered golden anchor on his left sleeve, completes the nautical fantasy. He poses in front of a series of tidal pools fenced in by the cliffs of Fécamp Bay, distantly visible in the painting's background—all described with loose brushwork that contrasts with the more tightly defined figure. The painting's disjuncture between figure and background highlights Renoir's stylistic transition in the mid-1880s, away from a purely impressionist style. Despite the outdoor setting, the portrait was likely painted in a studio with the use of background studies done on site.

Robert was the son of the mayor of Yport, the elder Robert Nunès, a relative of fellow impressionist painter Camille Pissarro. Yport, a small town on the Normandy coast of France, was close to several important impressionist painting sites, notably the beach resort town of Fécamp. Dr. Barnes initially purchased two portraits of the Nunès children, including one of Robert's sister, Aline, which was sold sometime in the 1930s.

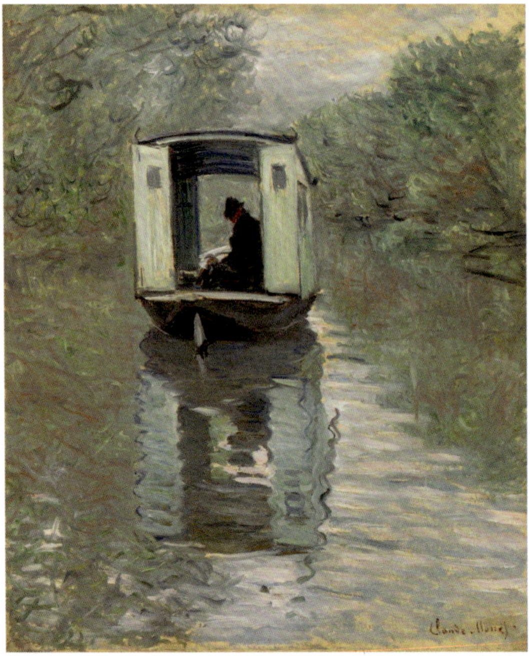

**CLAUDE MONET (FRENCH, 1840–1926)**
***THE STUDIO BOAT***
1876. Oil on canvas, 28 5/8 × 23 5/8 in. (72.7 × 60 cm). BF730

A boat bobs in the water, its doors flung open to allow a view through the structure. Within, a figure dressed in black leans over a newspaper. Trees enclose the space; only a small triangle of sky remains visible at the top of the painting. Sweeping horizontal brushwork in the lower half of the canvas mimics the rippling reflection of the boat as it floats along the river.

The curious structure was Monet's floating studio, here shown on the Seine near Argenteuil. The boat had an earlier precedent: French artist Charles-François Daubigny, a noted landscape painter and an influence on the impressionists, also painted outdoors in his boat *Le Bottin*. As an artist interested in fleeting, momentary outdoor scenes, Monet used his studio boat to capture many of these transitory images on site. Tucked away both in the boat and among the trees, the artist creates an intimate space for creative expression. Indeed, the figure reading may be a self-portrait.

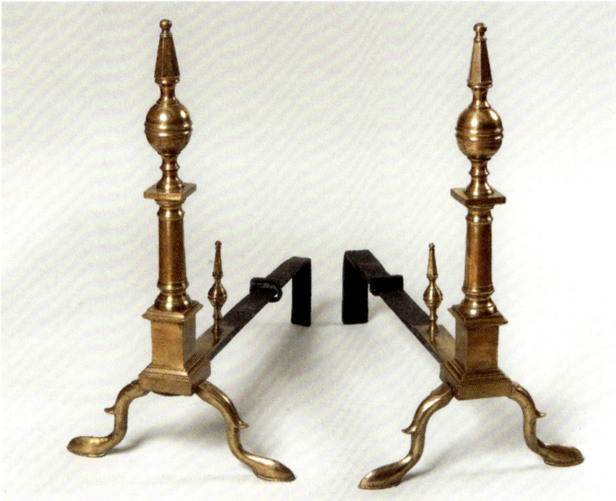

***ANDIRONS*** **(AMERICAN)**

Unidentified maker. 18th or 19th century. Copper alloy and iron, approx. 22½ × 12¾ × 23¼ in. (57 × 32.4 × 59 cm) each. 01.09.24a,b

Andirons typically were manufactured in pairs to hold logs in an open fireplace. The logs would rest on horizontal billet bars, which in this pair are made of exposed iron. The andirons' ornamental features, clad in a copper alloy, include cabriole legs with spurs at the knees and pointed feet; square plinths surmounted by colonettes; finials composed of steeple-shaped shafts on balls with turned lines; and log stops that echo the finials on a smaller scale. The andirons' overall design combines architectural, anthropomorphic, and vegetal elements that complement other objects in the ensemble—such as the fictive architecture and floral motifs of the Pennsylvania German chest they bracket, as well as the sinuous wrought-iron double hinges or the standing figure in Renoir's *Girl with a Jump Rope* on the wall above.

Dr. Barnes displayed twenty-three andiron pairs throughout his ensembles as framing devices and exemplars of craftsmanship. He emphasized that such "commonplace objects" were critical to his educational mission: "I believe I am on my way to show…that there is no essential aesthetic difference between the forms of the great painters and sculptors, and those of the iron-workers."

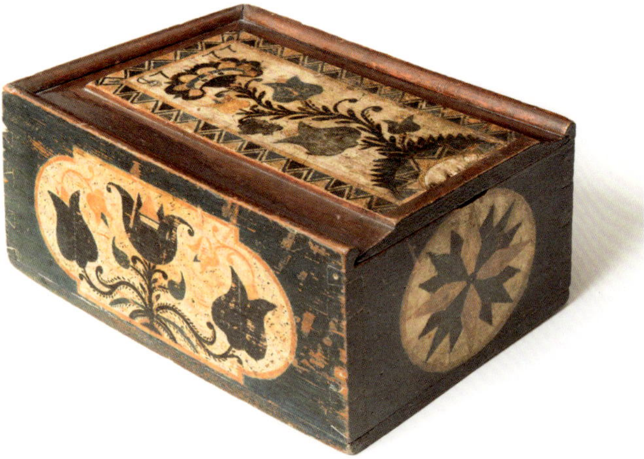

***CANDLE BOX*** **(AMERICAN, PENNSYLVANIA GERMAN)**
Unidentified maker. 1777. Painted pine, 14 ¼ × 6 7⁄16 × 8 11⁄16 in. (36.2 × 16.4 × 22.1 cm). 01.09.40

Though candles were essential in eighteenth-century households, they were rather expensive, and candlemaking itself was a laborious endeavor. As such, families would store their candles in small boxes like this one, protected from the elements and pests that might be attracted to their ingredients. The most common candles at the time were made of tallow, a solid animal fat, and could soften or bend in the summer heat.

The construction of this candle box, with handmade dovetails visible on the front, mimics that of Pennsylvania German blanket chests. This box, however, has a lid that slides into grooves on either side of its top. The elaborate decoration, including tulips and other popular motifs, is an example of how Pennsylvania Germans embellished even the most utilitarian of objects.

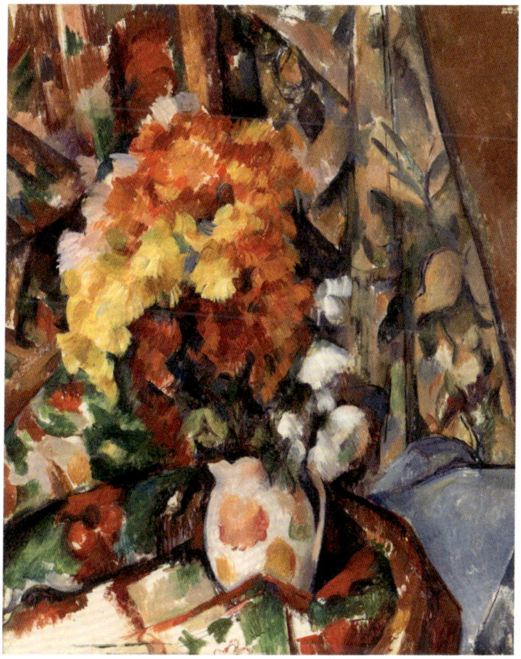

**PAUL CÉZANNE (FRENCH, 1839–1906)**
***THE FLOWERED VASE***
1896–98. Oil on canvas, 27¾ × 23 in. (70.5 × 58.4 cm). BF44

Cézanne painted this richly colored pitcher of chrysanthemums in his studio. The work shows his skillful use of props arranged around a circular wood table. Hanging to the left, the patterned drapery colored in green, red, and orange is actually a rug. The curtain decorated with leaves, which disappears behind the table to the right, has a role in many of the artist's late still lifes, and even portraits. The white milk pitcher at the center of the painting, another studio favorite, looks as if it may topple over.

This floral still life is a mixture of patterns offset by only a few swaths of solid color—at right the brown of a wall shows beyond the curtain, and below that a folded blue fabric departs from the colors used elsewhere in the composition. Cézanne's brushstrokes describing the chrysanthemums flare out in various directions, creating fan-shaped clusters of color and a sense of three-dimensionality. In contrast, the flowers in the patterned curtain are flatter, their forms following the surface of the fabric.

# ROOM 10

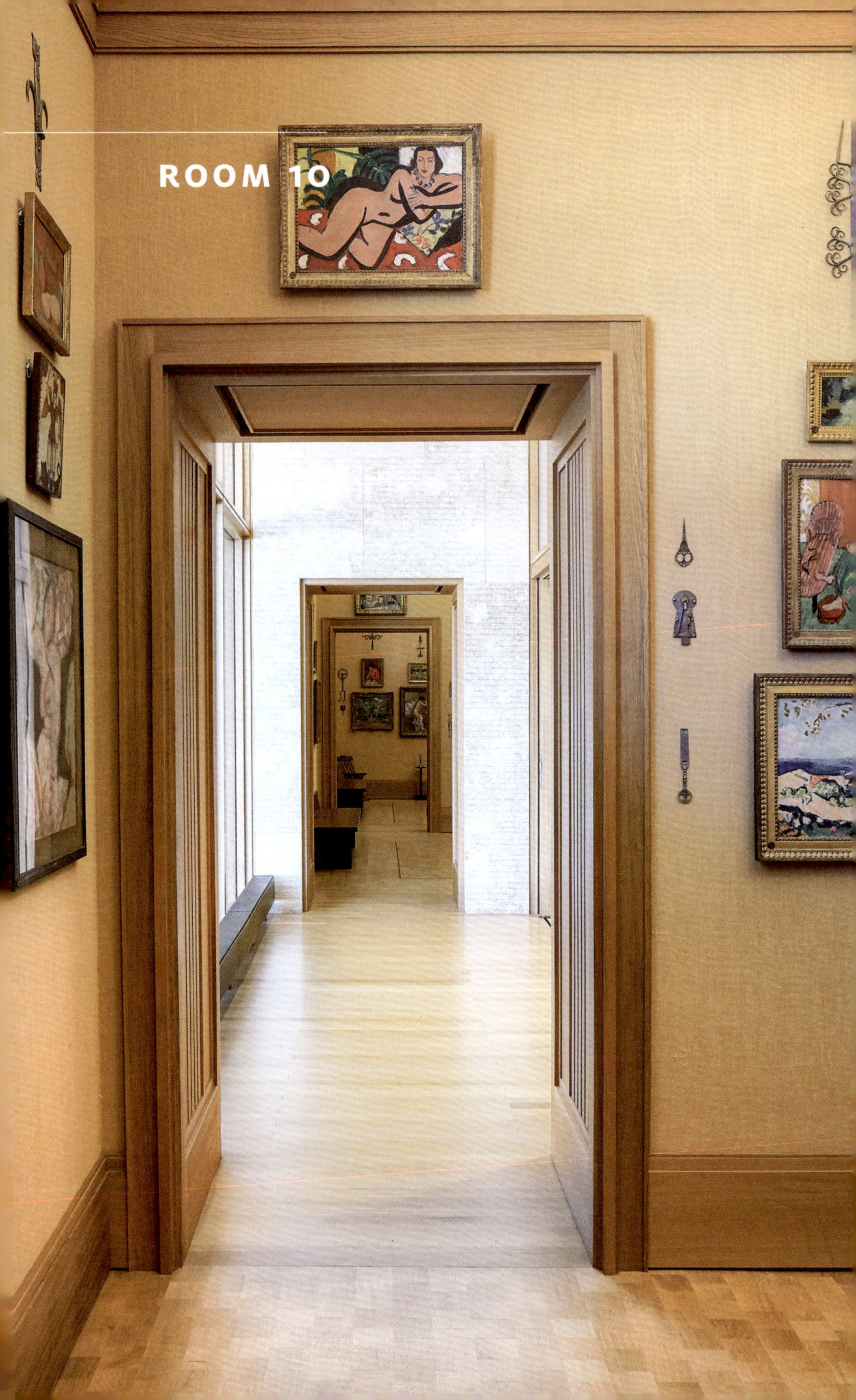

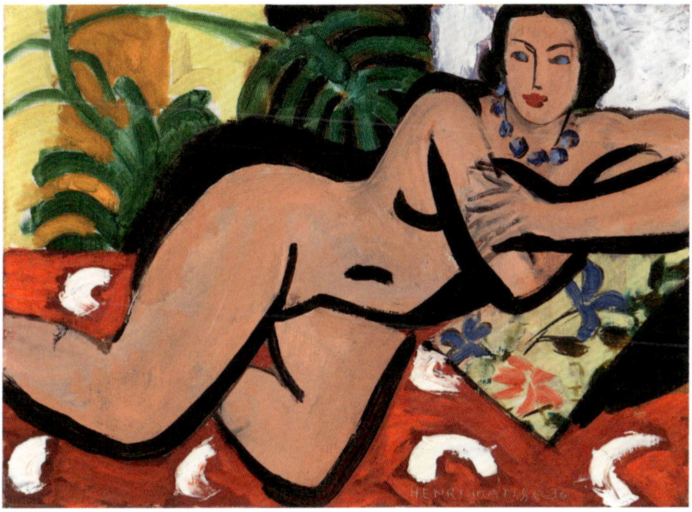

**HENRI MATISSE (FRENCH, 1869–1954)**
***RECLINING NUDE WITH BLUE EYES***
1936. Oil on canvas, 13 × 18⅛ in. (33 × 46 cm). BF955

Matisse's assistant Lydia Delectorskaya modeled for this painting. In the 1930s, Matisse began using photography in his painting process, and after each posing session, Delectorskaya would photograph the work in progress. The images show how Matisse refined the composition. For example, he added vertical sections to the background and a thick black outline to the figure, emphasizing the two-dimensional surface of the canvas.

While Matisse continually reworked details, the basic format of the reclining nude remained constant. This jewellike canvas was one of several that Matisse made in the mid-1930s to explore various solutions to the same pictorial problem. Although small in scale, the painting feels expansive because of the juxtaposition of the vivid color blocks and the way the figure extends beyond the frame.

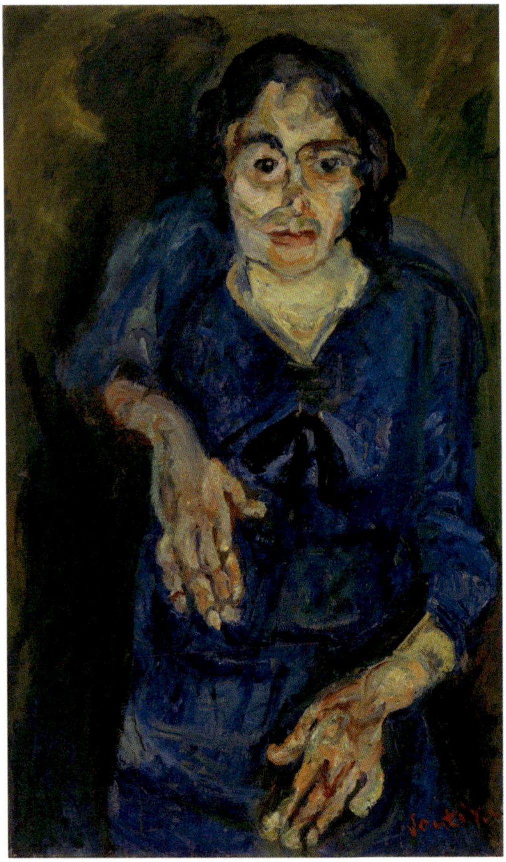

**CHAÏM SOUTINE (RUSSIAN, ACTIVE IN FRANCE, 1893–1943)**
***WOMAN IN BLUE***
c. 1919. Oil on canvas, 39 ½ × 23 ¾ in. (100.3 × 60.3 cm). BF886

Soutine's portrait of this unknown woman displays his characteristic asymmetries and distortions. Her shoulders are hunched and lopsided, with her right arm hiked up, elbow resting on a chair. Her upper right arm is shortened, while her left arm stretches as if boneless. The woman's oversize hands and elongated fingers dominate the composition. Their lurid flesh tones—a web of red-brown, yellow-orange, blue, and green brushstrokes—are echoed in the woman's face, which reflects her blue dress and the green background.

Though the contorted forms speak to Soutine's intensely personal vision, the picture gives a strong sense of the sitter's individuality and psychology. Her dark gaze is pensive as she stares out past the viewer. Perhaps her thoughts are reflected in the swirling turmoil of brushstrokes that capture her presence.

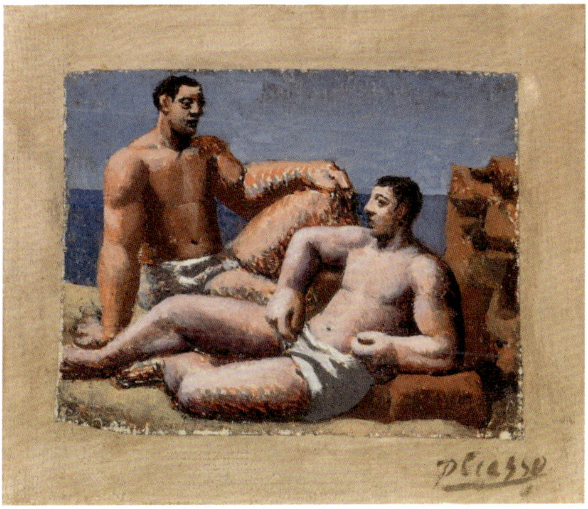

**PABLO PICASSO (SPANISH, 1881–1973)**
***TWO FIGURES***
c. 1921. Oil on canvas, 5½ × 6¾ in. (14 × 17.1 cm). BF283

The monumentality of the two bathers in this work belies its small scale. Their thick limbs and torsos look as if they were carved from stone, and the bather on the left is similar in color to the red-brown rock on the right, emphasizing his massive, stolid presence. The figures are like relief sculpture, set against the flat blue planes of the sea and sky.

Picasso produced a series of works in the early 1920s depicting figures on a beach, lounging and basking in the sun. He was spending summers on the French Riviera, and his new bathing pictures evoked the landscape and classical art of the Mediterranean. The artist's interest in Greco-Roman antiquity following World War I was part of a broader "return to order" movement in France. Given the trauma of war, many artists sought comfort in tradition. Picasso, nevertheless, employed this new Mediterranean classicism side by side with cubism.

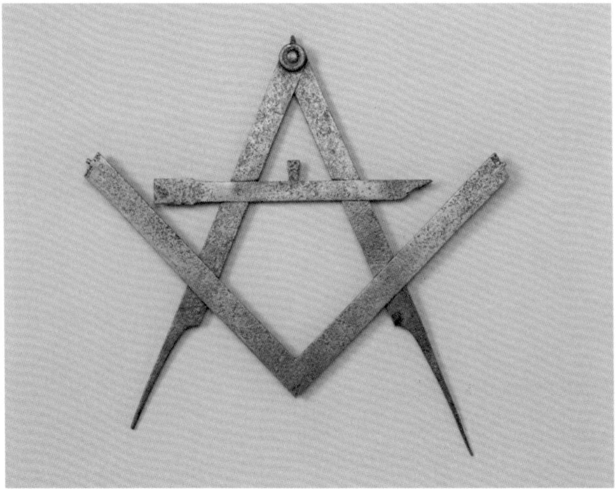

***EMBLEM*** **(FRENCH)**
Unidentified maker. 19th century. Iron, 9¾ × 10½ × ⅜ in. (24.8 × 26.7 × 1 cm).
01.10.21

The three "tools" constituting this metalwork are flat and nonfunctional, riveted together to form a decorative design. The compass—shaped as an inverted "V," with pointed ends—and the ninety-degree square are emblems historically associated with freemasons. For this group of fraternal organizations, which trace their origins to late-medieval stonemasonry guilds, the compass symbolizes restraint and the square morality and virtue. The third, smaller tool is a twibil, used specifically for timber joinery. Its presence indicates that this was likely a guild emblem for woodworkers rather than freemasons, though it would have expressed similar symbolic values when hung in their guildhall. The emblem's display at the Barnes Foundation invites further layers of interpretation, such as the correspondence between the square and the gridded background of Henri Matisse's *Reclining Odalisque* on this wall, or between the twibil and the wooden furniture and frames.

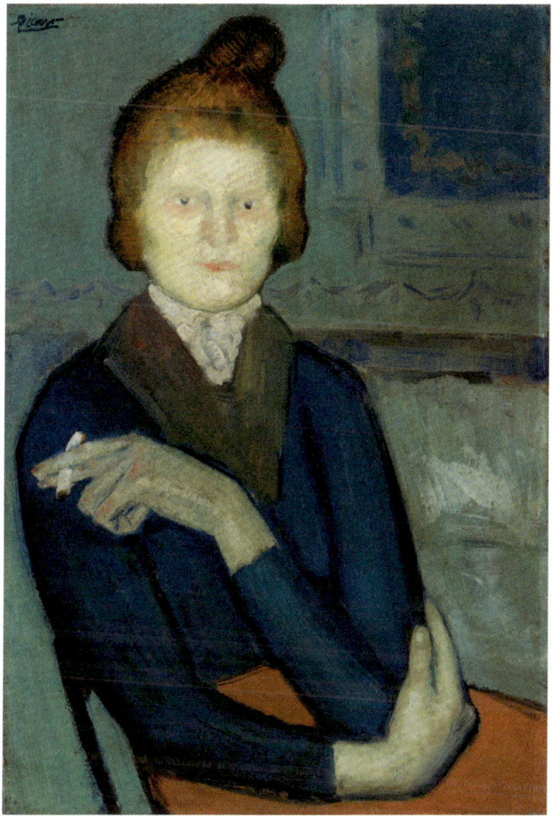

**PABLO PICASSO (SPANISH, 1881–1973)**
***YOUNG WOMAN HOLDING A CIGARETTE***
1901. Oil on canvas, 29 × 20⅛ in. (73.7 × 51.1 cm). BF318

A woman sits alone at a café, cigarette in hand. She stares past the viewer with red-rimmed eyes set in a cadaver-white face. Her tightly set lips and body language, with one arm crossed over her chest and the other grasping her elbow, convey a guarded expression. Picasso painted this picture in 1901, an important year for him. In February, a close friend ended his own life, leaving the artist deeply shaken. He then had his first solo show in Paris—a critical success that launched his career. The works he displayed there synthesized the influences of artists like Degas, Manet, Van Gogh, and Toulouse-Lautrec. This picture takes on a theme associated with these artists but also shows Picasso developing a new style that would come to be known as his Blue Period. Processing his friend's death, Picasso began painting subjects from the margins of society in melancholic tones and elongated forms.

This was one of the first paintings to enter Dr. Barnes's collection. It was part of a group of works purchased by William Glackens on his behalf in Paris in 1912.

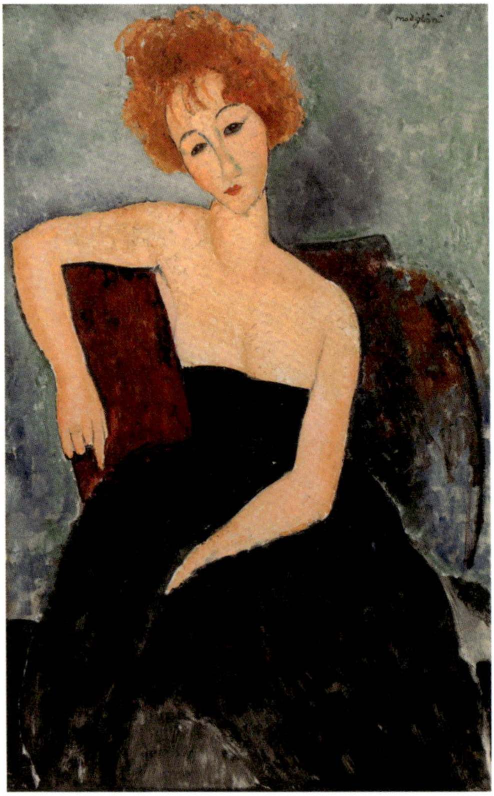

**AMEDEO MODIGLIANI (ITALIAN, 1884–1920)**
***REDHEADED GIRL IN EVENING DRESS***
1918. Oil on canvas, 45¾ × 28¾ in. (116.2 × 73 cm). BF206

A stylish young woman stares confidently from this painting, as if to appraise the viewer, an arm propped casually on the back of her chair. Her low-cut strapless gown hovers precariously at her bust. Vigorous brush marks describe her ivory flesh.

If this portrait highlights the sensuality of its sitter, it also acknowledges her status as a modern woman. In early twentieth-century Paris, her short auburn hair and painted red lips would have been daring fashion choices. Modeling was a controversial profession at the time—some models were also sex workers—but it was a relatively lucrative profession. By posing for Modigliani, perhaps this unidentified sitter achieved a degree of financial independence.

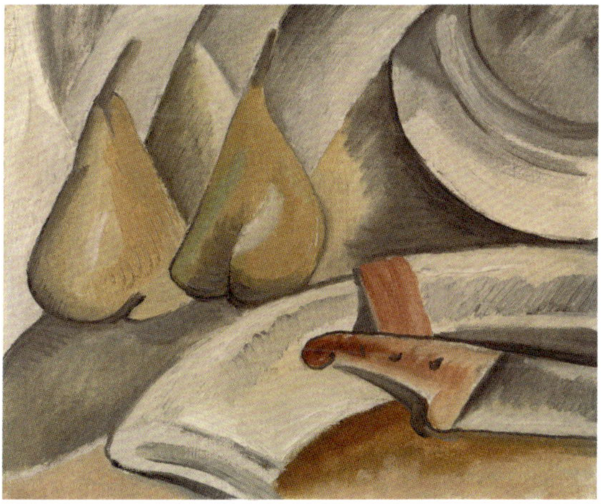

**GEORGES BRAQUE (FRENCH, 1882–1963)**
***NAPKIN, KNIFE, AND PEARS***
1908. Oil on canvas, 8 ⁹⁄₁₆ × 10 ⁹⁄₁₆ in. (21.7 × 26.9 cm). BF437

This small still life dates from a time in which, influenced by Cézanne, Braque and Picasso developed a new approach to painting. Cubism, as it soon became known, simplified objects, landscapes, and figures into their fundamental geometric forms, conveying the real-life experience of seeing them from multiple angles. Here, Braque limits himself to kitchen and studio objects like those favored by Cézanne: three pears sit behind a folded napkin and a knife, with part of a plate visible in the background.

*Napkin, Knife, and Pears* may be a preparatory work for another painting or part of Braque's broader investigations into composition. It does resemble the lower half of a larger still life, *Plate and Fruit Dish* (1908, private collection). His restrained choice of color, typical of this moment in his career, would grow increasingly somber in the next few years.

# ROOM 11

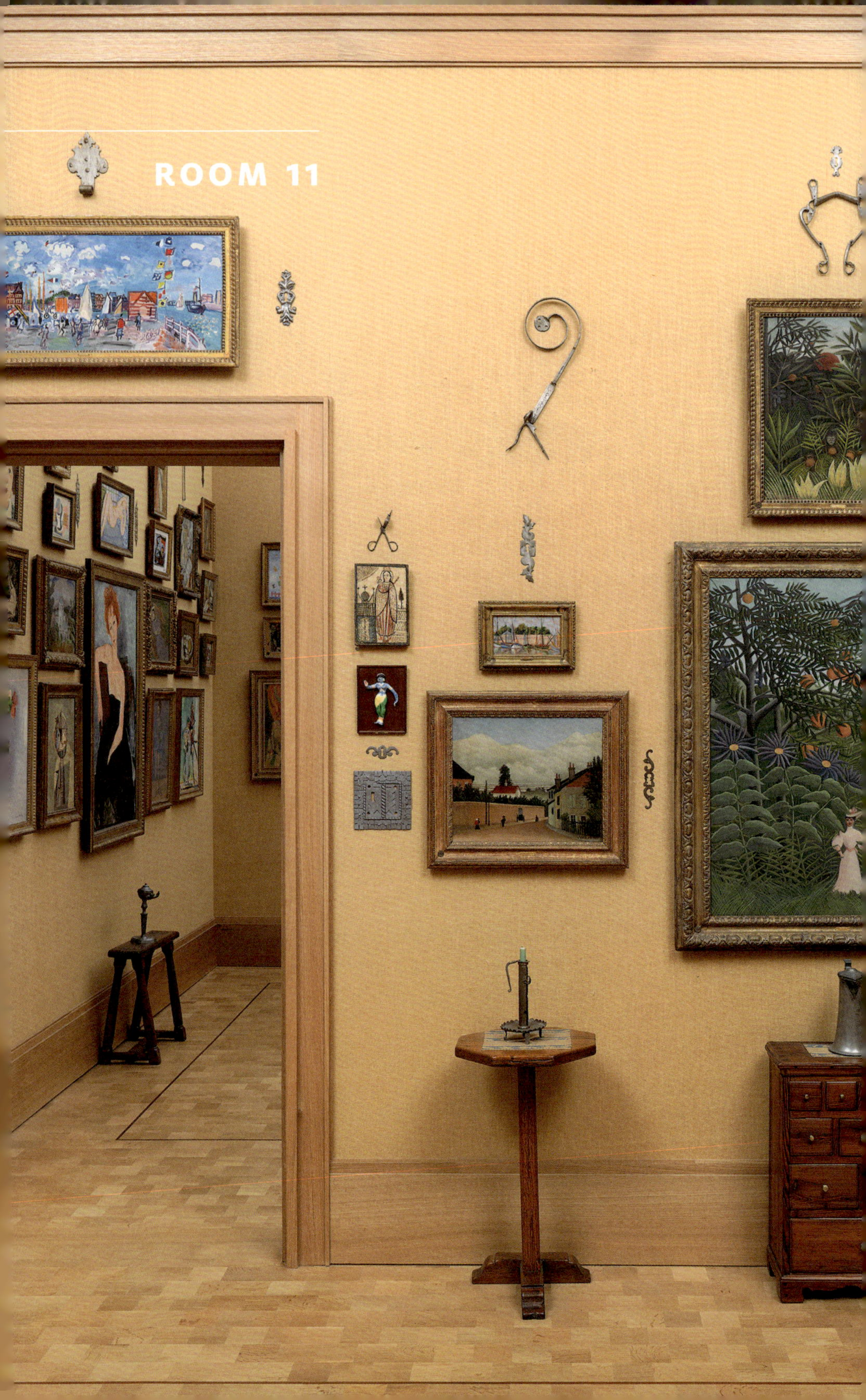

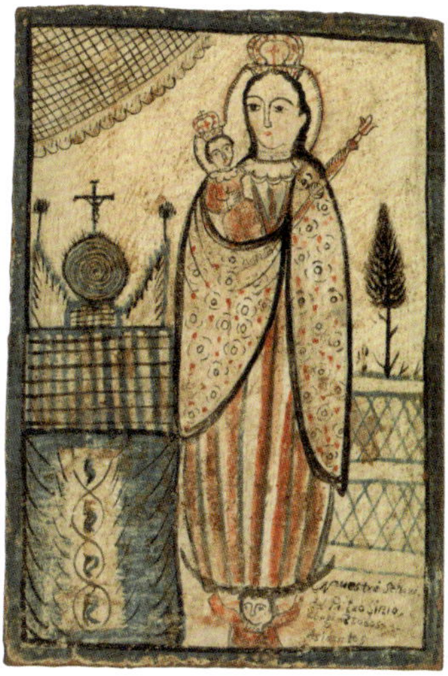

**PEDRO ANTONIO FRESQUIS (MEXICAN, 1749–1831)**
***OUR LADY OF PROTECTION***
c. 1815. Water-based paint on wood panel, 9⅜ × 6½ in. (23.8 × 16.5 cm). BF1019

*Retablos*, devotional paintings of Catholic religious figures, were common works by New Mexican religious painters (*santeros*) in the sixteenth through nineteenth centuries. Small, mobile paintings on metal or wood panels, *retablos* could be used by worshipers for private prayer in a home or chapel. Here, the Virgin Mary envelops the Infant Christ in the protective folds of her robe. The divinity of both figures is expressed through the halos around their heads and by the angel who holds the crescent moon on which Mary stands. Both wear crowns and elaborate robes with frilled collars, and Mary holds a scepter, symbolizing her role as Queen of Heaven. The figures are set within a tiled garden that contains an altar covered in a checkered cloth, surmounted with a monstrance (the vessel that holds the Eucharist) and protected by the curtain above. This image of the Virgin and Christ Child was used to invoke divine protection or offer gratitude for recovery from injury or illness. An inscription in the bottom right corner reads, “Our Lady of Protection assiduously pleads for everyone.” The idyllic garden with an altar suggests a scene of quiet serenity and privacy that perhaps helped to comfort the worshiper.

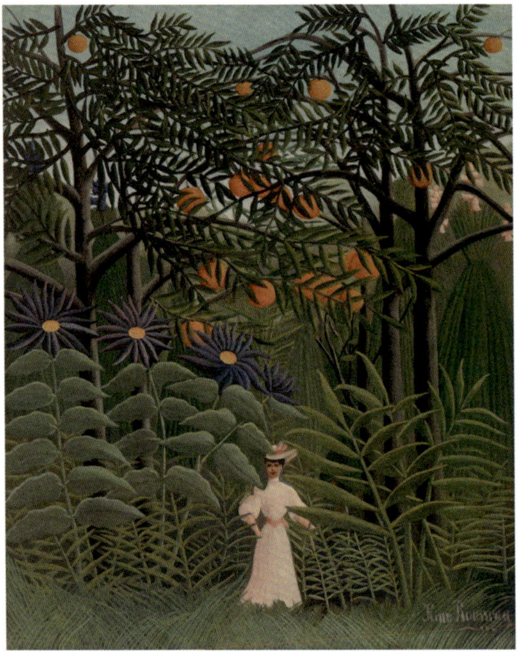

**HENRI ROUSSEAU (FRENCH, 1844–1910)**
***WOMAN WALKING IN AN EXOTIC FOREST***
1905. Oil on canvas, 39⅜ × 31¾ in. (100 × 80.6 cm). BF388

A well-dressed woman appears, incongruously, in the heart of a verdant forest, dwarfed by giant blue flowers and fruit-laden trees. As if lost, she peers out from behind the leaves, while long grass obscures her feet. Admirers suggested that Rousseau did his military service in Mexico, and that this experience inspired his jungle scenes, but in reality Rousseau never left France. Instead he was inspired by his love of Paris's botanical garden. "When I enter those hothouses and I see those strange plants from exotic countries," he told a journalist in 1910, "it seems to me that I enter a dream. I feel like a completely different man." Perhaps his elegant model, so clearly dressed for the city, is in a similar state of reverie.

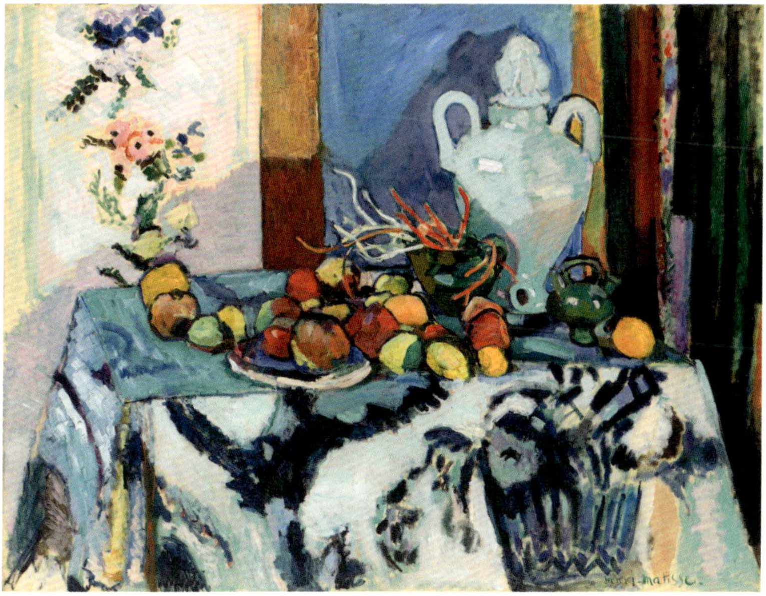

**HENRI MATISSE (FRENCH, 1869–1954)**

***BLUE STILL LIFE***

1907. Oil on canvas, 35 5⁄16 × 45 15⁄16 in. (89.7 × 116.7 cm). BF185

This work's overall blue palette comes from the tablecloth, a French fabric printed with garlands and baskets of flowers. Though Matisse purchased the commonplace cloth from a Paris junk shop, after spotting it from atop a city bus, it became a source of inspiration for him, appearing as a major element in paintings for more than a dozen years.

Here, the fabric's dark and light blues are echoed in the two-handled jar as well as the background wall. Matisse contrasts these cool hues with the bright reds and yellows of the fruit and the soft pinks of the folding screen. The garlands in the cloth create an arabesque-like structure—the patterns and objects form an undulating rhythm that weaves the foreground and background together, collapsing space. In the cloth's upper left corner, for example, a branch of the garland continues into the leaf design on the folding screen, creating a push-pull effect between dimensions.

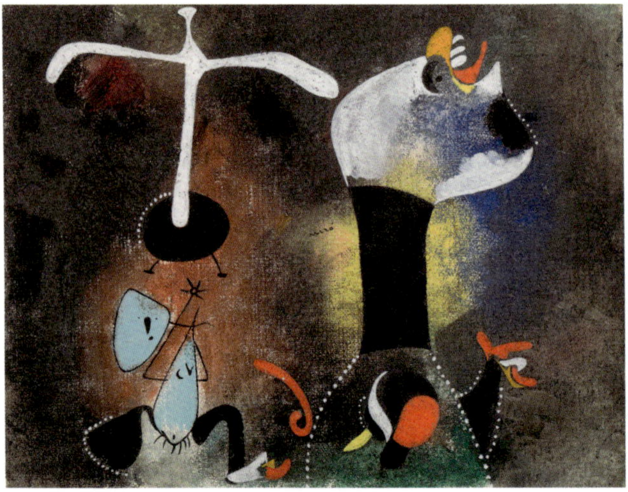

**JOAN MIRÓ (SPANISH, 1893–1983)**
***GROUP OF WOMEN***
July 15, 1938. Oil on canvas, 10 7/8 × 14 in. (27.6 × 35.6 cm). BF1188

Miró, who was from Barcelona, made this small work during the Spanish Civil War (1936–39), when General Francisco Franco's fascist regime overthrew the Republican government of Spain. He depicts flailing figures against a smoky background, evoking the calamity of aerial bombings, which newspapers of the day reported on and documented in photographs. This painting is part of a series Miró produced within a two-week span and uncharacteristically labeled with specific dates—perhaps his personal attempt to chronicle the war.

The figures here echo those in Picasso's monumental painting *Guernica* (1937, Reina Sofía Museum, Madrid), which infamously portrayed the bombing of a Basque town. Here, the woman on the right looks toward the sky, her tongue stretched into a scream, a likely reference to the wailing mother holding her dead child in *Guernica*.

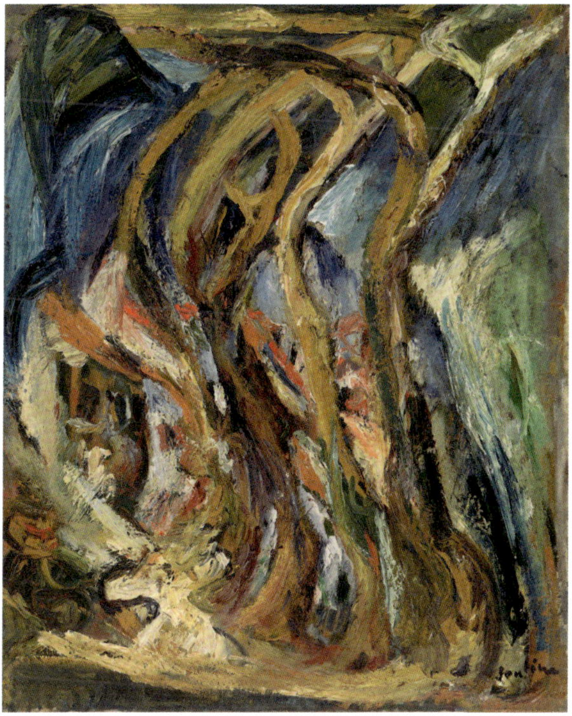

**CHAÏM SOUTINE (RUSSIAN, ACTIVE IN FRANCE, 1893–1943)**
***GROUP OF TREES***
c. 1922. Oil on canvas, 28 ⅞ × 23 ⅞ in. (73.3 × 60.6 cm). BF331

Around 1918, toward the end of World War I, Soutine's dealer Léopold Zborowski encouraged the artist to leave Paris and visit the South of France for a change of pace. Soutine, who was raised in a shtetl in modern-day Belarus, had been living with other immigrant artists in poor, bohemian Montparnasse since 1913. Financed by Zborowski, Soutine escaped to the countryside, traveling between Cagnes-sur-Mer on the French Riviera and Céret in the Pyrenees for the next few years.

Toward the end of his travels, he painted this picture of white buildings with red roofs seen through a screen of trees. Thick passages of paint and heavily distorted forms give a sense of turbulence and disturbance, yet the frenetic brushwork and saturated color convey an energy and joy that Soutine perhaps felt in the sun-drenched south. The same towns and landscapes had inspired other artists before him, including Renoir, Picasso, and Braque.

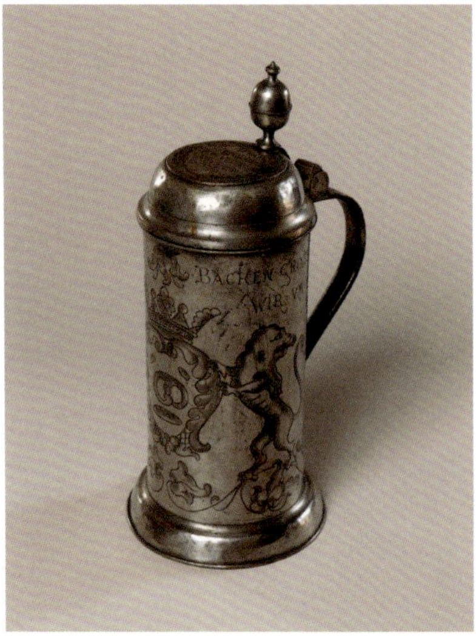

***TANKARD* (GERMAN, SWISS, OR AUSTRIAN)**
Unidentified maker. 1766/92. Pewter, 12 ¾ × 5 ¾ × 7 ⅞ in. (32.4 × 14.6 × 20 cm). 01.11.60

This drinking vessel, probably used for beer or cider, bears the emblem of the bakers' guild: a pretzel and three loaves of bread set within a foliate border topped by a jeweled crown, with lions rampant (standing in profile), claws unsheathed, to either side. Two cheery inscriptions in German announce the hopes of both patron and pewterer. The inscription surrounding the emblem reads: "May God in Heaven bless the field / Bake big bread so that we may make a little money." The one on the lid, encircled by a wreath of grain, declares: "Long live a well-crafted tankard, AD 1792."

Surprisingly, the Barnes tankard seems to have received its engraving some twenty-six years after the vessel was made, as the interior is stamped with the year 1766. It was probably made for private enjoyment (those designed for guild ceremonies were usually 18–20 inches high) and later repurposed for communal use. Its oath "Long live a well-crafted tankard" upholds the Barnes Foundation's equal privileging of the designs of "fine" and "useful" objects.

# ROOM 12

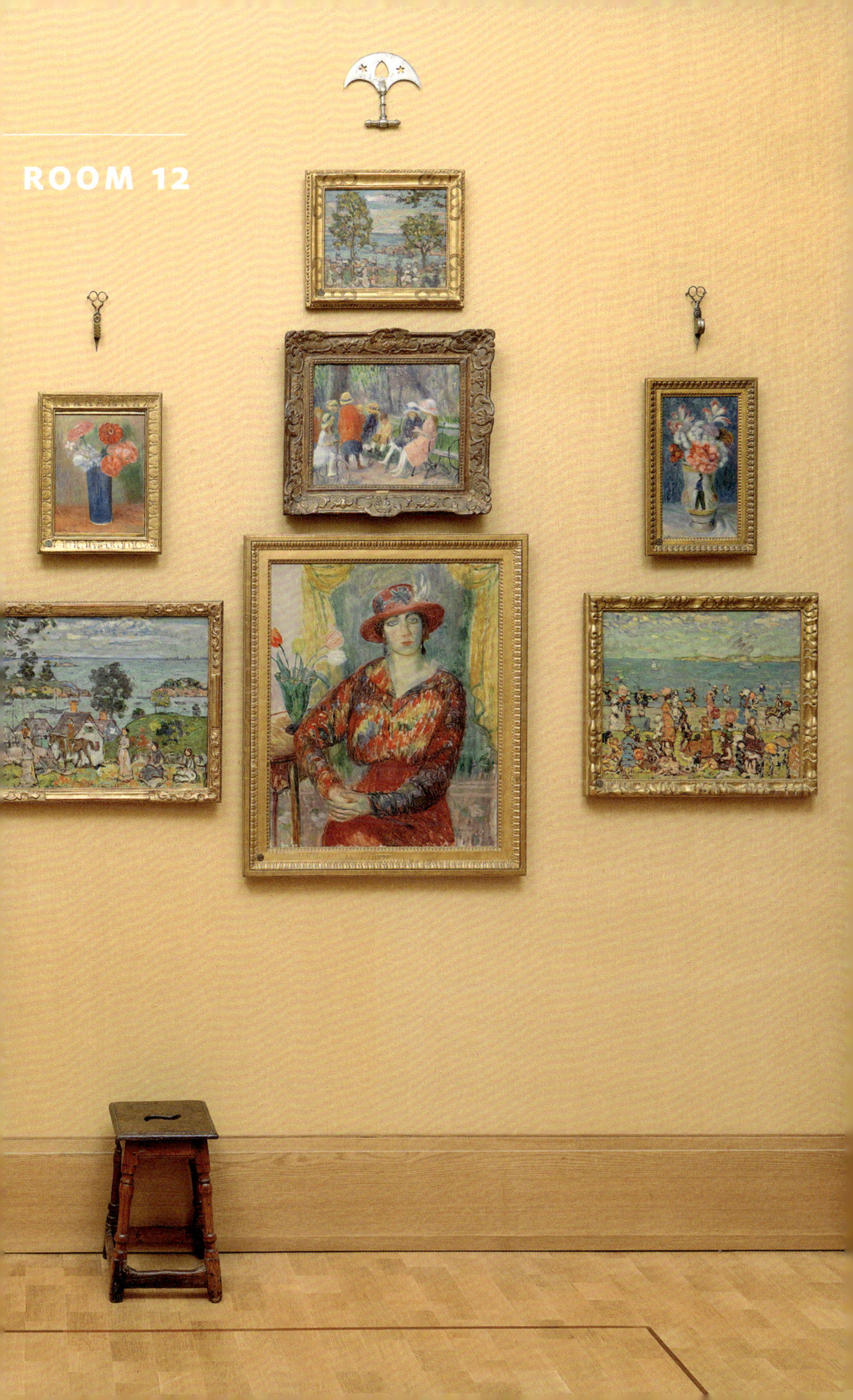

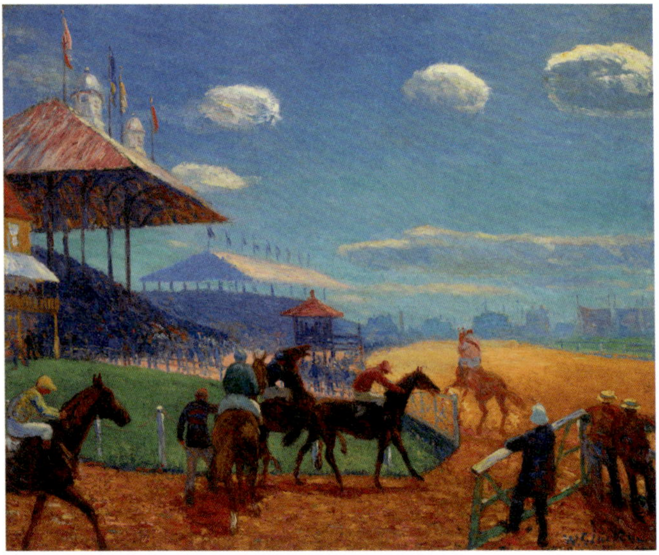

**WILLIAM JAMES GLACKENS (AMERICAN, 1870–1938)**
***RACE TRACK***
1907–9. Oil on canvas, 26⅛ × 32¼ in. (66.4 × 81.9 cm). BF138

*Race Track* was a game-changing painting for both Glackens and his close friend Dr. Barnes. In the two years he worked on it, Glackens pivoted from the somber tones of his urban realist works to the bolder, nonnaturalistic colors of emergent European and American art. Yet he remained committed to scenes of everyday life, with an emphasis on leisure pursuits. Here, he captured jockeys in colorful silks and spirited mounts trotting, capering, and bolting at the Brighton Beach Race Track in Brooklyn. Under a brilliant blue sky, the bright orange course stretches into the distance, marked by the grandstands' pitched roofs and red, yellow, and blue pennants. Glackens underscored the venue's urban context by including tall buildings and smokestacks in the background.

The rainbow palette of *Race Track* surprised Dr. Barnes, provoking him to investigate modern art. The painting, acquired in 1913, became a cornerstone of his collection as the talisman that had initiated him into a new world of perception and meaning.

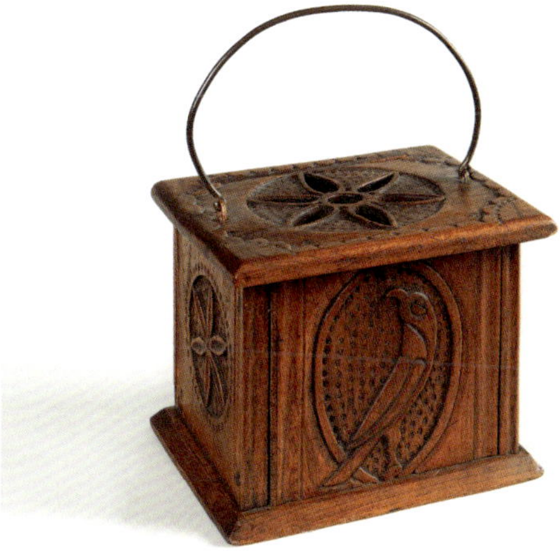

***FOOT WARMER* (PROBABLY AMERICAN)**
Unidentified maker. Probably 18th or 19th century. Wood, copper alloy, and iron; 8 × 9½ × 7½ in. (20.3 × 24.1 × 19.1 cm). 01.12.07

Homes and public spaces were generally poorly heated prior to the mid-1800s. Foot warmers were popular devices for keeping comfortable at home, in carriages or sleighs, and at church and other gathering places. These portable boxes have metal trays inside to hold hot coals—accessed, in this case, by a sliding back panel—and holes for ventilation. The front of this one features a stylized goldfinch whose body, bill, and wings echo the contours of the oval in which it is set. The top features an engrailed border as well as ventilation holes in a pinwheel design that recurs on the sides.

As displayed in the Barnes Foundation, the box rests upon an elegantly carved pine footstool and, in turn, supports a copper teakettle whose florid and stippled designs complement the box's own. Stacked at a diagonal in the corner, these three American domestic objects almost present a microcosm of the materials and motifs found in Room 12—from the wood panels of Horace Pippin (see page 117), to Albert H. Nulty's Pennsylvania German–style doves, to the vegetal motifs of the wrought-iron hinges and escutcheons.

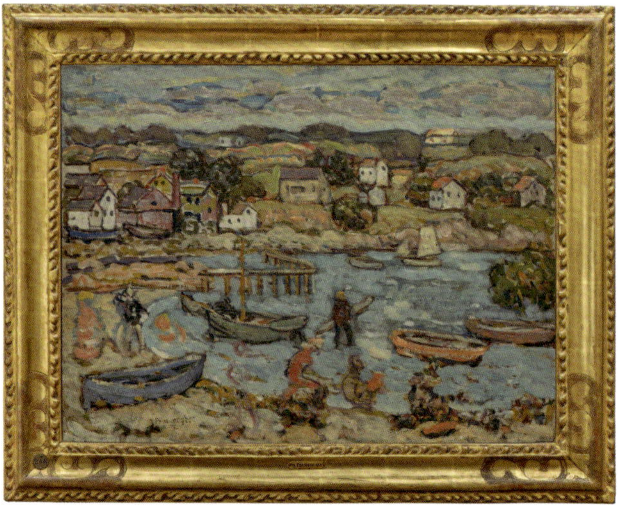

**MAURICE BRAZIL PRENDERGAST (AMERICAN, 1858–1924)**
***MARBLEHEAD HARBOR***
c. 1918–1920. Oil on canvas, 18 × 24⅛ in. (45.7 × 61.3 cm). BF216

**CHARLES PRENDERGAST (AMERICAN, 1863–1948)**
***FRAME***
20th century. Carved wood with gesso, red bole, and gold leaf; 23½ × 29½ × 1¼ in. (59.7 × 74.9 × 3.2 cm). BF216fr

A few figures, probably fishermen, wade amid rowboats or crouch at the water's edge in the coastal town of Marblehead, Massachusetts. On the far shore, multicolor clapboard houses nestle between equally vivid trees and hills, and the cool light of the purple, silver, and yellow sky suggests the coming of evening or autumn. Maurice Prendergast, a pioneer of American modernism, was a key artist in Dr. Barnes's collection. Influenced by contemporary European art, he used bright, contrasting colors and flat pattern-like forms to capture the beaches and parks of the Northeast. This painting was the last work by the artist acquired by Dr. Barnes.

The frame was made by Maurice's younger brother, Charles, an artist and skilled woodworker. Dr. Barnes bought more than fifty frames from the younger Prendergast, who modeled his designs on eighteenth-century Venetian examples. Many feature the incised C scrolls shown here, a reinterpretation of vegetal motifs that Prendergast called his "sausage" pattern.

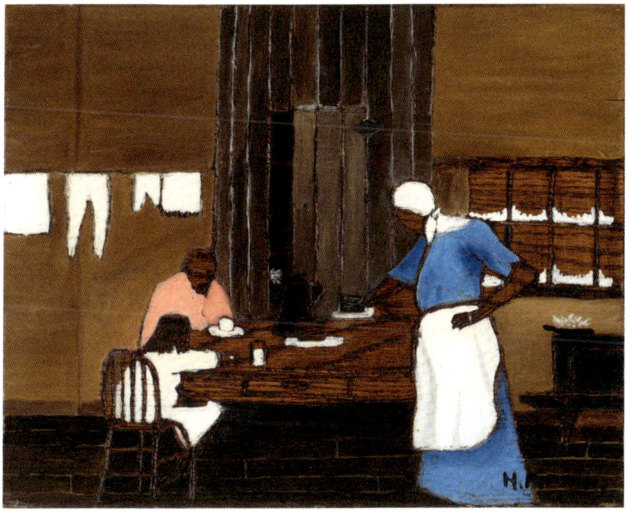

**HORACE PIPPIN (AMERICAN, 1888–1946)**

***SUPPER TIME***

c. 1940. Oil on burnt-wood panel, 12 × 15⅛ in. (30.5 × 38.4 cm). BF985

An African American artist from West Chester, Pennsylvania, Pippin was interested in depicting the everyday life of Black people, as evidenced by this work showing a family having a meal at home.

Pippin, who was self-taught, often painted on wood, carving his composition with a hot poker before adding color. Here, burnt-wood lines shape the chair, windowpanes, door panels, and contours of the figures. Pippin leaves much of the wood exposed, making it an active part of the composition. Unpainted wood establishes the table and the view through the window; it also forms the skin of all three figures. Vibrant blues and pinks enhance the figures, but the scattering of white—in the hanging laundry, cups and saucers, and snow piled on the windowpanes—is what ties the work together.

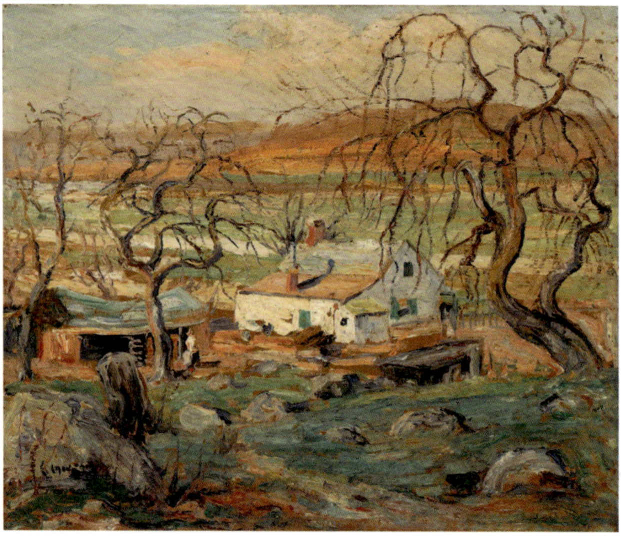

**ERNEST LAWSON (AMERICAN, 1873–1939)**
***LANDSCAPE WITH GNARLED TREES***
c. 1910. Oil on commercial wallboard, 20 × 23⅞ in. (50.8 × 60.6 cm). BF389

This rural landscape in upstate New York—Lawson's adopted home—shows winter melting into spring. The white clapboard cottage and its outbuildings nestle among rocky hills and the bare, writhing trees of the title. They look out on a pale green meadow, striped with white, toward distant mountains shrouded in purple haze.

Lawson, who was born in Nova Scotia and studied in Kansas City and Mexico City, had moved to New York in 1891. Two years later, he journeyed to France in search of paintings by Paul Cézanne and Alfred Sisley. While in Paris he lived with the English author W. Somerset Maugham, who based the character Frederick Lawson in his novel *Of Human Bondage* (1915) on the artist.

William Glackens introduced Lawson to Dr. Barnes in 1912, just before Barnes began collecting modern art in Paris. Lawson's rugged application of rich, unctuous pigment, sinuous drawing, and vivid, light-saturated colors struck a responsive chord and opened the way for Barnes's appreciation of the powerful color rhythms of artists whom he would soon encounter in Paris, especially the young Chaïm Soutine (see pages 60, 100, 111, 163).

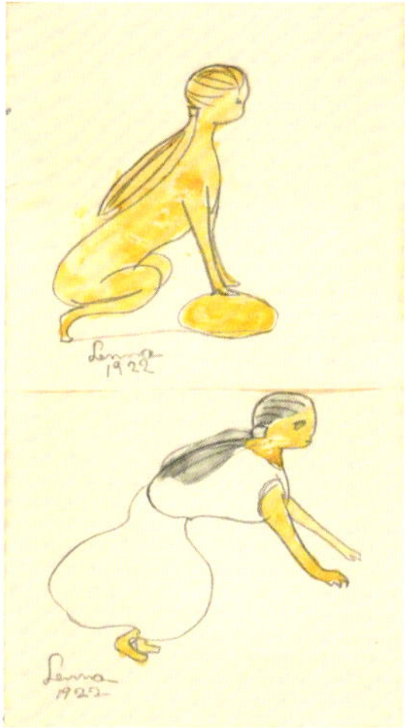

**LENNA GLACKENS (AMERICAN, 1913–1943)**
***TWO FIGURES—SPHINX***
1922. Graphite and watercolor on two leaves of wove paper, 7 × 4 in. (17.8 × 10.2 cm). BF758

This small watercolor sketch shows two sphinxes in profile, one above the other. The lower sphinx wears a white dress, while the upper one is nude and rests her hands on what appears to be a boulder; each is signed and dated “Lenna 1922.” The artist was the daughter of Dr. Barnes's dear friend William Glackens, whose *Race Track* (see page 114) on the adjacent wall had sparked Barnes's interest in modern art. The ponytails worn by Lenna's sphinxes—an amusing addition to these mythical monsters—remind viewers that she was only nine years old when she created them.

In one respect, Dr. Barnes's display of Lenna's *Two Figures—Sphinx* offers a tender tribute to his friendship and ideological camaraderie with her father. In addition, the display of children's art is related to Dr. Barnes's interest in self-taught artists. He believed in the force of their original, unmediated creative visions.

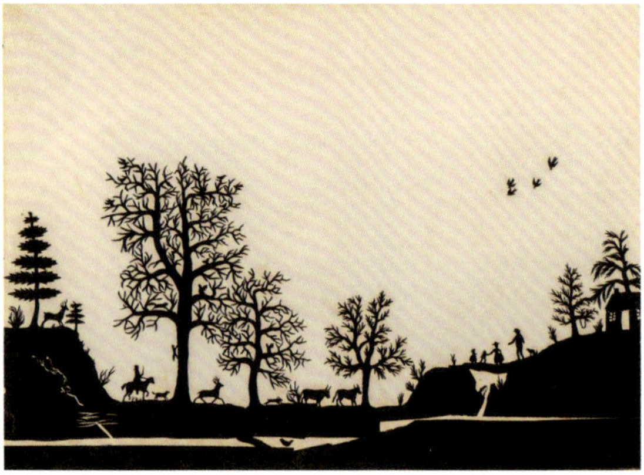

**SUSAN CRAY (AMERICAN, ACTIVE MID-19TH CENTURY)**
***NEW JERSEY CUT-OUT***
1843. Cut-out wove paper with glossy black coating mounted on cream wove paper, 10 × 14 in. (25.4 × 35.6 cm). BF1182

Little is known about the American artist Susan Cray, but her use of cut black-coated paper mounted on a cream-colored background connects her scene of rural New Jersey to the paper-cutting traditions of silhouettes that first emerged in France, Germany, and Switzerland in the 1700s. At left, a hunter and his dog pursue squirrels, deer, and a rabbit through a forest; on the right, a family crosses a bridge over a waterfall to approach their home, perched cozily on a hill.

In mid-nineteenth-century America, nature and the home were viewed as refuges from the modern industrial world—places where spiritual values could be cultivated, and thus appropriate subjects for women's artistic production.

# ROOM 13

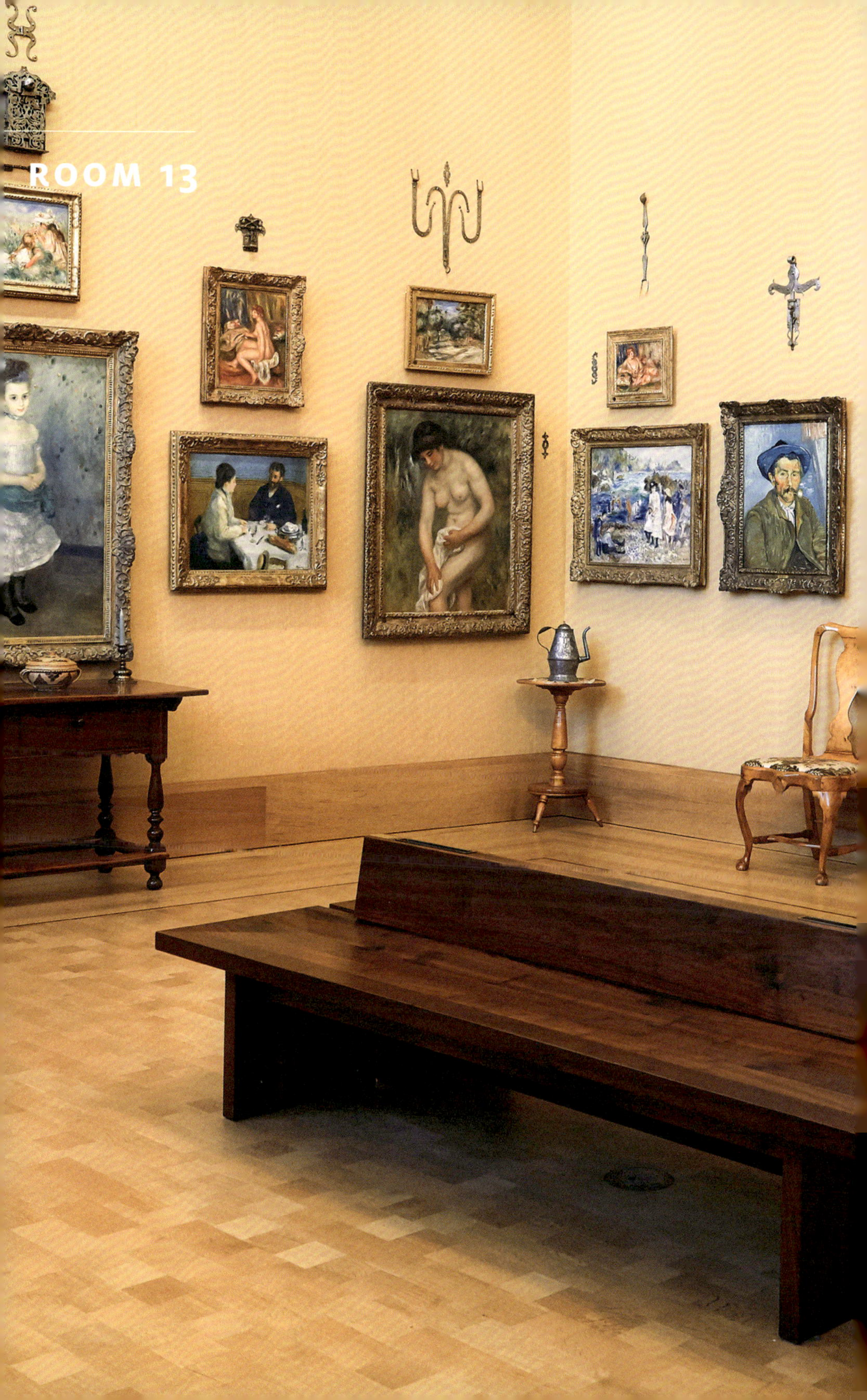

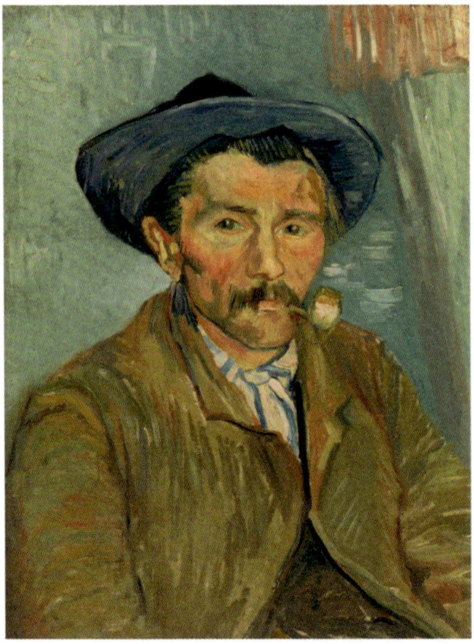

**VINCENT VAN GOGH (DUTCH, 1853–1890)**
***THE SMOKER***
1888. Oil on canvas, 24 ¾ × 18 ¾ in. (62.9 × 47.6 cm). BF119

Van Gogh often painted the residents of Arles during his time in the South of France. He aimed to create portraits of working people as regal as those of saints and rulers. Here, he depicts a pipe-smoking man with a hat that resembles a deep blue halo. The man's half-length figure takes up most of the canvas, and he looks out at the viewer, puffing smoke from his pipe. The figure of the smoker derives from seventeenth-century Dutch genre painting, which Van Gogh, who was from the Netherlands, would have considered part of his own heritage.

Although this man represents a type, Van Gogh also captures the sitter's individuality. His calm yet penetrating gaze is accentuated by dashes of bright green paint around his pupils, and his ruddy cheeks, suggesting work outdoors, are sculpted from red and pink brushstrokes. Quick, loose strokes describe his brown coat and striped shirt, with some of the ground layer exposed as highlights. Areas of thin paint use the canvas's texture to suggest the coat's rough fabric.

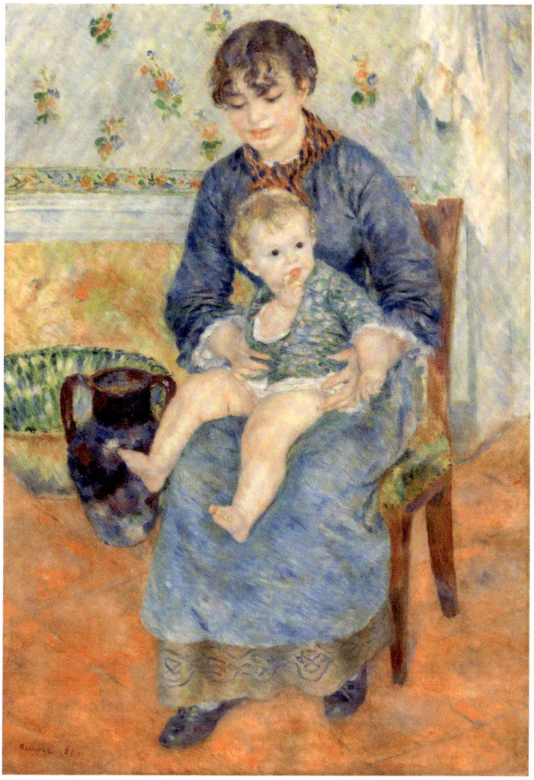

**PIERRE-AUGUSTE RENOIR (FRENCH, 1841–1919)**

***YOUNG MOTHER***

1881. Oil on canvas, 47¾ × 33¾ in. (121.3 × 85.7 cm). BF15

Painted in Naples, Italy, during Renoir's visit there in the autumn of 1881, this work marked the beginning of a stylistic shift in the artist's career, as he moved away from earlier impressionist concerns such as instantaneity to pursue simplified, monumentalized forms. The artist sets the mother and child closer to the picture plane than in his earlier portraits, and both figures have firmer outlines. There is also greater contrast between figures and background, especially noticeable in the cool colors of the garments, the rose tones of the floor and chair, and the glowing pink flowers of the wallpaper.

The baby squirms on his mother's lap, fleshy legs splayed on either side of her knee. Her hands come up to hold him protectively around his hips. The woman gazes down at the child, whose animated face counters the pleasant passivity of her expression. Viewed within the context of his Naples visit and the city's plethora of religious imagery, the painting becomes a contemporary Madonna and Child, something Renoir himself noted when he mentioned to son Jean that "in Italy, every woman nursing a child is a Raphael Madonna."

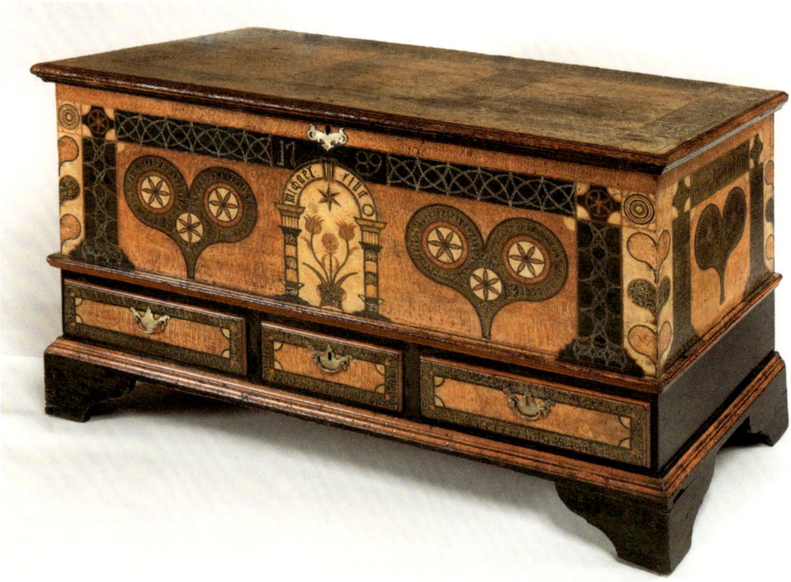

**ATTRIBUTED TO JOHN BIEBER (AMERICAN, 1763–1825)**
***CHEST OVER DRAWERS***
1789. Painted pine and copper alloy, 30 3/16 × 52 1/2 × 23 1/2 in. (76.7 × 133.4 × 59.7 cm). 01.13.18

Pennsylvania German chests served as storage for household goods or personal belongings; they could also provide seating, which might explain the abraded paint on the top of this one. The artists who painted these chests used rulers, compasses, templates, and stamps to create symmetrical designs; the hearts with encircled rosettes shown here were likely made with a compass. Many of the decorative motifs were adapted from European designs and can be seen elsewhere in Pennsylvania German furniture, in the manuscript art known as Fraktur, and even on the sides of barns.

This chest was made for a man named Michael Fink—note the inscription in the central arch—probably by John Bieber, whose father, Jacob, also made furniture. The large hearts flanking the arch were a signature of the younger Bieber, likely modified from a design by his father.

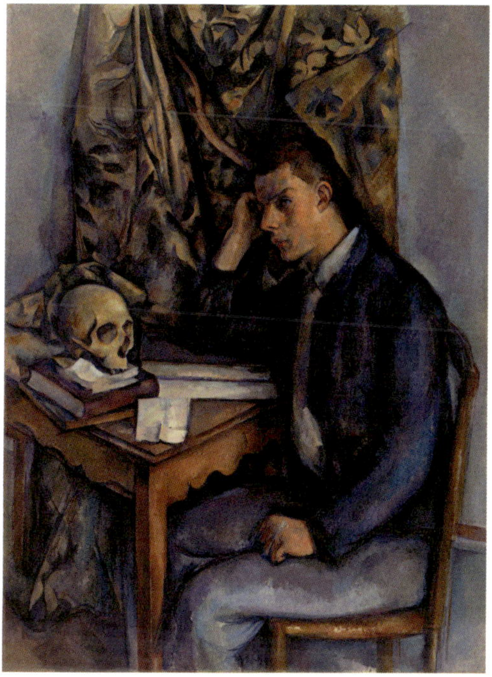

**PAUL CÉZANNE (FRENCH, 1839–1906)**
***YOUNG MAN AND SKULL***
1896–98. Oil on canvas, 51 3/16 × 38 3/8 in. (130 × 97.5 cm). BF929

Seated at a desk, a young man stares out the left side of the canvas. He holds one hand in a taut fist against his left thigh, while he leans slightly into his other hand, held against his face. A skull perches atop the books and papers strewn across the small desk. A rich fabric cascades down, further enclosing the boy and skull. Featuring a range of brilliant purple and blue tones, the cool palette primes the viewer to meditate on the work's subject: melancholy, death, and the passing of time.

Cézanne's figure recalls the pose typical of the artistic allegory of Melancholia, one of the four temperaments associated with the bodily humors in ancient medical thought and linked with creativity. The skull too appears throughout the history of art, often placed in still-life paintings as a memento mori, or a reminder of death. In Provence, where Cézanne spent much of his life, the skull was a popular image in regional festivals. Cézanne featured the skull more often in his earlier work; his return to the subject here may have been motivated by life events, including his mother's death in 1897 and his own failing health.

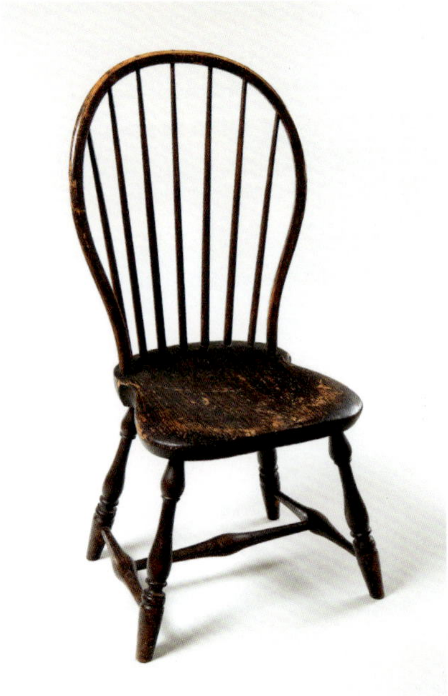

**_WINDSOR SIDE CHAIR_ (AMERICAN)**
Unidentified maker. 18th century.
Wood and paint, 37 × 19¾ × 17 in.
(94 × 50.2 × 43.2 cm). 01.13.42

Albert Barnes had a particular affinity for Windsor chairs as he claimed one of his ancestors used to make them. Characterized by a sculpted wood seat with a back featuring turned spindles, the Windsor chair originated in early eighteenth-century England. In America, it was first produced in the Philadelphia region, around the mid-eighteenth century. Beginning in 1935, Dr. Barnes bought dozens of the chairs in a variety of styles—including side chairs, armchairs, and settees with various seatbacks. He installed them in the collection galleries, his home just outside Philadelphia, and his country house, Ker-Feal.

This chair has a bow-shaped back with seven spindles and a shield-shaped seat. The lower half is more ornate, with double-baluster-and-spool legs connected by an H-shaped stretcher accented with central swells. Unlike most of the Windsor chairs collected by Dr. Barnes, this one retains some of its original dark paint. In the 1930s, chairs were regularly stripped to reveal the underlying wood; this example, along with the other Windsor side chair nearby, offers a glimpse at how these pieces would have looked in the eighteenth century.

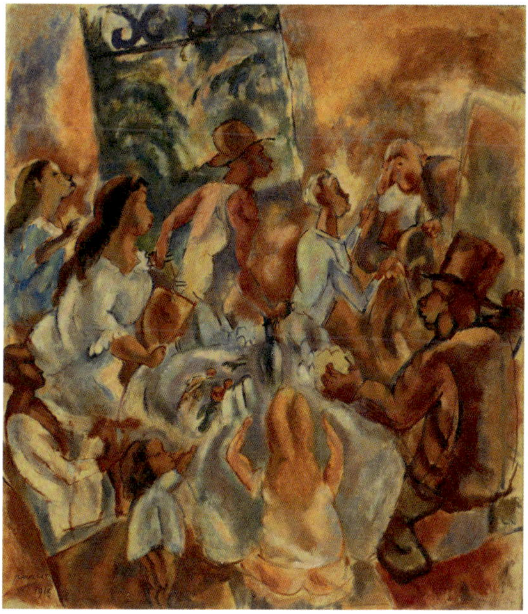

**JULES PASCIN (AMERICAN, ACTIVE IN FRANCE, 1885–1930)**

***CUBAN HOSPITALITY***

1915. Oil on canvas, 40 × 35 in. (101.6 × 88.9 cm). BF344

In *Cuban Hospitality* (alternatively titled *Creole Hospitality*), a group of children and adults rush toward a man entering the scene from the right, while several others sit around a table bearing a white tablecloth, a jug, and some produce. The subject of this painting is possibly explained by Pascin's title for a preparatory drawing: *La fin du déjeuner, ou le retardataire* (*The End of Lunch, or the Latecomer*; private collection). The jumbled, vertically stacked planes and the figures' schematic faces lend *Cuban Hospitality* a tumultuous motion and human intrigue that is idiosyncratically Pascin's.

Pascin was born in Bulgaria and moved to Paris in 1905. With the outbreak of World War I in 1914, Pascin emigrated to the United States. He traveled through the southeastern states and to Cuba, then subject to considerable US involvement in its political and economic affairs. The artist was drawn to the rhythms of everyday life among the people of mixed heritage and African descent in these places. To express his experiences, Pascin began to integrate ideas from cubism and West African figural sculpture.

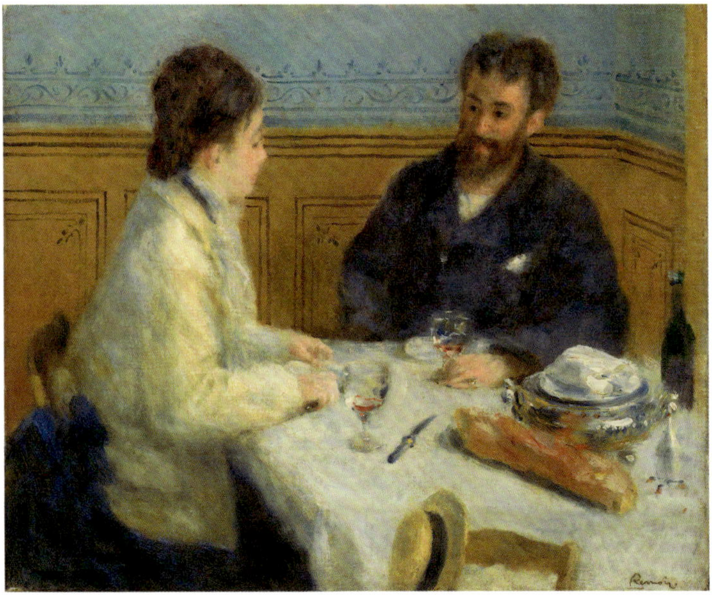

**PIERRE-AUGUSTE RENOIR (FRENCH, 1841–1919)**
***LUNCHEON***
1875. Oil on canvas, 19 ⅜ × 23 ⅝ in. (49.2 × 60 cm). BF45

A boater hat hanging on the chair in the foreground suggests that this couple is probably breaking for lunch during a canoe outing. In the late nineteenth century, boating had become a popular leisure activity for Parisians looking to escape the city, and many restaurants had cropped up along the banks of the Seine. This quiet and intimate scene is one of several that Renoir painted of boating parties and luncheons during the late 1870s and early 1880s.

Renoir paints the meal on the table with delicate vivacity. A glinting soup tureen reflects the warm tones of the baguette beside it. A few dashes of red paint describe the last sips of red wine in their glasses. A yellow daub on the handle of the bread knife echoes the gold ring on the man's little finger, creating a diagonal through the composition. The entire scene is unified by the patterned light-blue wallpaper and paneled brown dado.

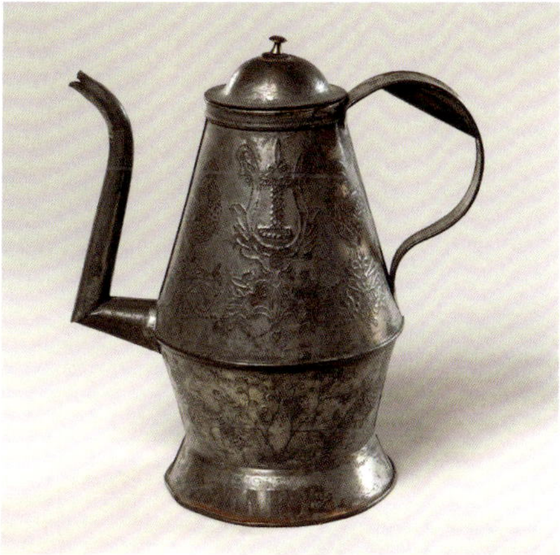

**WILLOUGHBY SHADE (AMERICAN, ACTIVE 1840–1866)**

***COFFEEPOT***

1840s. Tin over sheet iron and copper alloy, 10 ¾ × 6 ¼ × 10 in. (27.3 × 15.9 × 25.4 cm). 01.13.01

This tinned sheet-iron coffeepot bears the elegant decoration of a lyre flanked by birds (probably peahens) and foliate motifs, most likely adapted from Pennsylvania German art. The curving forms of the domed lid, rounded handle, and goosenecked spout complement the angularity of the double-conical body. The name of the coffeepot's original owner, Mary Weisner, is stamped in large capital letters around its flared base; the name of its maker, the Pennsylvanian master tinsmith Willoughby Shade, adorns the top of its handle.

Coffee had gained popularity in America following the Boston Tea Party of 1773, when citizens of the colonial port city boarded British ships waiting in the harbor and threw their tea cargo overboard. The drink thereafter became associated with American national values and was widely enjoyed by the time Shade fashioned this handsome pot in the 1840s.

# MEZZANINE AND BALCONY

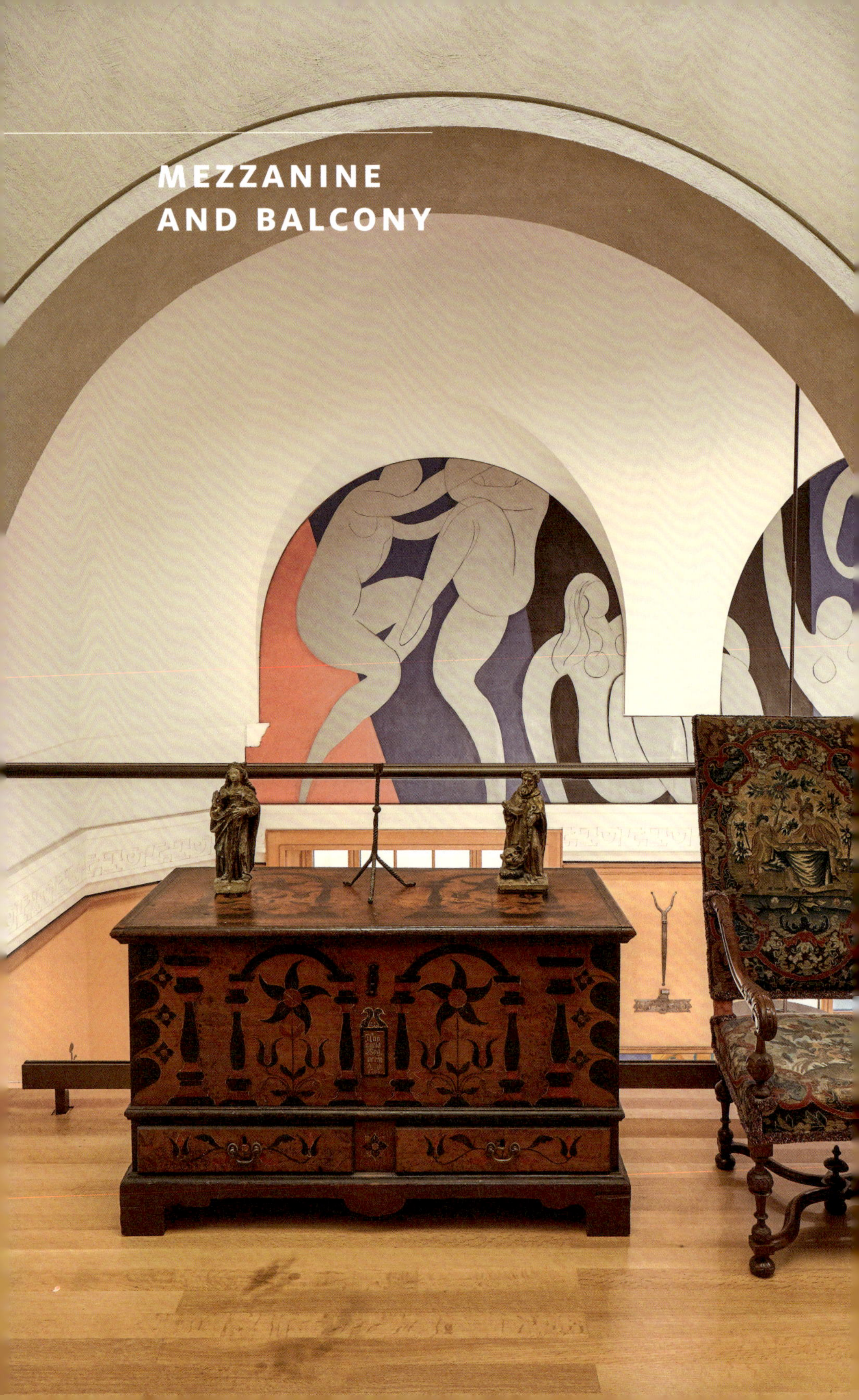

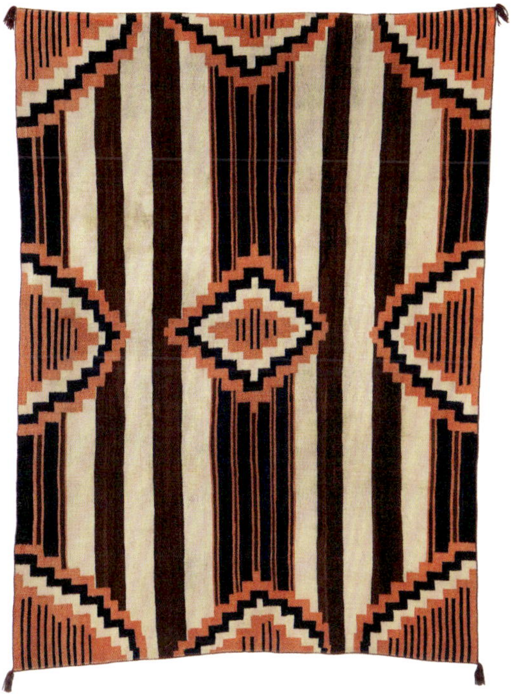

**_THIRD PHASE CHIEF BLANKET_ (NAVAJO)**
Unidentified maker. c. 1880–90. Wool, 72⅞ × 53½ in. (185.1 × 135.9 cm). 01.24.04

Navajo textiles are famously known for their bold colors and designs, as can be seen in this large blanket. Traditionally, textiles of this type were made by Navajo women, who used enormous vertical looms that allowed the creation of large works that could take months or even years to weave. This example features dyed indigo blue, red, and black yarns and natural white yarns. The design includes a stepped diamond motif in the center and stepped half diamonds along the edges. The contrasting colors and geometric patterns create an optical illusion, with the motifs appearing to float above the background field. The high quality of the weaving and balanced symmetry of pattern and color suggest the Navajo concept of *hózhó*, the sacred beauty and balance between the human, natural, and spirit worlds. While this work is described as a chief blanket, the term refers to this striped style of garment. Navajo textiles were often multifunctional, used not only as blankets but also as serapes, door covers, wall hangings, and rugs. This textile may have functioned in any of these roles.

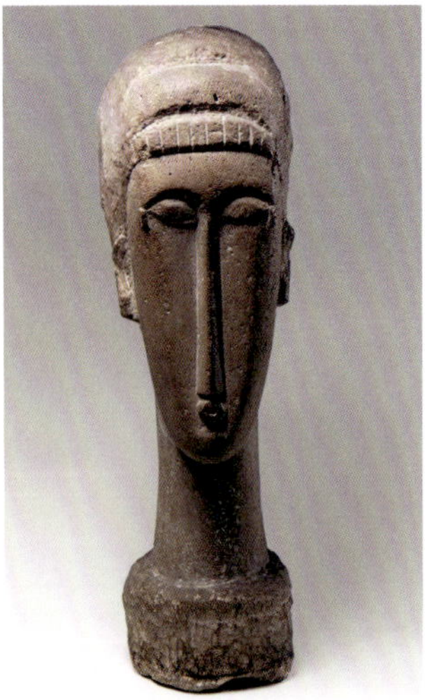

**AMEDEO MODIGLIANI (ITALIAN, 1884–1920)**
***HEAD***
1911–12. Limestone, 25½ × 7½ × 9 in. (64.8 × 19.1 × 22.9 cm). A249

A broad range of art and ethnography informed the elongated profile, rectangular nose, and orblike eyes of this sculpture. At the time it was made, Modigliani was in contact with the Romanian sculptor Constantin Brancusi, but he was also interested in ancient Egypt, and in sculpture from Africa and Asia. Rather than model the figure in wax or clay, Modigliani worked directly on the stone, a technique favored by progressive artists at the time.

Modigliani had ambitions to create an elaborate stone temple, and he may have made this work with that project in mind. Fellow sculptor Jacob Epstein recalled that the artist would light candles and place them on his carved heads, creating a templelike effect. But this chapter in the artist's career proved short-lived. During a brief, intense period of around two years, he produced approximately twenty-five carved works.

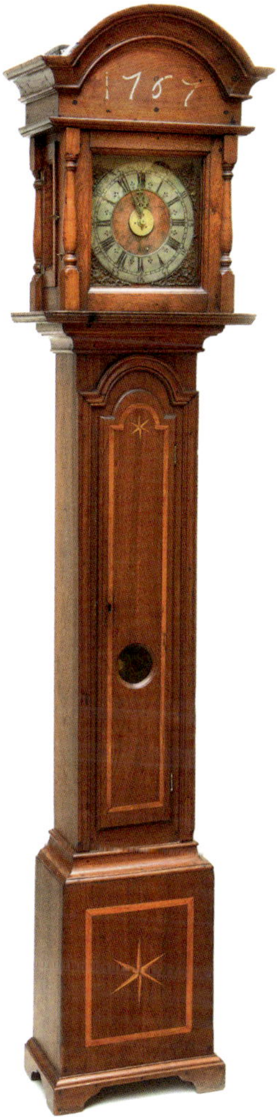

***TALL CASE CLOCK*** **(AMERICAN)**

Unidentified maker. 1767. Walnut, tulip, glass, and copper alloy; 89 ⅛ × 19 ¾ × 10 ¾ in. (226.4 × 50.2 × 27.3 cm). 01.24.25

The mechanical works of this tall chain-wound case clock were made by a specialist who had trained most likely in Germany or Switzerland. Its dial is made of brass and painted iron; the spandrels feature elegant wrought-pewter floral designs. In the chapter ring are Roman numerals for the hours, arabic ones for the minutes, and abstract designs of dots and lines. At center is an engraved brass alarm-setting disk. The clock's alarm bell, winding chain, and gear wheels are visible through lateral access windows in the case.

Another craftsperson would have constructed the case to the clock owner's tastes. This one is walnut inlaid with what may be cherry, with a backboard of pine or poplar. Like many tall clock cases, it assimilates forms of classical architecture. In the bonnet, framing the dial, four spindles evoke columns and support an arched pediment inscribed with the date 1767. The trunk reiterates this arch shape three times, calling attention to the window revealing the pendulum. Inlaid, six-pointed stars—echoing the dial—grace the door as well as the base.

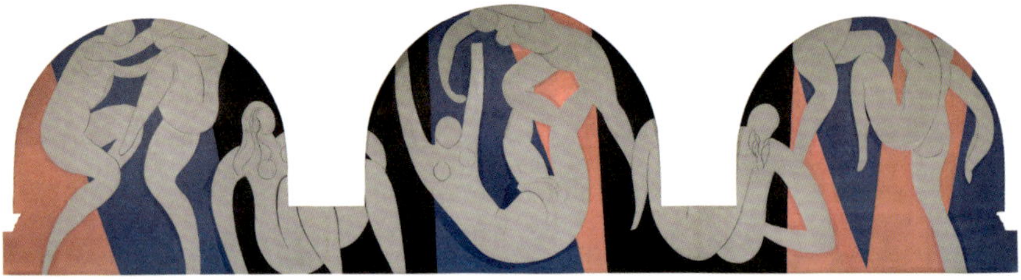

**HENRI MATISSE (FRENCH, 1869–1954)**

***THE DANCE***

1932–33. Oil on canvas; three panels: (left): 133 ¾ × 173 ¾ in. (339.7 × 441.3 cm); (center): 140 ⅛ × 198 ⅛ in. (355.9 × 503.2 cm); (right): 133 ⅜ × 173 in. (338.8 × 439.4 cm). 2001.25.50a,b,c

By the time Matisse paid his first visit to the Barnes Foundation in 1930, Dr. Barnes had already acquired twenty-five of the artist's paintings. Impressed by Barnes's collection, and his unusual approach to display, Matisse quickly agreed to take on this site-specific commission for the galleries in Merion. A second trip to the United States in December of that year allowed him to study the space. Preferring to work in France—where he had rented a garage to accommodate the process—Matisse left with scaled paper templates of the architectural lunettes.

The artist settled quickly on a theme of interlinked figures—an idea he had visited in several earlier works—and he used paper cutouts to determine the arrangement of colors. With the help of a housepainter, blocks of blue, pink, black, and gray became flawless painted surfaces. However, after working for more than a year on the mural, Matisse realized that he had miscalculated the dimensions and had no choice but to start over. Adding new figures to the composition, he amended his design to fit the space, finishing work in 1933. After installing the mural in the gallery, the artist declared, "It has a splendor that one can't imagine unless one sees it," a statement that holds true today.

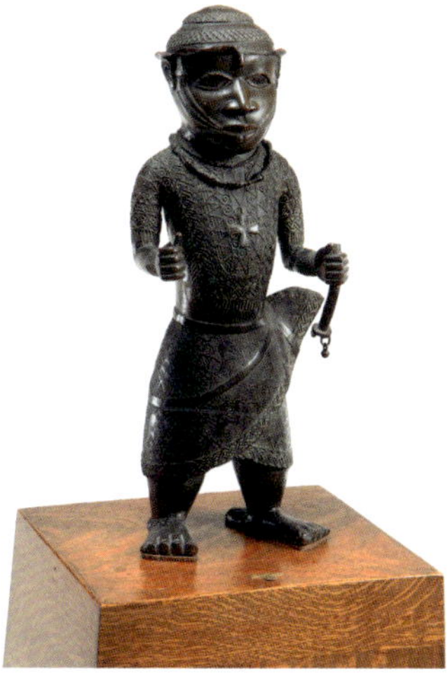

***STANDING MALE FIGURE* (BENIN KINGDOM, EDO)**
Unidentified artist. 16th century. Copper alloy, 22 ¼ × 9 ¼ × 8 ¾ in. (56.5 × 23.5 × 22.2 cm). A230

This small-scale sculpture was made by an artist working for the king (*oba*) of Benin, an empire that flourished in present-day Nigeria from around 1400 to 1897, when it was sacked by British forces. Works of cast bronze (an alloy of copper and tin) such as this example documented life at the Benin court and glorified the power and wealth of the *oba*. The figure may represent a priest or messenger. In its original sixteenth-century context, the solid bronze figure would have been placed alongside carved ivory tusks, commemorative bronze heads and bells, and other artworks on the memorial altar of an *oba* of Benin. To create this sculpture, the artist made a finely detailed wax model to form a mold for casting. The damask pattern on the skirt was etched into the model, and the lace garment that ties behind the figure was formed with delicately rolled wax pieces or with molten wax dropped from above. Benin sculptures of standing officials are rare, and only eleven such figures are known in museum collections today.

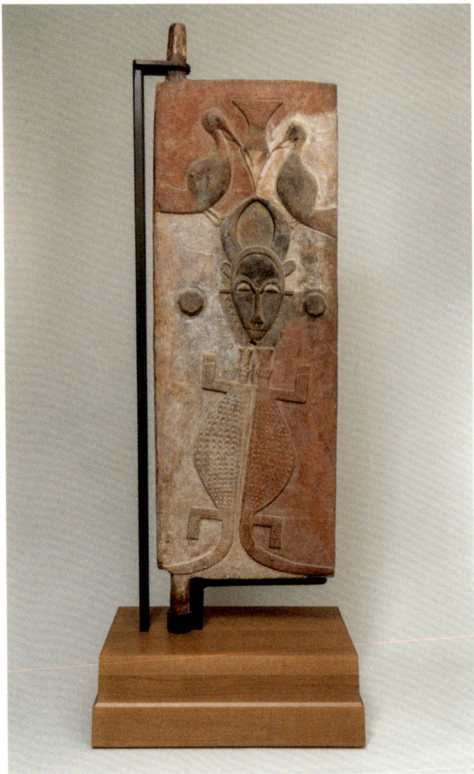

**_DOOR FOR AN INNER ROOM (BAULE)_**

Unidentified maker. Late 19th century. Wood and pigment, 61½ × 20 × 2 in. (156.2 × 50.8 × 5.1 cm). A238

Made by the Baule peoples of Ivory Coast in Africa in the late nineteenth century, this door probably stood at the entrance to a village courtyard. Just below the chin of the mask is a small hole through which a door pull would have been affixed. It is uncertain whether the motifs on the front—two birds, two crocodiles, and a mask—have symbolic significance.

Dr. Barnes purchased the door in the 1920s and was so taken by it that he had a tile version immortalized on the facade of the original gallery building in Merion, Pennsylvania. When the Barnes Foundation moved to Philadelphia in 2012, the architects Tod Williams and Billie Tsien installed a metal etching of the Baule door at the entryway of the building as homage to the original galleries.

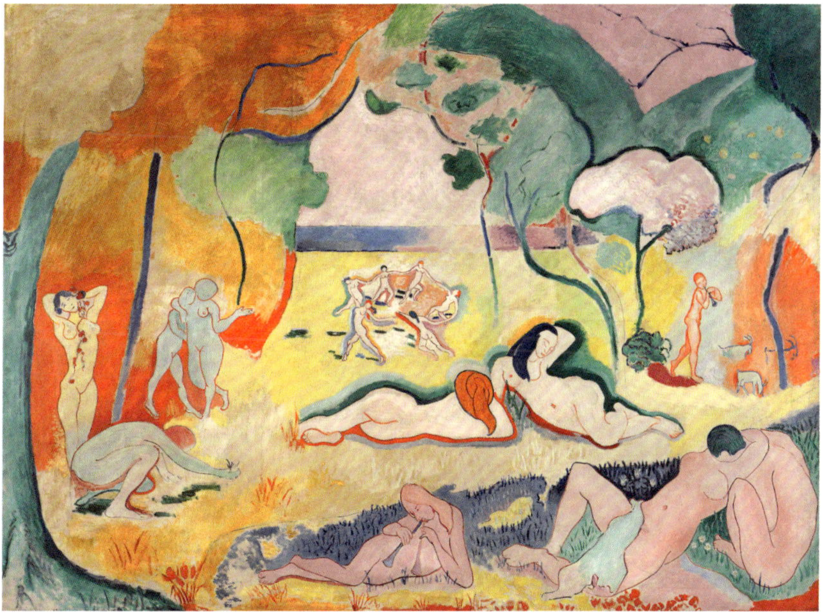

**HENRI MATISSE (FRENCH, 1869–1954)**
***LE BONHEUR DE VIVRE (THE JOY OF LIFE)***
1905–6. Oil on canvas, 69½ × 94¾ in. (176.5 × 240.7 cm). BF719

Matisse reinterpreted the age-old theme of arcadia to produce this watershed painting in the history of European modernism. Drawing on influences from Renaissance painting to advertising posters, he blended tradition and contemporary culture in a provocative way. When he exhibited the work in Paris in 1906, audiences were shocked by the execution—the nonnaturalistic colors, the jarring shifts in scale, and the distorted anatomies. The two figures in the right foreground, for example, seem to fuse into a monstrous form. The reclining nudes in the center, outlined in dark green and bright scarlet, look as if they are pasted to the stagelike background. The small scale of the ring of dancers further highlights the spatial inconsistency.

The painting's expressive arrangement of colors and forms reflects Matisse's "decorative" approach to composition. The work's title indicates the sense of happiness (*bonheur*) or contentment that Matisse aimed to convey with his bright palette and melodic, undulating lines.

# ROOM 14

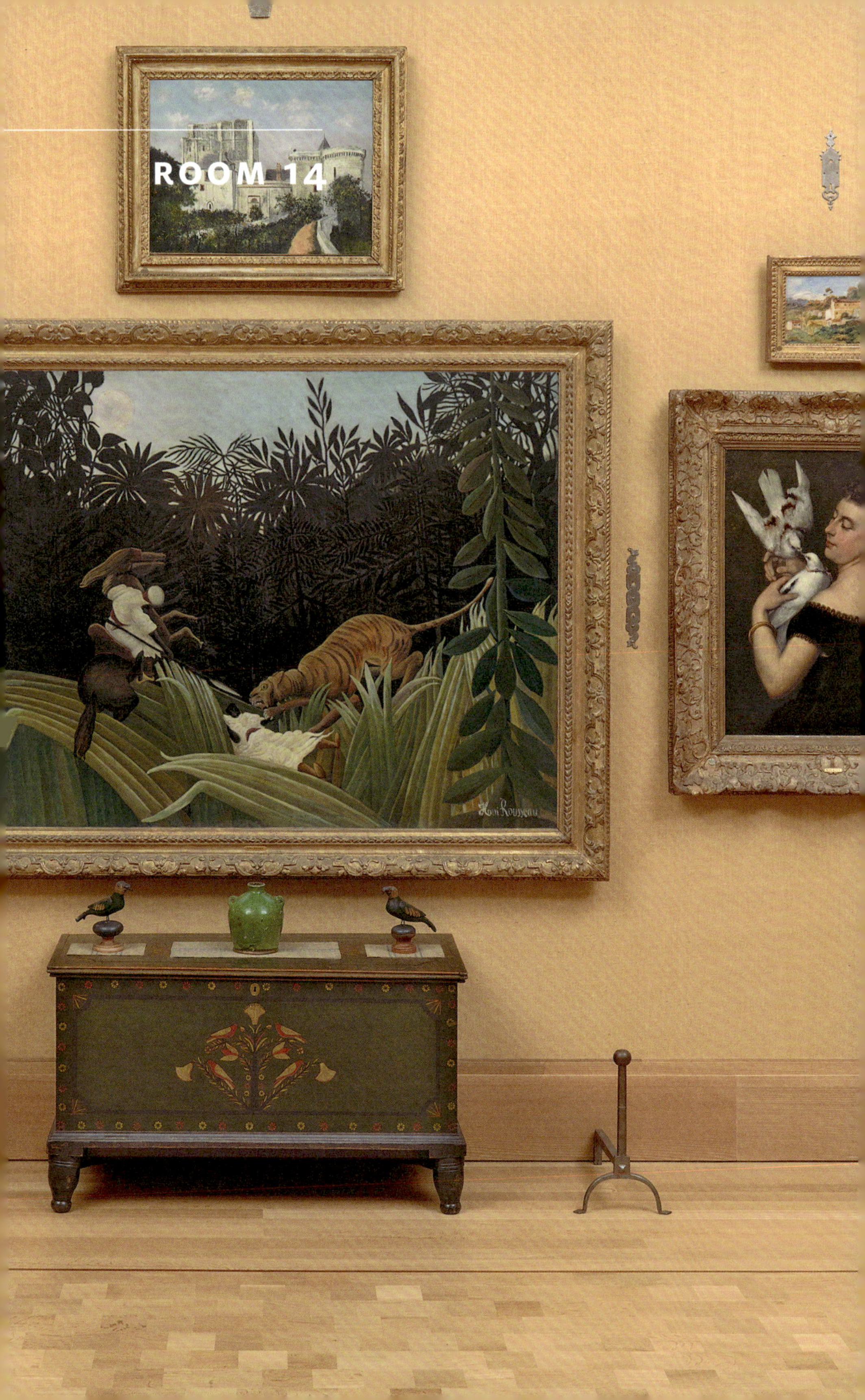

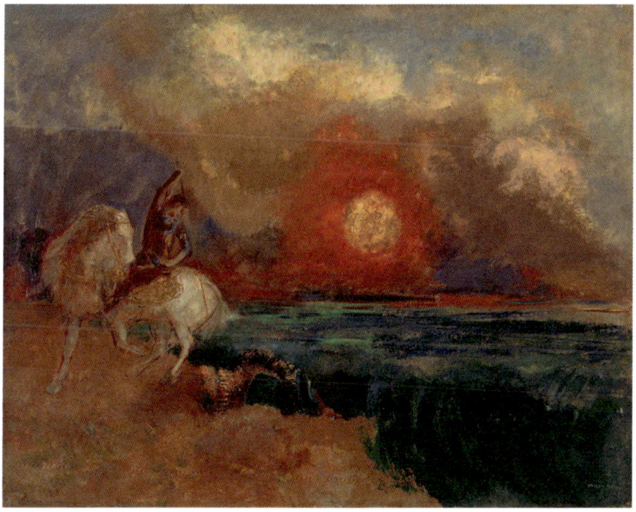

**ODILON REDON (FRENCH, 1840–1916)**
***SAINT GEORGE AND THE DRAGON***
c. 1909–10. Oil on paperboard, 21 × 26 ¾ in. (53.3 × 67.9 cm). BF2093

Redon drew from religion, mythology, and literature to develop his own mystical vision in his art. This painting shows Saint George, a Roman soldier who, according to Christian legend, heroically killed a dragon that was terrorizing a Libyan city; the citizens, in gratitude, converted to Christianity. Redon presents the climactic moment of the slaying but pushes it off to the side. The roiling landscape occupies most of the canvas. Redon uses color to convey the story's drama—a hot red sun burns on the horizon, its rays dissolving into an emerald-green ocean. The land seems to curl over the water, like a wave spraying bits of brown foam. Heavy clouds described with textured brushwork fill the sky.

Redon established his career in the late nineteenth century with black charcoal drawings of fantastical creatures. In his late work, like the present canvas, he turned to oil to explore the expressive potential of rich color in his hazy, dreamlike images.

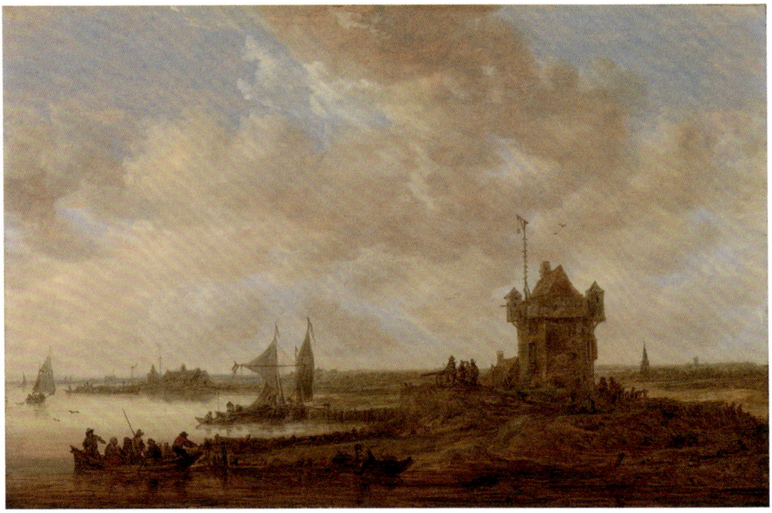

**JAN VAN GOYEN (DUTCH, 1596–1656)**
***THE SQUARE WATCH-TOWER***
1651. Oil on panel, 22¾ × 35¼ in. (57.8 × 89.5 cm). BF843

Van Goyen studied under six different masters and traveled regularly throughout the Netherlands, settling in The Hague in 1632. He helped to develop a new approach to Dutch landscape painting that focused on local subjects such as fishing grounds, canals, and rivers and used a palette of primarily browns, grays, greens, and yellows.

A blue and pink sky dominates the composition and provides a bright, contrasting background for the brown and gray tones of the watchtower and the boats lining the river. The low horizon, common in the artist's work, gives the painting a sense of expansiveness and depth. The light appears to come from the upper left, perhaps at dawn or dusk, as a boat arrives at the shore in the foreground—a ferry filled with soldiers relieving those gathered around the tower's cannon. The location of this painting has not been identified, and Van Goyen is known to have altered landscapes to fit his compositions. Thus, the scene may be invented or it may be representative of a type of place in the Netherlands. The painting exemplifies how the artist's style changed later in his career to incorporate greater luminosity in the use of color while retaining the monochromatic tones of his earlier works.

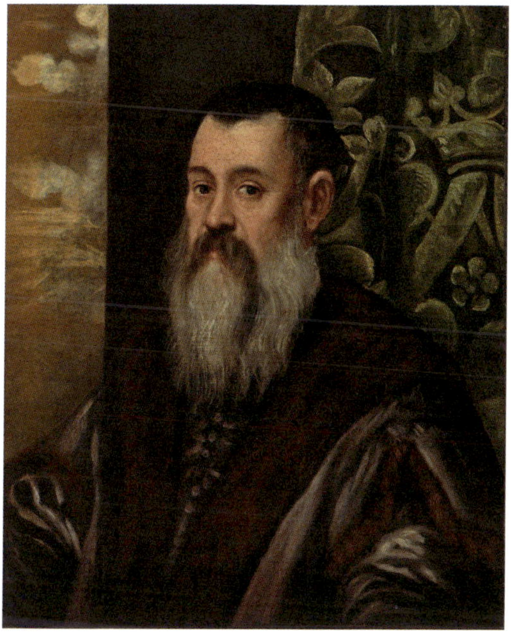

**TINTORETTO (JACOPO ROBUSTI) (ITALIAN, 1519–1594)**
***PORTRAIT OF A GENTLEMAN***
Mid-16th century. Oil on canvas (later mounted to fiberboard), 37 7/8 × 32 1/2 in. (96.2 × 82.6 cm). BF836

The sitter, shown from the waist up, is likely a patrician from Venice. Portraiture had traditionally been reserved for the nobility and was a sign of high status by virtue of its cost. By the middle of the sixteenth century, however, tradesmen and artisans regularly commissioned portraits of themselves, and thus the way in which the sitter was portrayed and the size of the portrait became signs of status. Large portraits and rich garb often indicated the sitter's importance.

This composition follows a format that Tintoretto and his studio used often for portraiture: the sitter is portrayed in three-quarter view, turning toward the viewer. Behind him, green drapery hangs at his left, and to his right is an upright architectural form and a distant landscape. Tintoretto, who took this name to refer to his father's profession as a dyer (*tintore* in Italian), employed a large workshop in the city of Venice that included several of his children and appears to have been collaborative in nature. This workshop practice and Tintoretto's ability to market himself allowed the artist to produce a vast number of commissions for Venice's churches, government buildings, private residences, and confraternities.

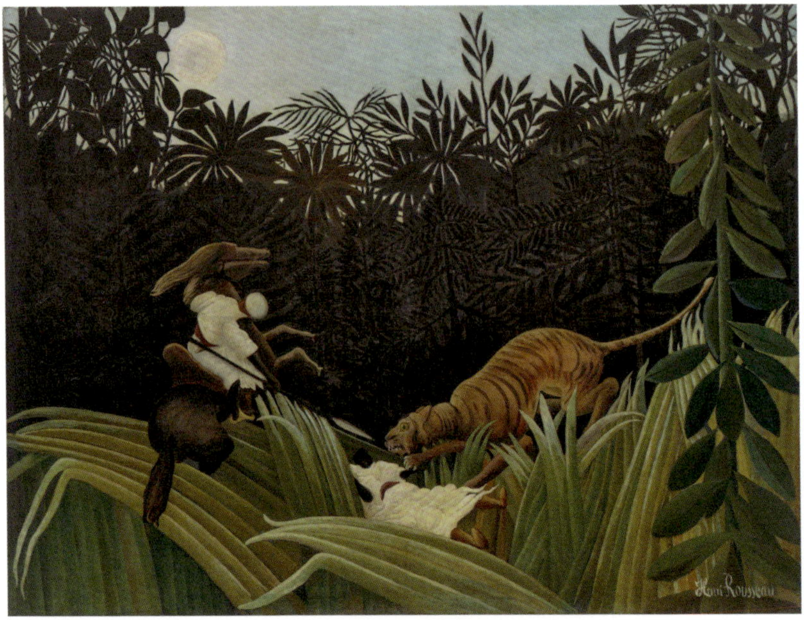

**HENRI ROUSSEAU (FRENCH, 1844–1910)**
***SCOUTS ATTACKED BY A TIGER***
1904. Oil on canvas, $47\frac{7}{8} \times 63\frac{3}{4}$ in. ($121.6 \times 161.9$ cm). BF584

Eerily large grasses part to reveal a tumultuous battle in which a huge tiger mauls its victim, claws outstretched, eye wide open. Another man, clutching at the reins of his rearing horse, fights back as he thrusts a spear at the animal. A large plant in the right foreground acts like a curtain, framing the bloody encounter, which plays out against a backdrop of decorative fronds.

Rousseau lived in an era of colonial expansion. He had briefly been a sales representative for a lowbrow illustrated newspaper, *Le petit journal*, which often featured tales of fear and wonder set in distant parts of France's then-empire. The artist sometimes found inspiration from this imagery, using it as a springboard for his original compositions. Deliberately or not, here he furthered the fantasy of colonialist power by rendering the scouts anonymous, their faces hidden from view.

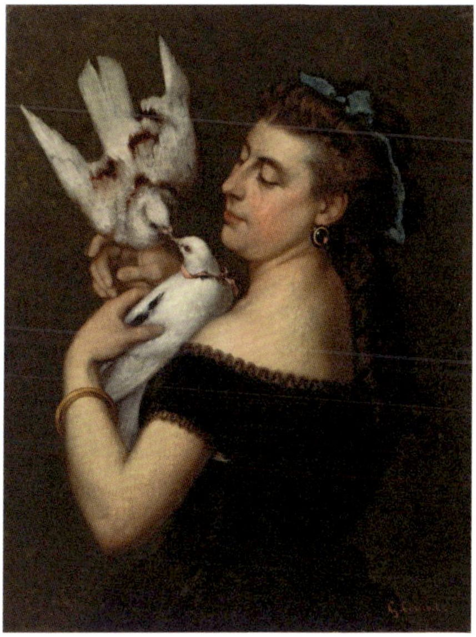

**GUSTAVE COURBET (FRENCH, 1819–1877)**
***WOMAN WITH PIGEONS***
Mid-1860s. Oil on canvas, 31 ⅜ × 23 ⅞ in. (79.7 × 60.6 cm). BF824

This enigmatic canvas lies somewhere between a portrait, an erotic painting, and a genre scene of everyday life. A woman dressed in black with a blue ribbon in her hair holds a pigeon in her left hand while another perches on her right index finger. They are perhaps her pets, as birds were popular household animals during the nineteenth century. The monochromatic background, however, gives no clues to indicate a domestic interior setting. Instead the painting focuses on textures and the sense of touch: the pigeon gently held to the woman's breast, feathers pressing against flesh; the soft curve of her bare shoulder; the gleam of her earring; the shine of her bangle; the silk ribbons against chestnut hair and white plumage.

In this sensual setting, the pair of birds could be understood as a symbol of love or carnality. The pigeon perched on the woman's finger reaches down to graze beaks with the other pigeon while the woman looks on with a slight smile.

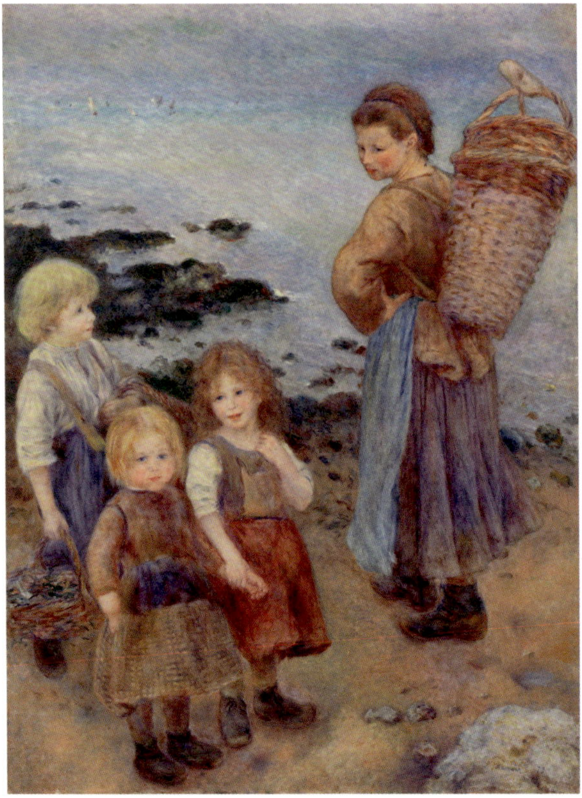

**PIERRE-AUGUSTE RENOIR (FRENCH, 1841–1919)**

***MUSSEL-FISHERS AT BERNEVAL***

1879. Oil on canvas, 69⅜ × 51¼ in. (176.2 × 130.2 cm). BF989

Renoir painted this work while visiting his friend Paul Berard in the late summer of 1879 at Berard's family home near Dieppe, France. The four figures, likely a group of fisherman's children, are depicted standing on Berard's private beach, Berneval-sur-Mer. The eldest turns to gaze at her younger siblings, the metallic end of a mussel stick peeking out from the deep baskets on her back. Both her protective regard for her younger siblings and her heavier burden imply her role of greater responsibility. A young blond boy, with his own basket full of collected mussels, gazes back at her. Two young girls stand at the painting's edge; it is only the youngest of the group who looks out toward the viewer. Despite its humble topic, Renoir submitted the painting to the Paris Salon of 1880, where it was exhibited. Its scale and softer tonalities indicate the work was likely executed in the studio rather than outdoors as was typical for the impressionists.

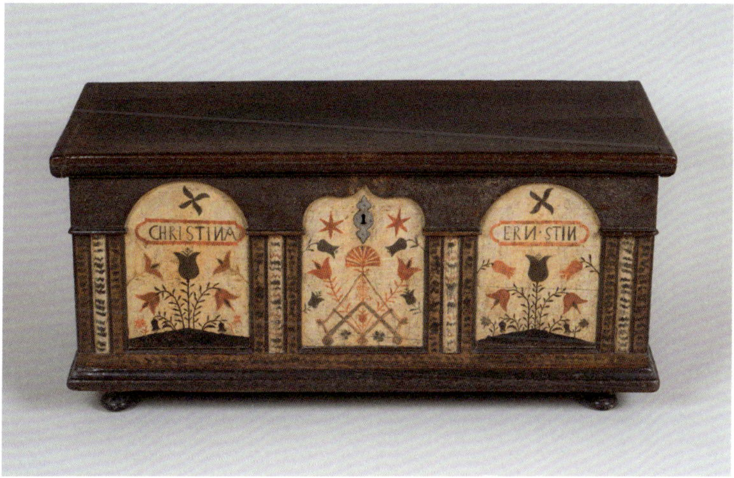


**_CHEST_ (AMERICAN, PENNSYLVANIA GERMAN)**
Unidentified maker. 18th century. Painted wood, 24 ⅞ × 54 ¼ × 23 ¾ in. (63.2 × 137.8 × 60.3 cm). 01.14.38

This Pennsylvania German furniture maker framed the decoration on the front of the chest with applied wood to create three-dimensional interest. The recessed arched panels were therefore not carved out but are actually the exposed surface of the constructed box. The applied wood on the front conceals a construction detail usually accentuated by furniture makers – the dovetails that keep the four sides in place. The chest's ball-shaped feet draw attention to the persistent influence of German construction on Pennsylvania German furniture and its independence from English style; this type of support was popular in Germany from the sixteenth century and persisted into the nineteenth century.

The center ogee arch frames the pointed lock escutcheon and is flanked on either side by rounded arches. Similar colors are used on all three arches to create a cohesive composition. While the painter created generally symmetrical compositions, the decorations vary slightly on each of the rounded arches. Within a red frame, the owner's name, "CHRISTINA ERNSTIN," is written with three reversed Ns—a feature that appears to be simply a reflection of the artist's personal style—while "in" is a feminization of Christina's last name, Ernst.

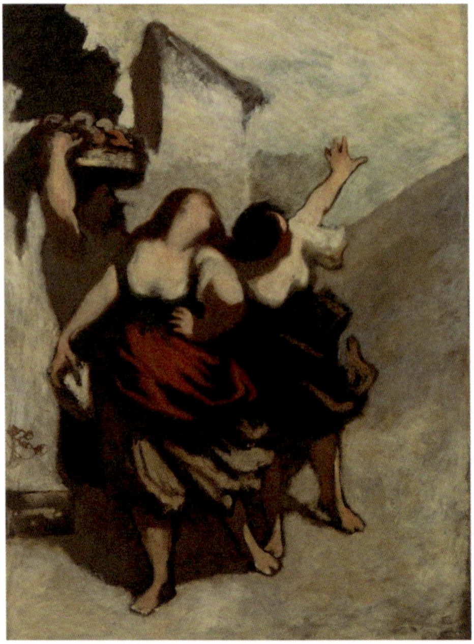

**HONORÉ DAUMIER (FRENCH, 1808–1879)**
***THE RIBALDS***
1848–49. Oil on canvas, 50¾ × 38 in. (128.9 × 96.5 cm). BF22

A noted caricaturist, Daumier was also adept at translating the foibles of nineteenth-century society onto canvas. Here, the artist focuses on a group of three women turned toward something beyond the canvas. A woman in a billowing skirt flings out her arm; another cranes her head, hand jauntily held on her hip; while a third looks on, holding a basket overflowing with produce.

The painting is a study for another work—*The Miller, His Son, and the Ass* (1849, Burrell Collection, Glasgow). Both take as their topic a fable from Aesop about a father and son who are taunted and mocked on their way to the market. Rather than focus on those figures, however, Daumier portrays their hecklers. Known for his own ribald sense of humor, the artist may have felt more in common with the women he depicted than with Aesop's father and son.

# ROOM 15

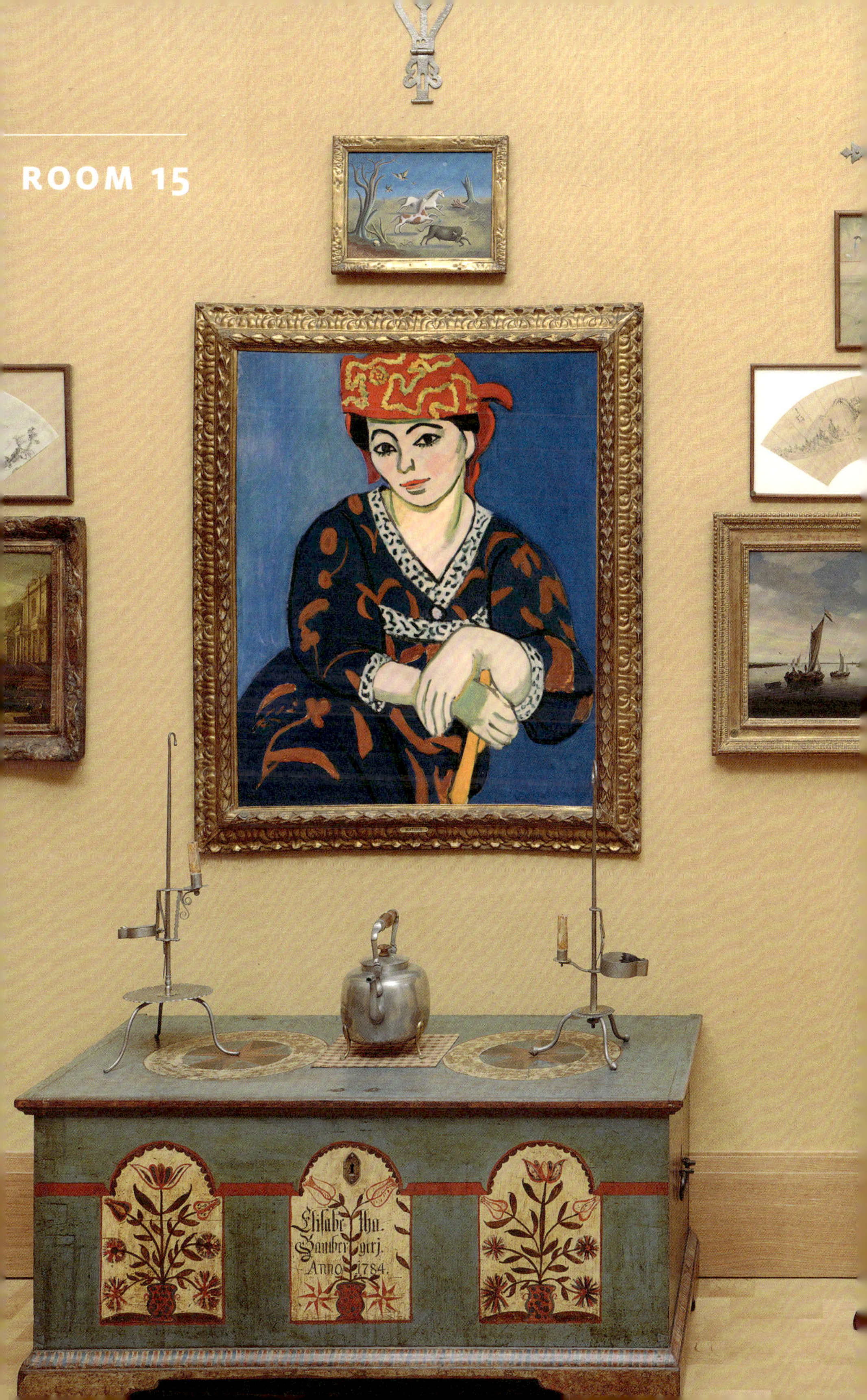

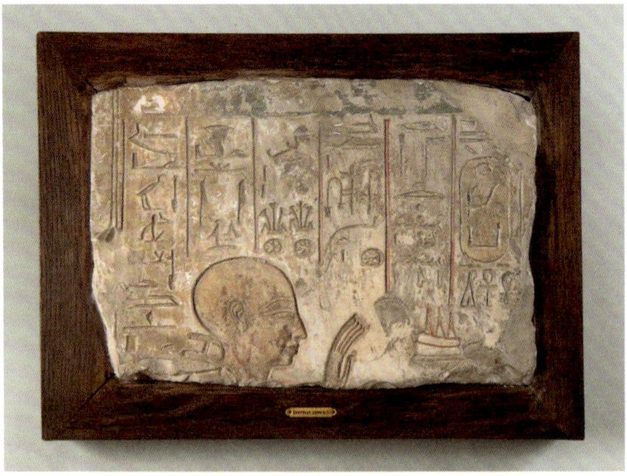

***RELIEF FROM THE TOMB OF KHAY* (EGYPTIAN)**
Unidentified artist. 1279–1213 BCE. Stone and pigment, 8 ¾ × 13 × 2 ⅝ in. (22.2 × 33 × 6.7 cm). A107

Khay was a mayor of the Egyptian city of Thebes (modern Luxor) and a vizier (head of the Egyptian bureaucracy) who served under the pharaoh Ramses II. This fragment probably formed part of a larger scene in the funerary chapel above Khay's tomb, where light would have cast dramatic shadows over the surface through a carving technique known as sunk relief. The scene shows the head and neck of Khay, who has the shaved head of a priest and wears an elaborate linen dress with a high collar. One of his hands is upraised in worship while the other, now missing, would have held the incense burner with three cones of incense, at the right. Seven columns (one of which is very fragmentary) of hieroglyphic text describe Khay making and presenting incense to the deified king Amenhotep I, whose name is written within the oval cartouche (an ornamental motif surrounding a royal name) on the far right. Originally, this scene would have included an image of Amenhotep I and his mother, Ahmose-Nefertari, to the right of the fragment, facing the worshiping figure of Khay. Traces of original red, brown, green, and yellow paint can be seen across the surface.

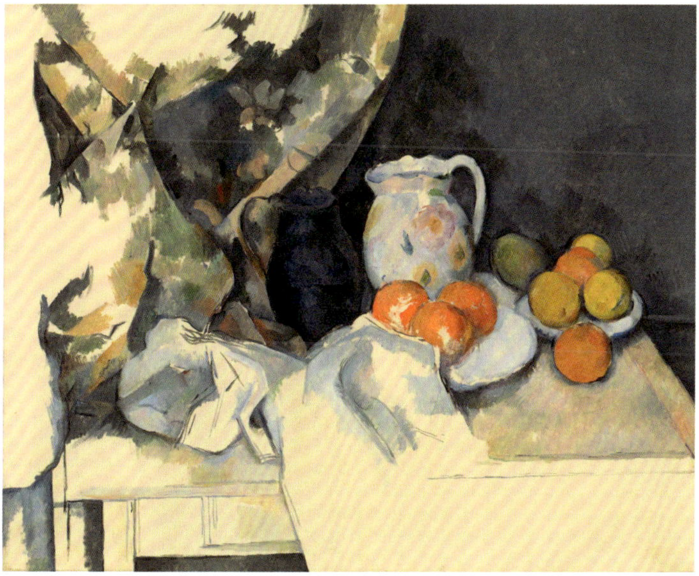

**PAUL CÉZANNE (FRENCH, 1839–1906)**
***STILL LIFE***
1892–94. Oil on canvas, 25⅝ × 32 in. (65.1 × 81.3 cm). BF148

While the unpainted canvas along the bottom and left edge suggests that this picture is unfinished, it is possible that Cézanne himself considered it a complete work. Just as striking as its exposed sections is the still life's off-center presentation—the table appears to pitch downward toward the left, and the fruit and pitcher rest precariously at the top of its surface.

The floral milk pitcher was from the kitchen of the Cézanne family's country estate, the Jas de Bouffan in Aix-en-Provence, where this work was painted. The pitcher appears in two other still lifes in the collection—*The Flowered Vase* (see page 97) and *Still Life*—and the artist later brought it, along with other props, from the Jas de Bouffan to his studio in Les Lauves in 1902. The foliated curtain to the left, which is only partially realized, frames the outside edge of the painting and complements the dark blue background on the right. Cézanne used personal and local objects—the two pitchers, the plain white plates, and even fruit (as with the oranges and lemons here)—in many of his still lifes, projecting an image of a Provençal kitchen interior, albeit one artistically arranged.

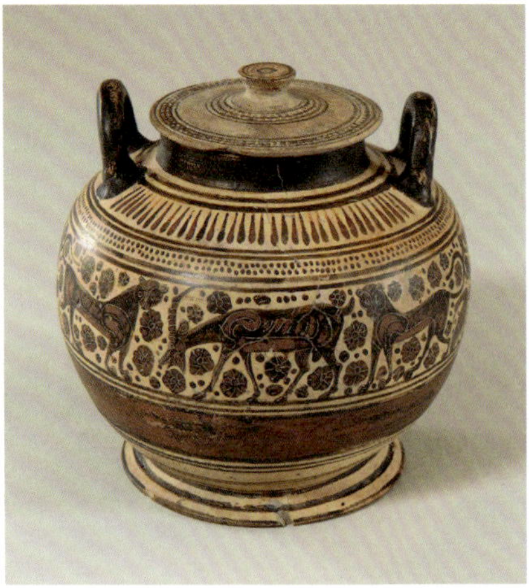

***CORINTHIAN PYXIS WITH LID* (GREEK)**

Unidentified maker. Early 6th century BCE. Earthenware, 6⅛ × 6⅝ in. (15.6 × 16.8 cm). A104ab

This small round ceramic jar was known in the ancient Greek world as a pyxis. Made sometime in the early sixth century BCE, it was formed using a potter's wheel. The painted and incised decoration that encircles the vessel is connected to the Greek city of Corinth, one of the major trading centers of the ancient Mediterranean. It was in cities such as Corinth that goods from the eastern Mediterranean and Mesopotamia would come into contact with the Greek world. Evidence of this ancient cosmopolitanism is visible in the panthers, goats, and ducks that march around the pyxis, motifs that were drawn from the Hittite and Assyrian empires. The lid, which does not match the jar, was made for a different object not in the collection. Dr. Barnes purchased the pyxis, along with the other ancient Greek ceramics in the collection, as a visual reminder of the continuity of artistic traditions that span the history of art.

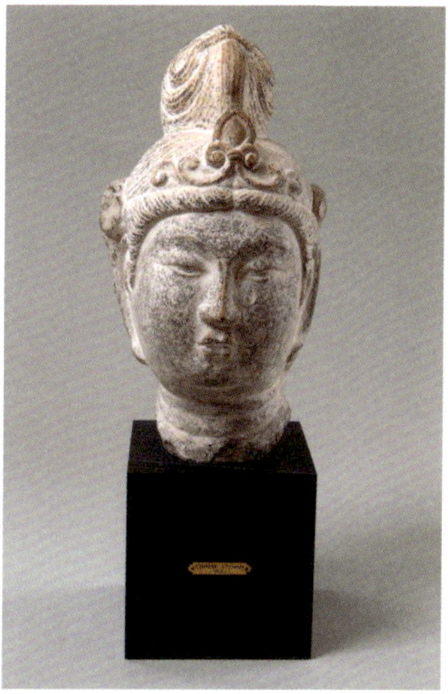

***HEAD OF A BODHISATTVA*** **(CHINESE)**

Unidentified artist. c. 710–720. Fine-grain buff-colored sandstone with traces of polychrome, 12 ¾ × 7 $^{3}/_{16}$ × 7 ¾ in. (32.4 × 18.3 × 19.7 cm). A142

This sandstone head represents a bodhisattva, a figure from Buddhist tradition who is on the path to enlightenment and devoted to helping others reach nirvana. Bodhisattvas can be distinguished from Buddhas by their princely appearance and elaborately coiffed hair, often styled with a crown, as in this sculpture.

This head belonged to a bodhisattva that once stood in the Buddhist cave temples at Tianlongshan ("heavenly dragon mountain"), in northern China. Used for retreat and meditation, the complex was filled with intricately carved and painted sculpture. This head retains traces of its original polychrome decoration, visible at the base of the crown of hair. After the fall of the Qing dynasty in the early 1900s, the caves were looted and the spoils were sold on the international art market. The body of this bodhisattva is currently in the Rietberg Museum in Zürich.

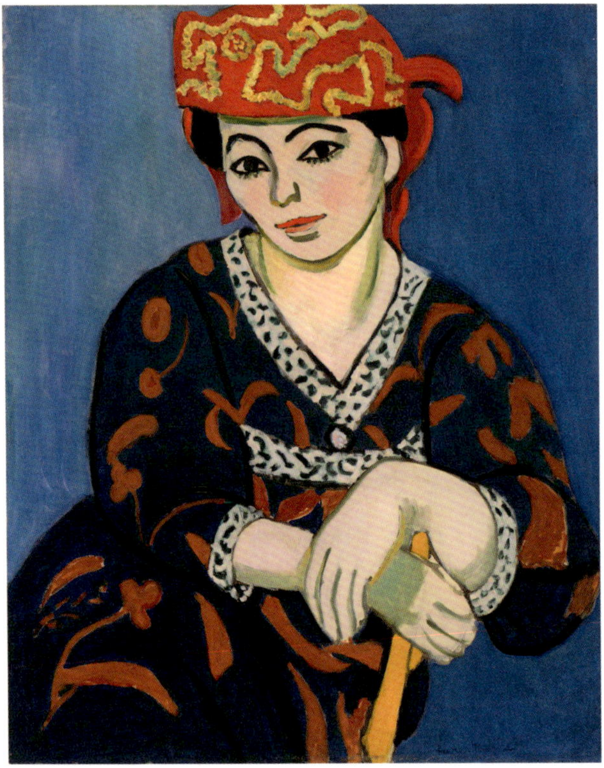

**HENRI MATISSE (FRENCH, 1869–1954)**
***RED MADRAS HEADDRESS***
1907. Oil on canvas, 39 3/8 × 31 7/8 in. (100 × 81 cm). BF448

Matisse's wife, Amélie, posed for this picture wearing a floral dress with lace trim and an ornate red-and-yellow cloth (madras) wrapped around her head. The model's dress and headwrap made it hard for critics to identify her ethnicity and class. When Matisse exhibited the picture in 1907, she was variously described as Creole, Maori, or Kanak. One even compared her to the type of woman pictured on labels of Martinican rum bottles.

This ethnic ambiguity reflects Matisse's approach to art during a time when France was aggressively expanding its colonial empire. He absorbed images and styles across cultures and eras, referencing Caribbean rum bottles, Fayum funerary portraits of Roman Egypt, Coptic textiles, Byzantine enamels, and portraits by Ingres, Van Gogh, Cézanne, and Gauguin. Matisse's sons were eight and nine years old while he worked on this painting, and he may have also borrowed the figure's graphic, simplified face from their coloring books. Matisse synthesized such influences into a cohesive decorative statement that reflected the complicated mix of cultures in the modern era.

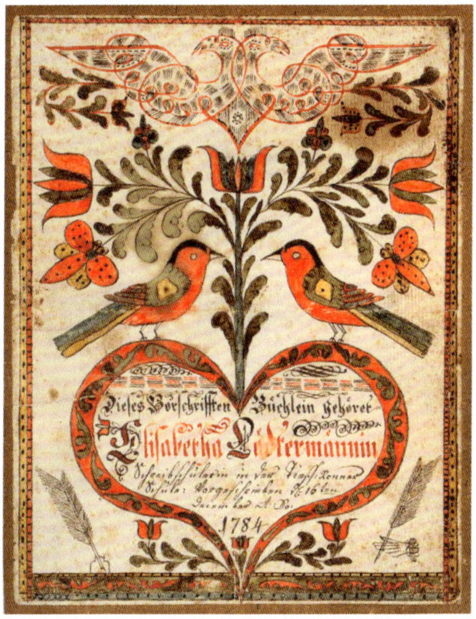

**JOHANN ADAM EYER (AMERICAN, 1755–1837)**

***COVER FOR A BOOK OF COPY MODELS***

1784. Watercolor, pen and iron gall ink, and pen and red watercolor on laid paper; 8 1/8 × 6 7/16 in. (20.6 × 16.4 cm). BF936

Eyer was a native of Bucks County, Pennsylvania, and a lifelong teacher. For most of his career, which predated the Free Public School Act of 1834, children attended schools affiliated with their church and took classes for reading, writing, grammar, arithmetic, and religious instruction. In areas populated by Pennsylvania Germans, classes were typically taught in German. This watercolor is the cover of a *Vorschrift*, or writing sample, teachers would give to students. Translated, the inscription reads, "This little book of writing models belongs to Elisabetha Lädtermann, pupil of writing in the Deep Run School, written out for her the 16th of December, Anno Domini 1784."

Eyer was a prolific Fraktur artist—the term Fraktur refers to manuscript art like this, which has origins in the German-speaking areas of Europe. The name acknowledges the fractured lettering of the typeface, but Fraktur also included intricate designs, such as the two birds facing each other above the heart framing the inscription.

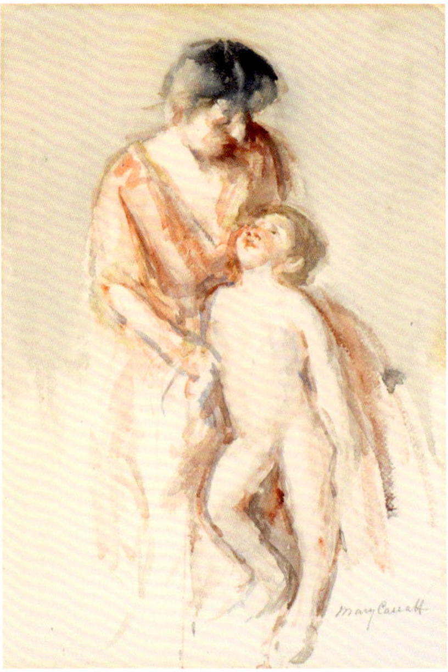

**MARY CASSATT (AMERICAN, ACTIVE IN FRANCE, 1844–1926)**
***WOMAN WITH NUDE BOY AT HER LEFT***
c. 1911–13. Watercolor on thick wove paper, 20⅞ × 13⅞ in. (53 × 35.2 cm). BF323

A skillful watercolorist, Cassatt was well known for her depictions of mothers and children. This work on paper gives clues to how she composed her portraits. Here, the artist uses loose, diagonal lines of warm pink and yellow to build up the drapery of the mother's dress. Blue outlining is visible on the boy's shoulder and the mother's hand, while the artist defines the boy's lower body in a thicker gray. The faces are the most fully realized section of the picture and also hold the key to the subjects' relationship. The child looks up into his mother's face while she gazes back at him with affection in a shared expression of familial love.

Cassatt was deeply connected to the Philadelphia region. Born outside Pittsburgh, she began studying art at the Pennsylvania Academy of the Fine Arts at the age of fifteen. Like William Glackens (see pages 32, 114, 201), who also studied at the academy and who advised Dr. Barnes on his early art acquisitions, Cassatt took up a role as art adviser, in her case to the prominent New York collectors Henry O. and Louisine Havemeyer.

# ROOM 16

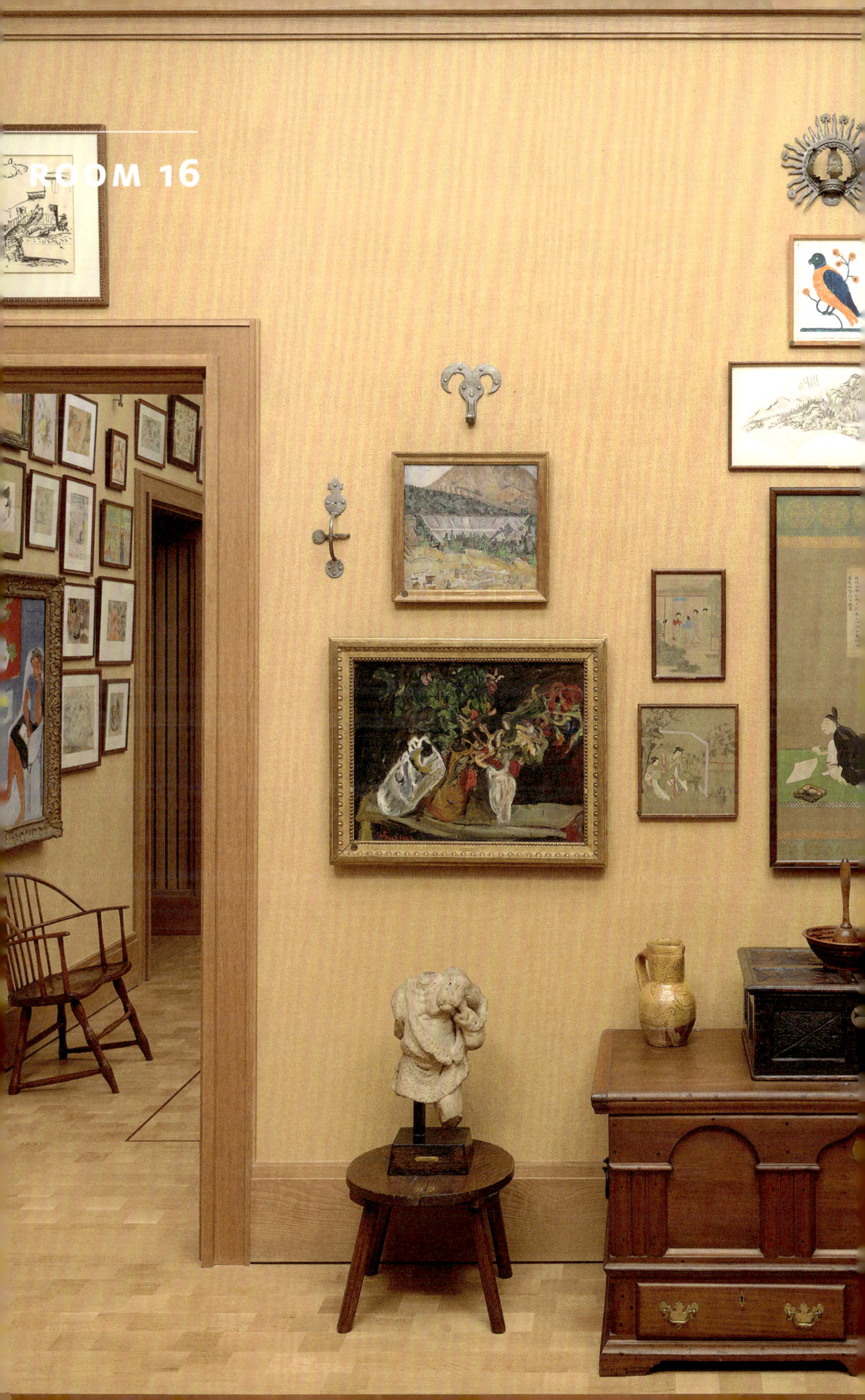

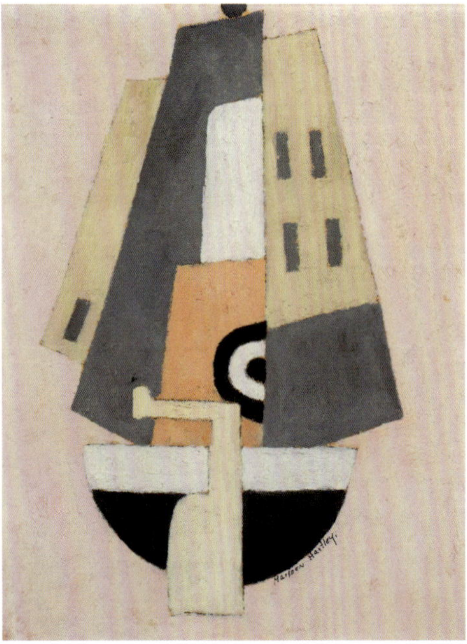

**MARSDEN HARTLEY (AMERICAN, 1877–1943)**

***MOVEMENT, BERMUDA***

1916. Oil on Beaver Board, 16 ⅛ × 11 ⅞ in. (41 × 30.2 cm). BF465

In *Movement, Bermuda*, Hartley abstracted the sails, hull, and rudder of a boat into compact series of geometric planes, rendered in subdued tones of pink, tan, and blue offset by black and white. The planes' color relations and truncation convey a sense of spatial recession. The sails have the effect of placid semaphores; the circular motifs provide a touch of drama that highlights the general flatness. The artist reiterated this scheme with subtle variations on another picture of the same title, also in the Barnes Foundation.

*Movement, Bermuda* (also known as *Black and White Hull*) was actually painted in Provincetown, Massachusetts, during the second half of 1916. Hartley traveled to Bermuda in December of that year, accompanied in both locations by his friend Charles Demuth (see pages 174, 191). Both artists used this time to experiment: Hartley, for instance, modulated his saturated palette to cool marine hues. When Dr. Barnes acquired the two *Movement, Bermuda* paintings in 1921, he hung them in his private office, writing to Hartley: "Demuth was here while I hung them and he agreed with me that outside of a few spots in my house there is probably nothing in America that can touch the wall in sheer, potent, exquisite, meaningful beauty."

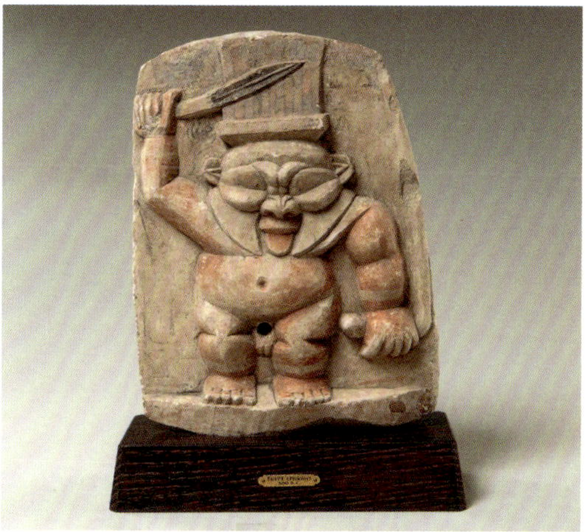

***VOTIVE PLAQUE OF THE GOD BES*** **(EGYPTIAN)**
Unidentified artist. 664–630 BCE. Limestone with red and black pigment, 9 ¾ × 7 ⅝ × 2 in. (24.8 × 19.4 × 5.1 cm). A48

The dwarf god Bes, believed to guard against evil forces, was a popular image in Egyptian household religion. This plaque may have been part of a domestic shrine, where Bes's imposing features would have kept malevolent spirits and dangerous creatures at bay. Carved in high relief, the somewhat crude execution and frontal view heightens the god's grotesque appearance, which features a squat, bearded face, ferocious grimace, and protruding tongue. He wears a feathered headdress and wields an upraised knife in one hand, preparing to behead the snake grasped in his other hand and the scorpion painted in black below the blade. A hole above his testicles originally held an erect phallus made of stone or a different material. Details such as the feathers in the headdress and pupils of the eyes are painted in red and black, and there are other traces of painted decoration in the background. Bes's monstrous face with animal-like ears was likely an early inspiration for Greek gorgons such as Medusa, who were also depicted in a frontal view with fierce, animalistic features.

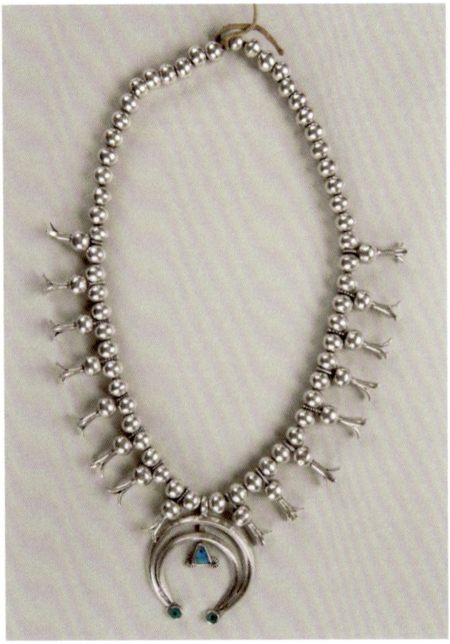

***SQUASH BLOSSOM NECKLACE* (NAVAJO)**

Unidentified maker. c. 1915. Silver alloy, turquoise, and rawhide; 15 × 3½ × ⅝ in. (38.1 × 8.9 × 1.6 cm). A79

Simple round silver beads are combined here with more elaborate beads fashioned in the shape of flaring "squash blossoms," a motif that may have been modeled after pomegranate designs from Spanish jewelry and textiles. The center of the necklace features a double silver crescent terminating in turquoise insets called *najas*, which frame a small triangular turquoise pendant. The *naja* (crescent) motif may also have originated in Spanish decorative arts, possibly from the silver crescents commonly found on horse bridles.

Navajo silversmiths often sourced silver from Mexican and Spanish silver coins, which they melted down and shaped through hammering and soldering. The beads in this necklace display a remarkably uniform appearance, but close inspection shows unique features that illustrate this handmade technique. While silver was a relatively new material in Navajo jewelry making, turquoise had long been used in their decorative arts. Its bright blue color was associated with water and sky, and its source from the earth related the mineral to earth spirits. Turquoise was believed to bring good fortune, bountiful harvests, and protection. The motif of a turquoise pendant hanging within the *najas*, as seen here, may have symbolized a child in its mother's womb.

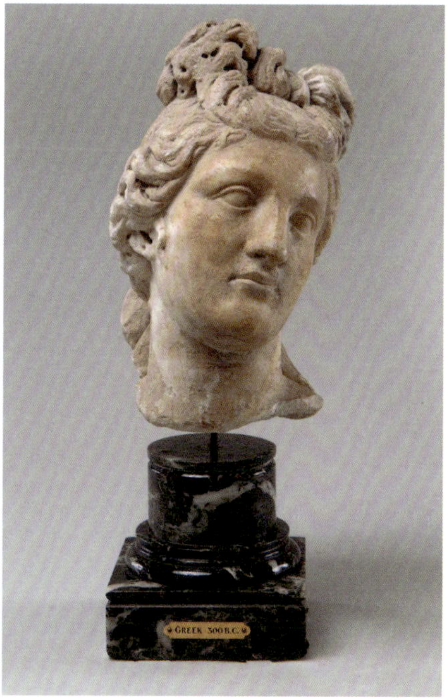


***FEMALE HEAD*** **(ROMAN)**

Unidentified artist. Possibly 1st–2nd century. Marble, 13 ⅜ × 6 ¼ × 6 ¾ in. (34 × 15.9 × 17.1 cm). A8

This fragmentary sculpture depicts a young woman with an elaborate hairstyle. Made sometime during the Roman Empire, perhaps in the first or second century, the sculpture likely represents Venus, the Roman goddess of love. The source of the sculpture's style, with its head tilted to the side and hair parted down the center and arranged in a bow, is borrowed from the famed ancient Greek sculpture known as the Aphrodite of Knidos, made in the fourth century BCE by Praxiteles. Copies of Praxiteles's masterpiece were exceptionally popular in ancient Rome and appeared in imperial palaces, aristocratic villas, and even public baths. It is not known where this example came from, but for Dr. Barnes it functioned as an important example of how the artistic traditions of the past built upon one another.

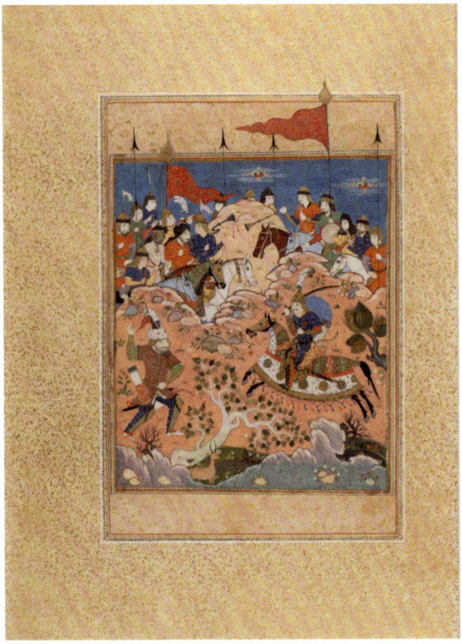

***RUSTAM CONFRONTS ASHKABUS*** **(PERSIAN)**
Unidentified artist. c. 1550. Opaque paint and gold on paper, 18¼ × 13 in. (46.4 × 33 cm). BF756

This miniature from a manuscript of the *Shahnameh (Book of Kings)* illustrates an episode from the battle between the Iranians and the Turanians. The Iranian hero Rostam, at lower left, has confronted his rival Ashkabus on foot. Rostam reaches for an arrow to shoot Ashkabus's ornately clad horse, after which he will kill Ashkabus himself. An epic poem, the *Shahnameh* recounts the mythic and historic past of the Persian Empire up to the Islamic conquest in the seventh century. This is one of three pages from the same manuscript in the Barnes collection; the others hang nearby on this wall. They were executed by workshops in sixteenth-century Shiraz, a major cultural center. When the miniatures were sold to Dr. Barnes, they had already been removed from the original manuscript and pasted onto new paper sheets speckled with gold.

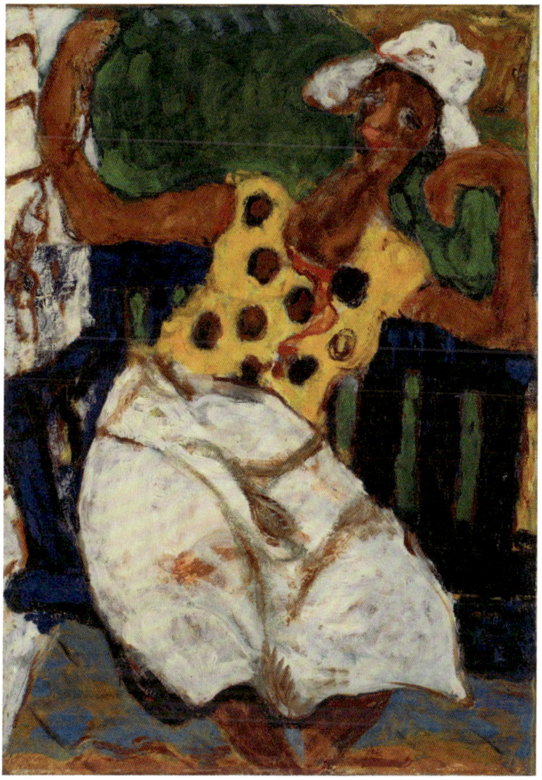

**LUIGI SETTANNI (AMERICAN, 1908–1984)**
***FIGURE***
c. 1939. Oil on canvas, 34¼ × 24½ in. (87 × 62.2 cm). BF2037

An African American woman sits on a porch swing, holding its chain with one hand and resting her head on the other. Her bright yellow shirt with dark polka dots forms the heart of the dynamic composition. Settanni, an Italian immigrant who was studying at the Barnes Foundation during this time, likely painted this canvas on a summer trip to New Orleans. The woman's sinuous pose suggests the heat and languor of the day.

The painting was previously titled *Topsy*, which may refer to the character of a young enslaved girl in Harriet Beecher Stowe's 1852 novel *Uncle Tom's Cabin*. Such a reference might indicate the stereotypes through which Settanni viewed his subject—childlike, happy-go-lucky, and redeemed through white intervention. The painting was never published with this title, however.

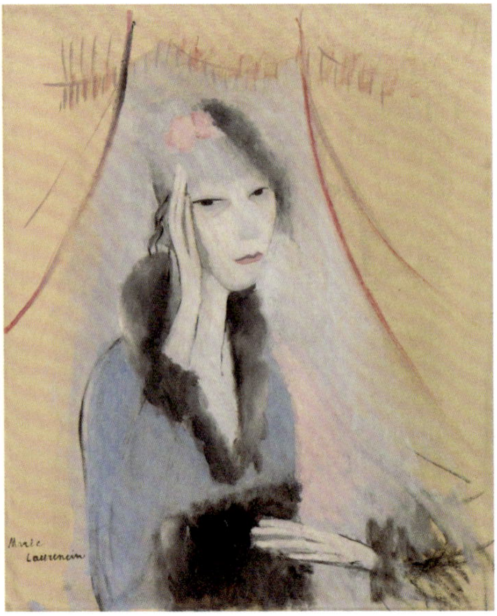

**MARIE LAURENCIN (FRENCH, 1885–1956)**
***WOMAN WITH MUFF***
c. 1914. Oil on canvas, 21½ × 18 in. (54.6 × 45.7 cm). BF384

Laurencin associated with many cubist artists and modern writers, despite not painting in a discernably cubist style. She instead used elongated and stylized forms to develop her signature motif of the willowy, ethereal woman-child who inhabits an almost exclusively feminine world. At the Autumn Salon in Paris in 1912, Laurencin participated in an ambitious ensemble of model domestic interiors called the *Maison Cubiste* (*Cubist Home*). She contributed four oval portrait heads of young women that crowned full-length mirrors in a model living room.

This painting treats a similar theme. A fashionably dressed woman holds a muff in one hand, adjusting her pink-ribboned hat with the other. Her elegant manner is apparent in her long neck and fingers. She is perhaps seated in a theater box, indicated by the parted curtain behind her. Laurencin's pink-and-blue palette and focus on fashionable women relates her work to eighteenth-century French painting of the rococo era.

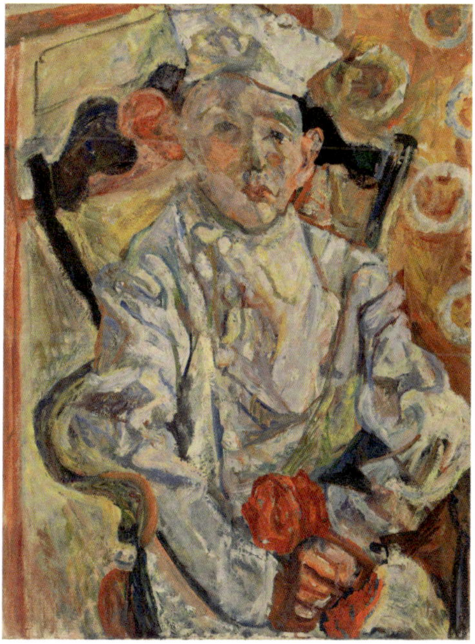

**CHAÏM SOUTINE (RUSSIAN, ACTIVE IN FRANCE, 1893–1943)**
***THE PASTRY CHEF (BAKER BOY)***
c. 1919. Oil on canvas, 26 × 20 1⁄16 in. (66 × 51 cm). BF442

Despite his exaggeratedly large ear and the tense way he clutches the red napkin in his lap, this teenage pastry cook, Rémi Zocchetto, was painted by Soutine with the dignity of a man of high social standing. In the late teens and early 1920s, the artist began a series of portraits featuring the staff of luxury restaurants and hotels. He strove to convey the humanity of these service workers; moreover, their uniforms interested him aesthetically. The boy's white jacket is a field of agitated brushwork, with slashes and swirls of yellows, blues, and greens suggesting its rumpled and heavily used appearance.

When Dr. Barnes saw this painting in Paris in 1922, he was struck by its expressive power. In short order, he proceeded to buy more than fifty additional works by Soutine, single-handedly establishing the artist's international career. Although Barnes later sold many of these paintings, Soutine remains a major presence in these galleries; the collection includes twenty-one canvases by the artist.

# ROOM 17

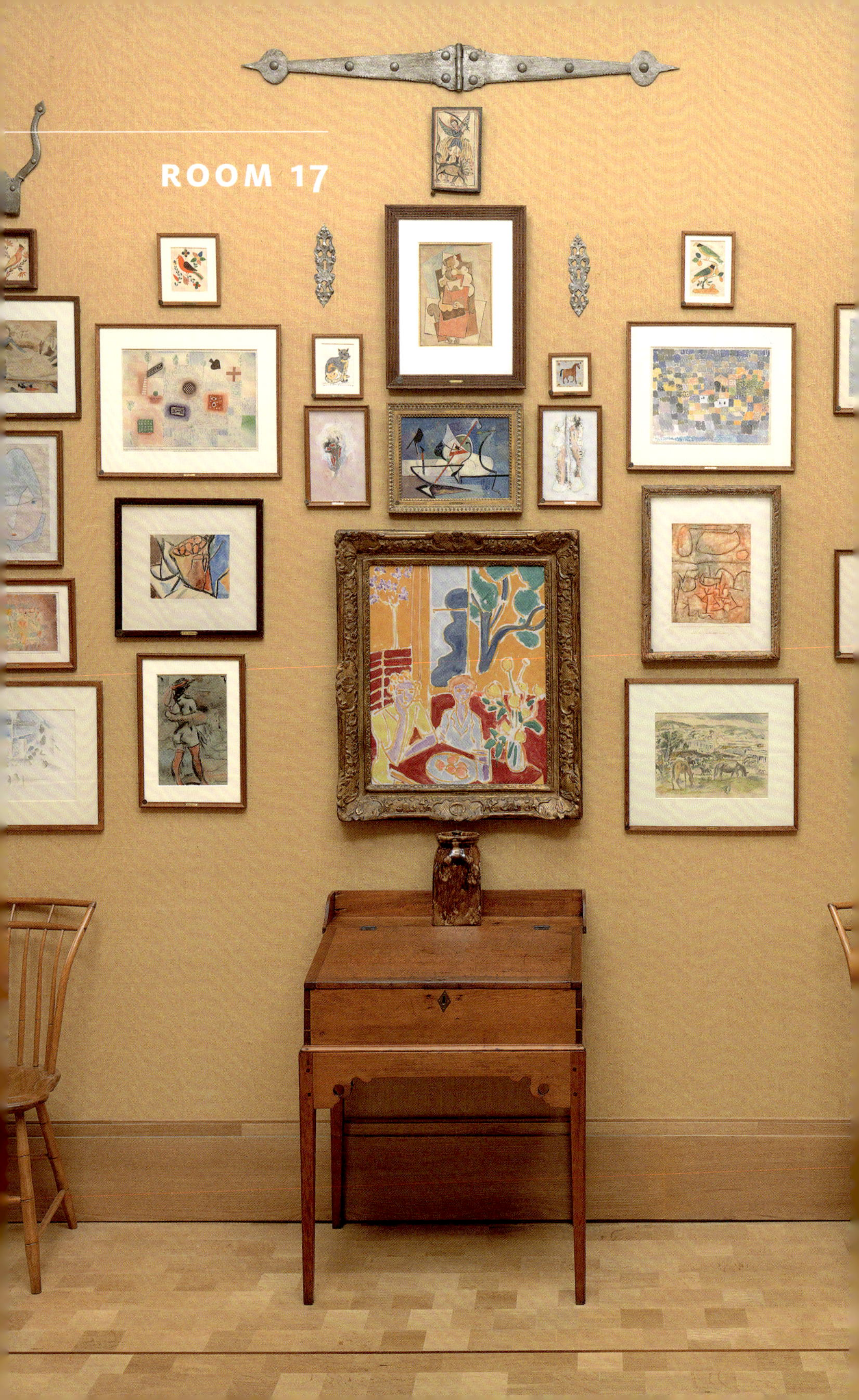

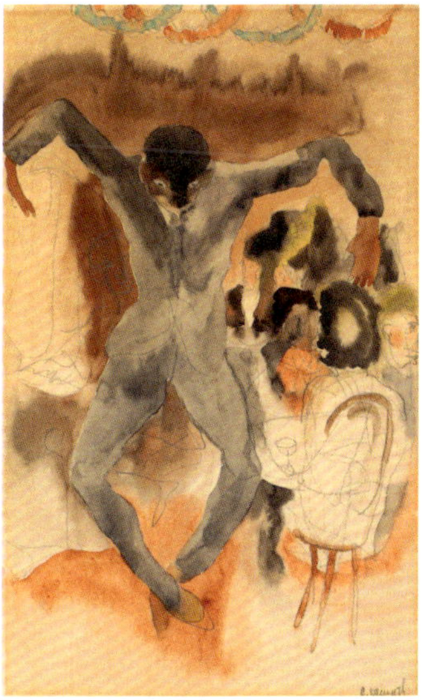

**CHARLES DEMUTH (AMERICAN, 1883–1935)**
***AT MARSHALL'S***
1917. Watercolor and graphite on laid paper, 13 × 8 in. (33 × 20.3 cm). BF741

Although he lived in rural Lancaster, Pennsylvania, Demuth regularly visited New York to meet up with friends and fellow artists at jazz clubs and hotel bars. This lively watercolor depicts a dancer at the Marshall Hotel, a Black-owned establishment in midtown Manhattan. The Marshall was a major center of African American cultural and intellectual life in early twentieth-century New York. Many white patrons also came to experience the music, discussions, and performances that would lay the foundation for the Harlem Renaissance. Demuth made this watercolor after Marshall's closed in 1913, offering a retrospective look at a place key to the birth of American modernism.

Demuth was adept with watercolor and used the pooling and bleeding of fluid washes to his advantage. In the dancer's gray suit, he painted wet-in-wet to create a sense of light and shadow raking across the figure. He also used the edges of washes to convey a smoky, shimmering atmosphere.

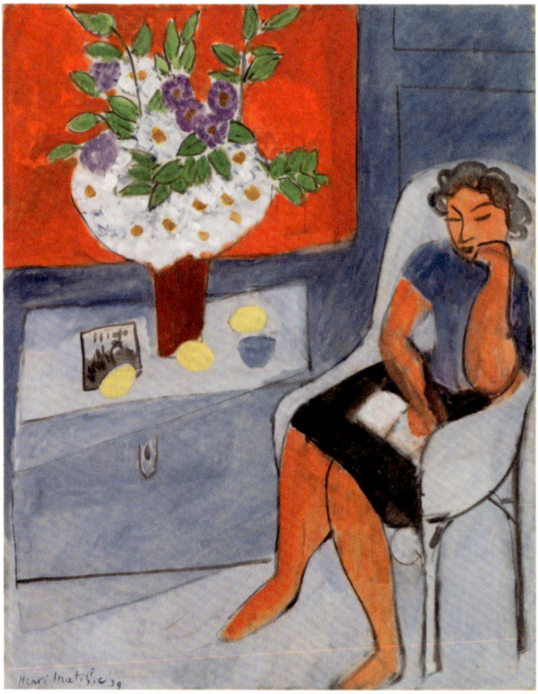

**HENRI MATISSE (FRENCH, 1869–1954)**
***FIGURE WITH BOUQUET***
1939. Oil on canvas, 36 7/16 × 28 15/16 in. (92.5 × 73.5 cm). BF980

"My models, human figures, are never just 'extras' in an interior. They are the principal theme of my work. I depend absolutely on my model," Matisse wrote in the summer of 1939, shortly before working on this painting. He developed the contemplative picture around the Hungarian model Wilma Javor's serene pose. In an earlier draft, which was photographed, the figure stared into the distance. In the final composition, however, she peruses a book, paralleling the viewer's own absorption in the scene.

Matisse left traces of these earlier states visible. The ghost of the model's lower right leg indicates a previous position closer to the chest, and the chest's own vestigial outline reveals its formerly diagonal orientation. By moving the chest flush with the wall and painting it a shade of blue that connects the floor and the wall, Matisse established a tonal region that tempers the joyously vibrant red square in the background, which would otherwise dominate the composition. The burst of bright color hints at the emotion beneath this tranquil scene.

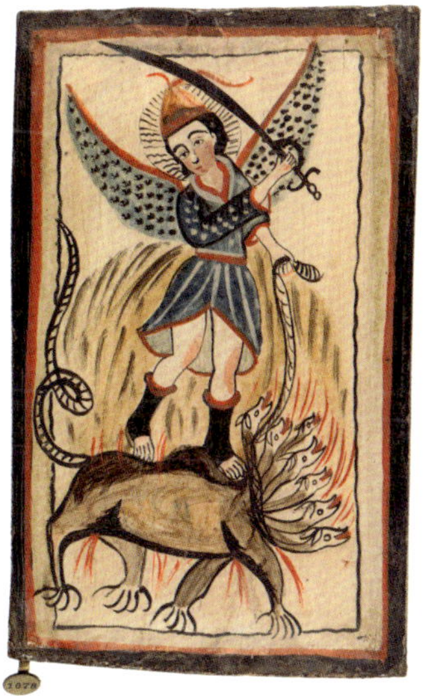

**JOSÉ RAFAEL ARAGON (MEXICAN, 1796–1862)**
***ARCHANGEL SAINT MICHAEL***
c. 1840. Water-based paint on wood panel, 8 ⅞ × 5 ⅞ in. (22.5 × 14.9 cm). BF1078

This small *retablo* (a painting of an important religious figure) is an example of the blending of Spanish, Mexican, and Pueblo artistic styles and subjects found in New Mexico. It depicts a dramatic scene from the New Testament story of the War of Heaven. The archangel Saint Michael, leader of the host of heaven, is seen in the act of slaying a multiheaded fire-spewing dragon, likely representing the fallen angel Satan. Michael is armed for battle, wearing armor and a plumed helmet and wielding a Spanish saber, which is raised above his head moments before he slaughters the dragon. While the subject is derived from Franciscan Catholicism, the stylized flat figures, bright hues, and bold and flowing brushstrokes are characteristic of Pueblo and Mexican painting traditions.

Aragon was a prolific religious painter (*santero*) in the region of New Mexico and created artworks, such as this *retablo*, for Franciscan missionary outposts. These missions worked to convert local Native American communities, including the Pueblo and Navajo peoples, to Catholicism as part of a strategy to more easily control the population.

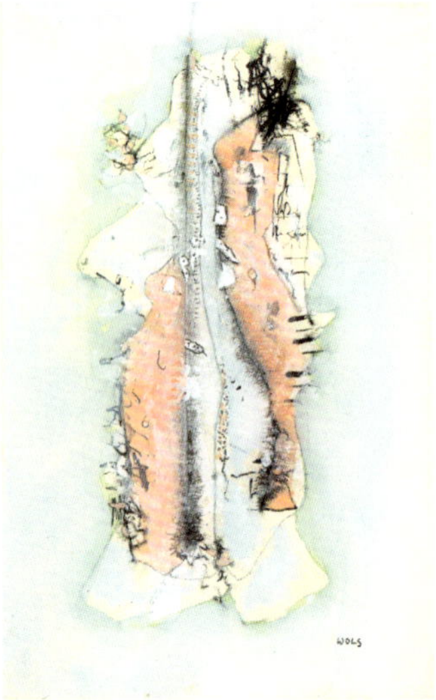

**WOLS (ALFRED OTTO WOLFGANG SCHULZE) (GERMAN, 1913–1951)**
***BIRD'S-EYE VIEW***
c. 1949. Gouache and pen and ink on wove paper, 6 ⅜ × 9 ¾ in. (16.2 × 24.8 cm).
BF2525

This tiny gouache (opaque watercolor) by the German artist Wols is among the latest and most abstract paintings in the collection. Irregular peach- and cream-colored areas form a vertical central motif, stitched together by fine lines of black ink. Some of these lines are short and regular, like the teeth of a zipper; others are longer and more chaotic, like the branching networks produced by static electricity or the dendrites of neurons. *Bird's-Eye View* might be read as an aerial view of a cityscape, an exercise in nonrepresentative abstraction, or a fragmented human body.

*Bird's-Eye View* is an example of *art informel*: abstract European painting of the late 1940s into the 1950s defined by a gestural technique and improvisation, and involving a desire for a fresh cultural start. But Wols's deliberate composition and delicate detail attest that this painting was not truly spontaneous. Its small size and allusive nature invite close, meditative looking—an experience that recalls the artist's statement that "a tiny sheet of paper can contain the world."

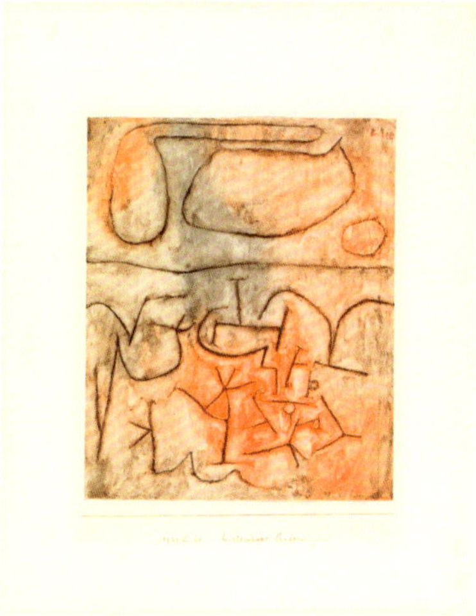

**PAUL KLEE (SWISS, 1879–1940)**
***HISTORIC GROUND***
1939. Watercolor with graphite underdrawing on wove paper; artist-mounted to paperboard; 10 9⁄16 × 8 3⁄4 in. (26.8 × 22.2 cm). BF2532

Below a wavering horizontal line, a cluster of jumbled forms evokes prehistoric or ancient symbols. During the 1930s, the decorated walls of Paleolithic caves were becoming increasingly well known; watercolor copies and photographic prints of the cave images featured in the exhibition *Prehistoric Rock Pictures in Europe and Africa*, presented in Frankfurt in 1936 and at the Museum of Modern Art, New York, in 1937. Klee called upon the viewer's knowledge of these discoveries by creating forms that mimic those found on cave walls. The title inscribed by the artist below the watercolor, along with its date, emphasizes Klee's reference to distant history.

In the early 1930s, Klee began suffering from an undiagnosed disease that affected his skin and other organs. At the same time, his art was coming under scrutiny in Germany with the increasing power of the National Socialists. He left Germany in 1933 to return to his native Switzerland, but by 1936 his output had been reduced to just twenty-five works. His health began to improve over the following years, and in 1939 he produced more than 1,200 works, including this watercolor, the most he had ever produced in a single year.

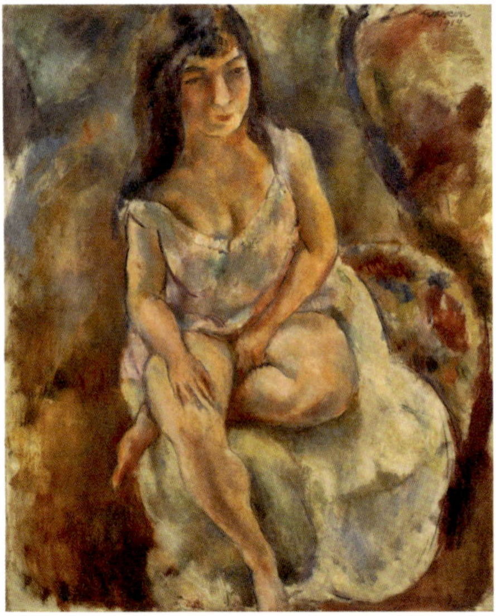

**JULES PASCIN (AMERICAN, ACTIVE IN FRANCE, 1885–1930)**
***SEATED GIRL IN CHEMISE***
1914. Oil on canvas, 28¾ × 23⅝ in. (73 × 60 cm). BF483

A woman wearing a loose-fitting pink chemise sits on a multicolor, partially shrouded ottoman next to a mirror. Her reflection is recorded in maroon and at an oblique tilt that exaggerates the viewer's high perspective. She sits on her left leg, tucking her left hand into her groin while resting her right hand upon her right thigh. While her ample body is exposed, her facial expression is inscrutable, perhaps registering boredom or contemplation.

Signed and dated "Pascin 1914" on the upper right, *Seated Girl in Chemise* is typical of the single-figure studies the Bulgarian-born artist produced in his adopted home of Paris, just prior to emigrating to the United States. His Parisian pictures, for the most part, presented his friends and surroundings in a distinctly personal style formed out of ideas from Renoir and Cézanne, as well as older European painters and prehistoric cave paintings. Dr. Barnes was impressed by Pascin's knowledge of art history and responded enthusiastically to his creative responses to tradition, remarking that Pascin had invented a unique amalgam of "interpenetrating colorplanes at all angles."

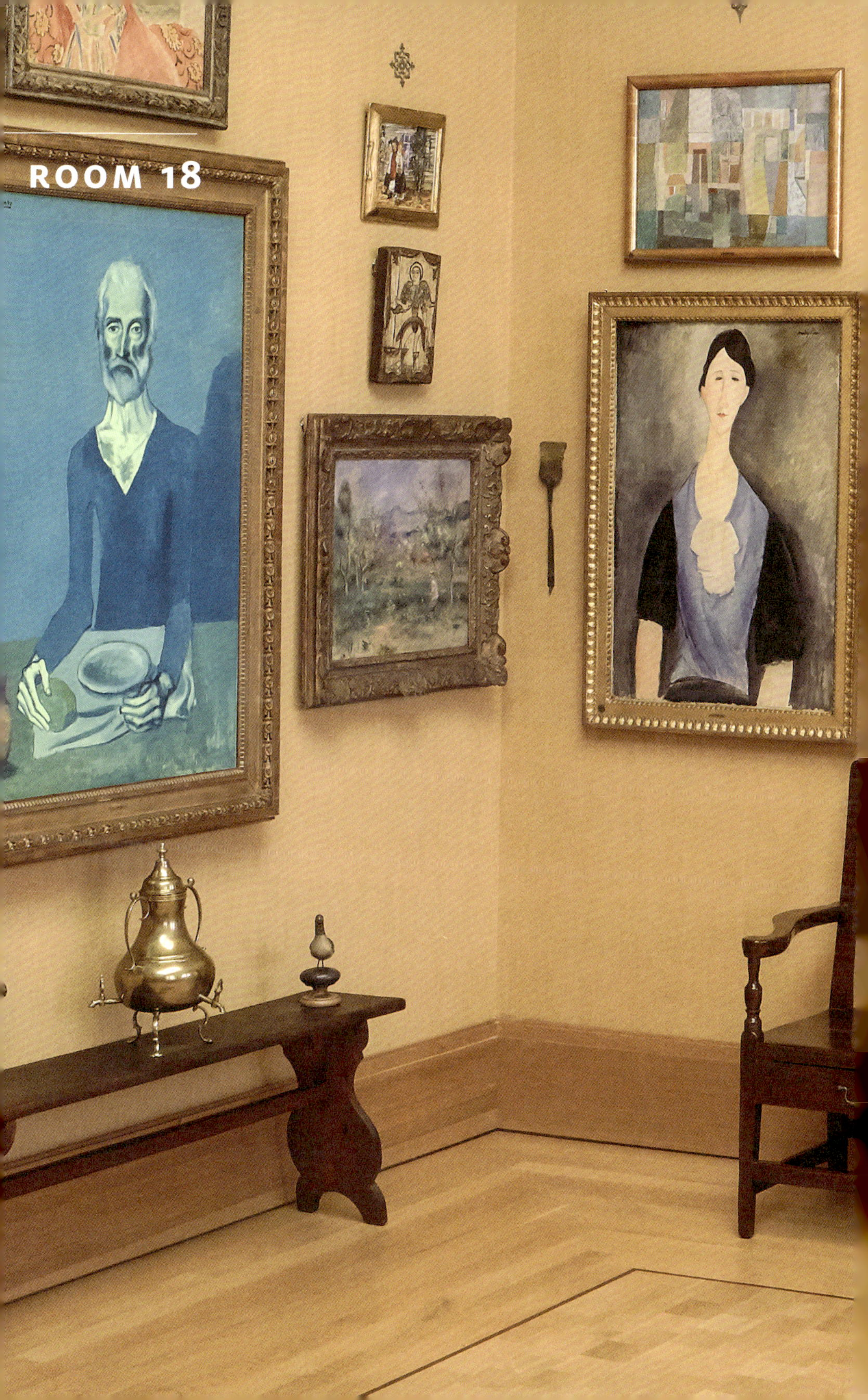
ROOM 18

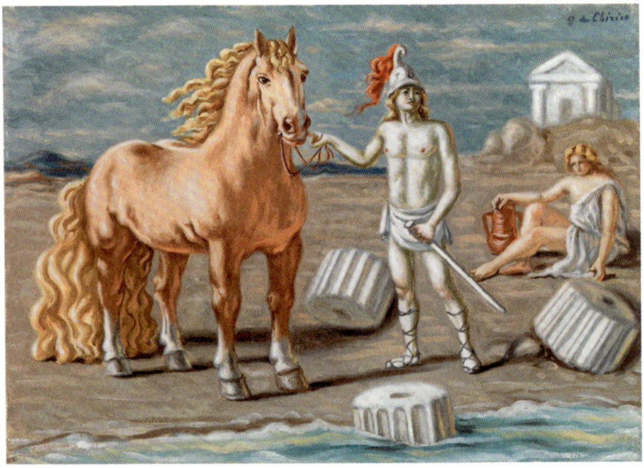

**GIORGIO DE CHIRICO (ITALIAN, 1888–1978)**
***ALEXANDROS***
1935. Oil on canvas (later mounted to hardboard), 19½ × 27⅝ in. (49.5 × 70.2 cm). BF960

De Chirico was an Italian artist, born in Greece, who drew much of his inspiration from ancient Mediterranean sources. Here, he depicts Alexander the Great, with the ruins of antiquity scattered around him, standing on a beach with his war horse Bucephalus. The scene appears to have been inspired by ancient accounts of how Alexander tamed the fearsome Bucephalus by turning his body toward the sun. The monumentally stocky horse basks in the sunshine as a statue-like Alexander stands at attention. Perhaps this is the calm before the two venture off to conquer neighboring lands.

The work was included in the artist's first US solo exhibition, in 1936 at New York's Julian Levy Gallery. Distinct from his so-called metaphysical works, which emphasize the mystery of empty architectural spaces, *Alexandros* celebrates the decorative aspects of baroque art, a period that De Chirico favored in the 1930s.

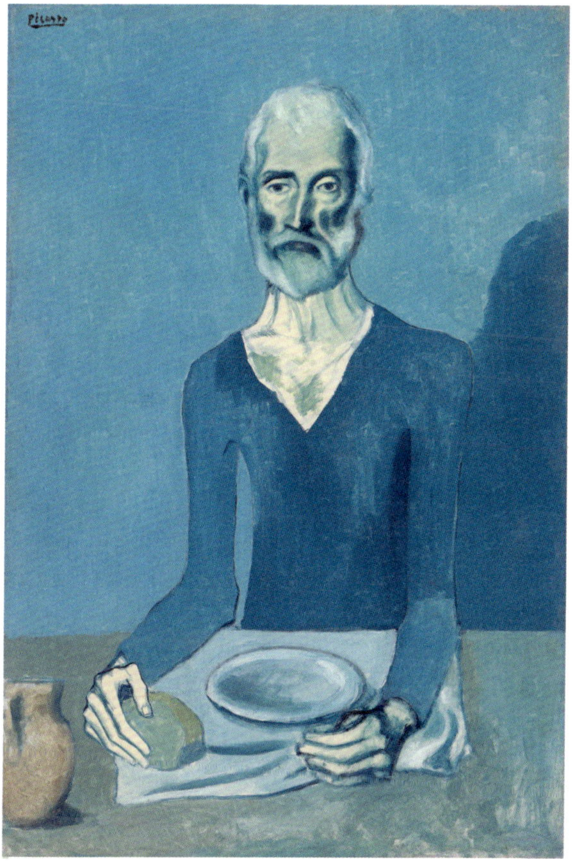

**PABLO PICASSO (SPANISH, 1881–1973)**

***THE ASCETIC***

1903. Oil on canvas, 46⅝ × 31¾ in. (118.4 × 80.6 cm). BF115

Between 1901 and 1904, during what is now called his Blue Period, Picasso pursued themes of suffering and alienation. He took the sick, the blind, the imprisoned, and the indigent as his subjects. The artist identified with marginalized people, as he struggled in the early years of his career.

Here, a man with a sunken, emaciated chest and hollow cheeks sits before a spare meal. The bread and pitcher provide the only contrast in the otherwise monochromatic palette, and may evoke the Eucharist, associating the elderly man's suffering with that of Christ. His vacant gaze, however, does not imply spiritual redemption, only inexorable poverty. Although the man faces the viewer, his unseeing eyes preclude intimacy or engagement, and the shadow behind him appears menacing. The elongation and distortion of his body suggests the deterioration of old age and poor health.

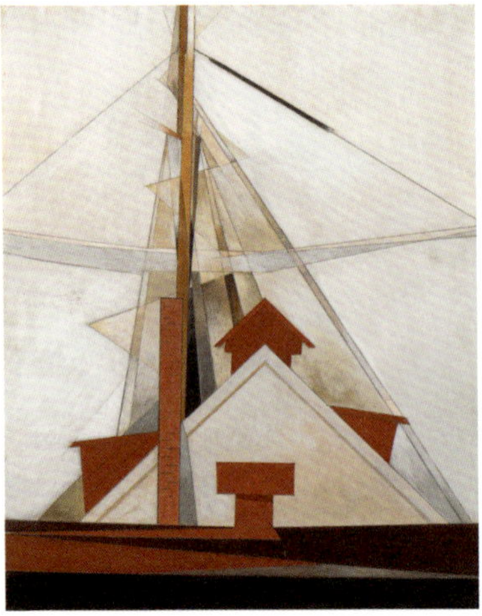

**CHARLES DEMUTH (AMERICAN, 1883–1935)**
***MASTS***
1919. Tempera on composition board, 19 7/8 × 16 5/16 in. (50.5 × 41.4 cm). BF343

Signed and dated "C. Demuth 1919 / Gloucester, Mass.," this painting was produced during the artist's summer stay at this seaside town. While Gloucester was a popular destination for summer holidays—not least among artists—*Masts* shows the city's industrial side, in a cubist-inspired style that came to be called precisionism. Overlapping shapes, many pyramidal, may read as a ship's mast, factory chimney, warehouse roof, radiating sails, and more. Incised, ruled pencil lines cut diagonally through the composition board like rays of light, creating faceted crystalline patterns enhanced by shifts in color and shading.

Demuth apparently was interested more in the style than the exact subject of *Masts*, which he exhibited in 1920 with the vague title *Chimnies* [sic], *Ventilators, or Whatever.* Like Dr. Barnes, Demuth was a prodigious and sophisticated reader, and his modernist literary tastes might account in part for the experimental style of his precisionist pictures and their enigmatic titles. For example, the companion painting to *Masts*—*Piano Mover's Holiday*—takes its name from the first line of a poem that Demuth dedicated to his close friend, the poet William Carlos Williams.

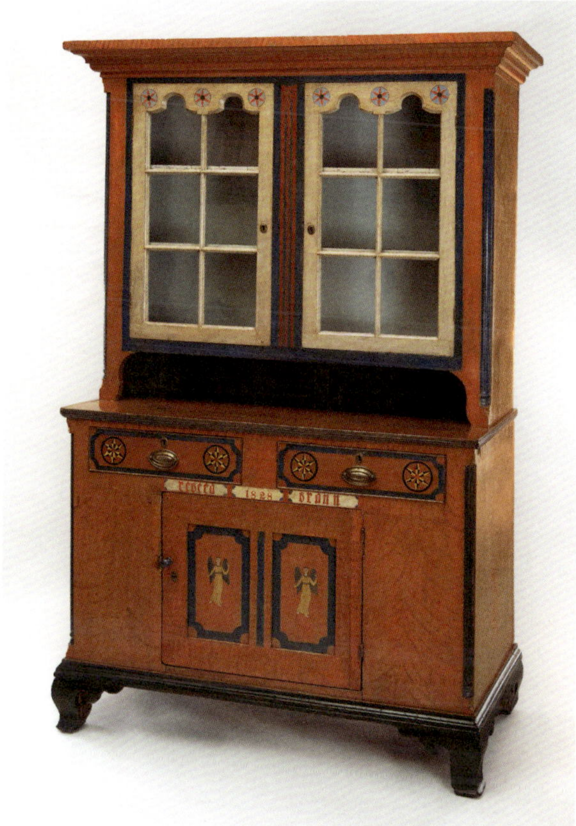

**WORKSHOP OF MICHAEL BRAUN (AMERICAN, 1772–1851)**

***CUPBOARD***

1828. Painted pine, 79½ × 49 × 21¼ in. (201.9 × 124.5 × 54 cm). 01.18.30

The remote Mahantango Valley, northwest of Philadelphia, was primarily connected to other Pennsylvania German communities through church membership, and its furniture has a distinctive style—noted for vibrant ground colors, stamped rosettes, and designs copied from Fraktur, a type of manuscript art. Painted decoration was a tradition brought to the area by south German immigrants, who utilized methods and designs from their homeland with materials common to southeastern Pennsylvania, including tulip, poplar, and pine.

An inscription above the lower cabinet door indicates that the cupboard was made for Rebecca Braun, the maker's daughter. Michael Braun and his workshop were responsible for a large body of work in the area; at least one son, John, joined his father in cabinetmaking and carpentry. Other decorative elements, such as the rosettes and six-pointed stars (sometimes called hex signs), were made with stamps, compasses, and rulers to create a uniform design. The angels are borrowed from a Fraktur design made for the poem "Concordia" around 1825.

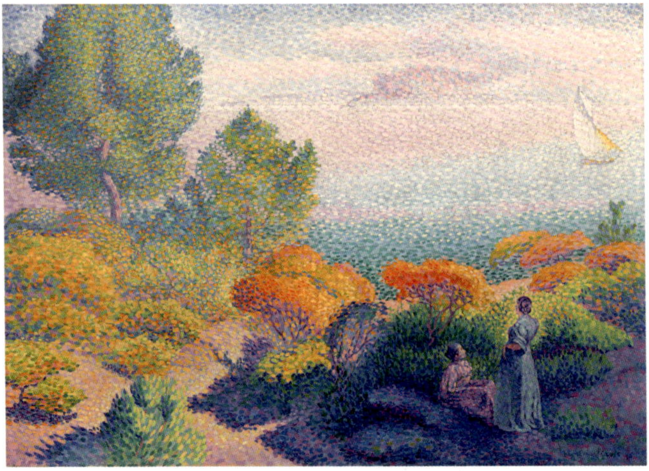

**HENRI EDMOND CROSS (FRENCH, 1856–1910)**
***TWO WOMEN BY THE SHORE, MEDITERRANEAN***
1896. Oil on canvas, 25⅝ × 36¼ in. (65.1 × 92.1 cm). BF436

Awash in strong Mediterranean light, a slightly sloping landscape is lush with dramatically colored vegetation. Green trees touched with golden brushstrokes break across the top of the canvas. In the middle ground, yellow flecked bushes proliferate on the left, while a series of fiery shrubs on the right gives way to the cool underbrush, where two women take refuge from the sun. They appear to gaze into the distance, perhaps at the white sail that punctuates the haze of pink water and clouds.

"I come back to the idea of chromatic harmonies," Cross once remarked, "created from nothing (so to speak) and outside nature, as a starting point." The artist's scintillating paint surface in this work demonstrates his interest in earlier nineteenth-century optical color theories, which proposed that adjacent hues combine in the viewer's eye to convey a purer sense of color. The painting also reflects Cross's anarchist political beliefs, presenting his vision of an imagined utopian society.

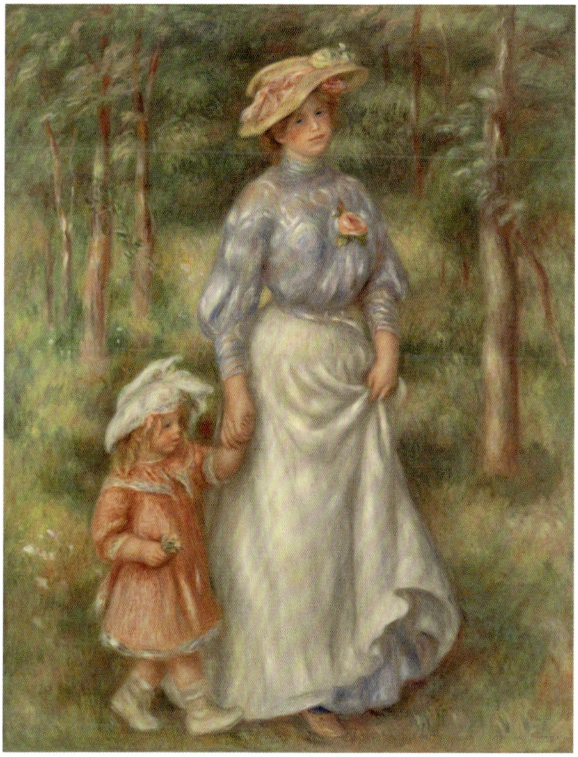

**PIERRE-AUGUSTE RENOIR (FRENCH, 1841–1919)**

***PROMENADE***

c. 1906. Oil on canvas, 64 ¾ × 50 15⁄16 in. (164.5 × 129.4 cm). BF571

The artist has painted his youngest son, Claude, walking with nursemaid Renée Jolivet. Claude, born in 1901 and nicknamed "Coco" by his family, is thus around the age of four or five in this portrait. The youngest of his three sons, Coco was among Renoir's preferred models in his later career, leading middle son Jean to describe his brother as "one of the most prolific inspirations my father ever had." The familial topic of the painting is highlighted by its location—the portrait was painted in Essoyes, the hometown of Renoir's wife, Aline.

Coco wears an outfit of pink and lace, characteristic of his garments in Renoir's other portraits of the child. The boy's distinctive blond tresses peek out from underneath a white bonnet. One hand clasps that of his nursemaid, and in the other he grasps a small bouquet of flowers, perhaps recently picked on their promenade. Jolivet's pinned flower and the pink ribbon on her hat echo Coco's coloring—a further visual cue to the connection between the two figures.

## ROOM 19

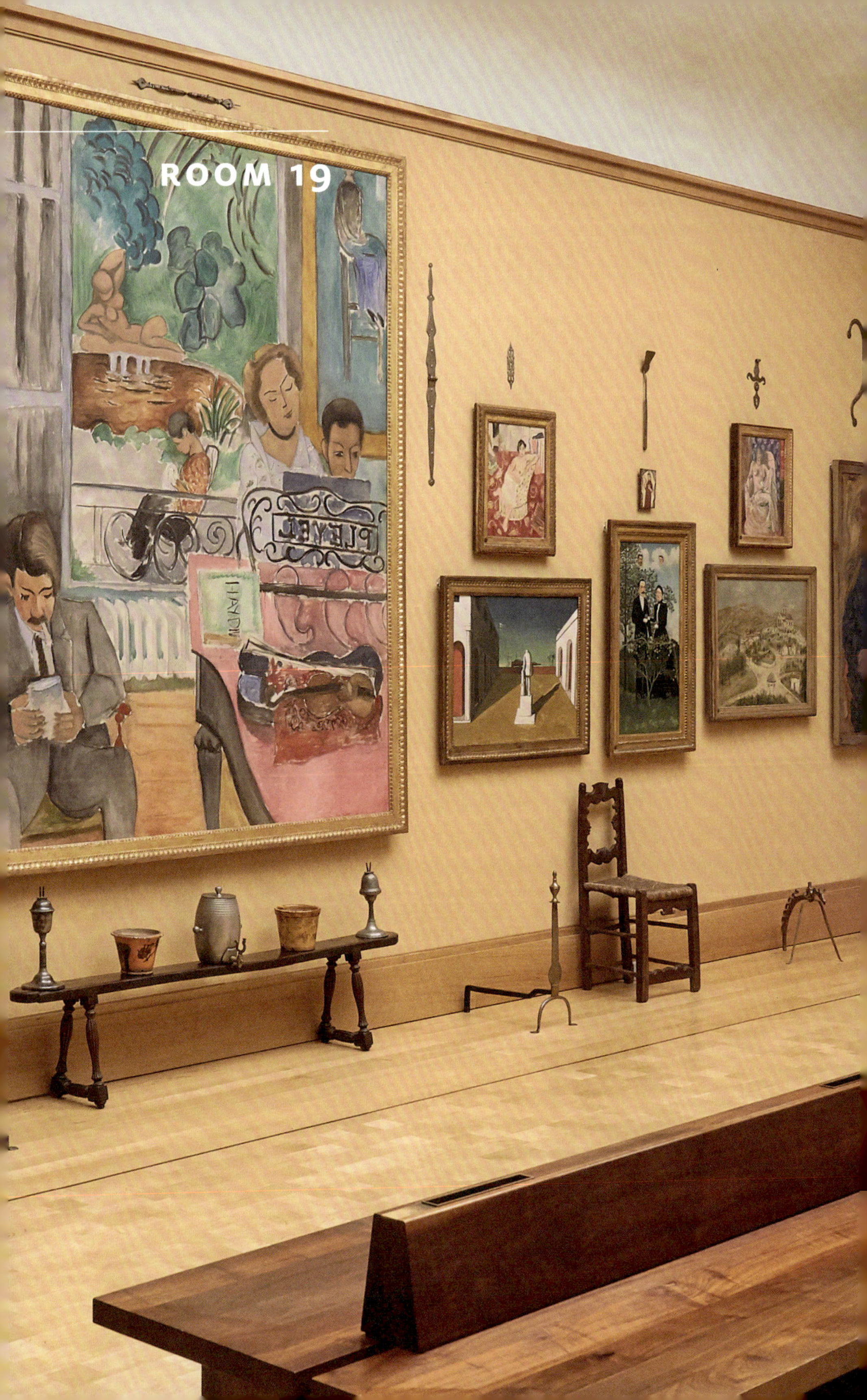

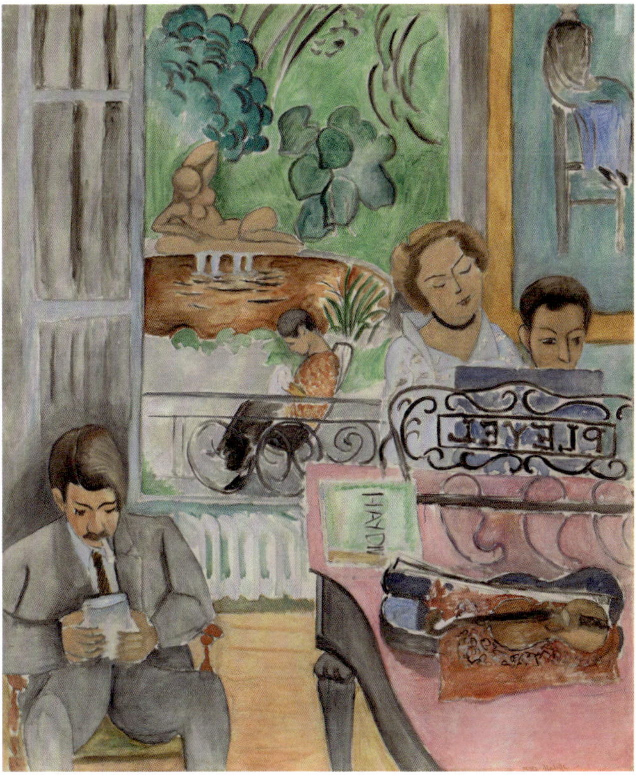

**HENRI MATISSE (FRENCH, 1869–1954)**
***THE MUSIC LESSON***
1917. Oil on canvas, 96½ × 83 in. (245.1 × 210.8 cm). BF717

Matisse set this portrait of his wife, daughter, and two sons in the living room of the family home in Issy-les-Moulineaux, France. Amélie, occupied with her knitting, sits in a rocking chair in the garden, just beyond the ironwork of the window grille. Jean reads a book while smoking a cigarette. On the right, Marguerite, wearing her characteristic black neckband, helps her brother Pierre practice the piano. Matisse's violin and case rest on the piano, next to a musical score by Haydn. The artist was an accomplished musician, and the instrument may have been his way of incorporating himself into the picture.

Matisse's own *Woman on a High Stool* (1914, Museum of Modern Art, New York) hangs on the wall behind the piano, and a terra-cotta cast of *Reclining Nude I (Aurora)* can be seen in the garden. On the surface, the scene projects cultured family domesticity. In reality, Jean had recently departed to fight in World War I. This portrait of family togetherness perhaps represents an unfulfilled wish on the artist's part.

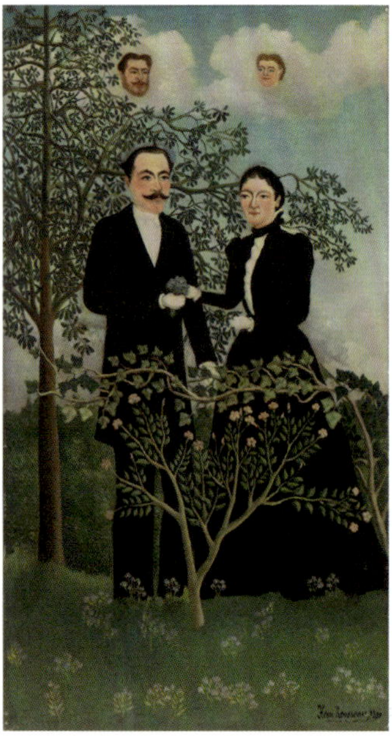

**HENRI ROUSSEAU (FRENCH, 1844–1910)**
***THE PAST AND THE PRESENT*, OR *PHILOSOPHICAL THOUGHT***
1899. Oil on canvas, 33¼ × 18½ in. (84.5 × 47 cm). BF582

After marrying his second wife, Josephine Noury, Rousseau made one of his "portrait-landscapes" to mark the occasion. These works functioned on two levels: they captured the likeness of the sitters, and placed them in a setting that revealed something of their life.

When asked about this painting, the artist remarked that it was "a bit Spiritualist." Both Rousseau and Noury had been widowed before they married in 1898. From 1868 to 1888, the artist had been married to Clémence Boitard, mother of his only surviving daughter. Here, he commemorates that earlier union, as well as his new wife's first marriage, by showing their late partners in the clouds above their heads. Hands touching, the new couple cradles a bunch of forget-me-nots—another clear reminder that, while they enjoy their present happiness, they treasure memories of times past.

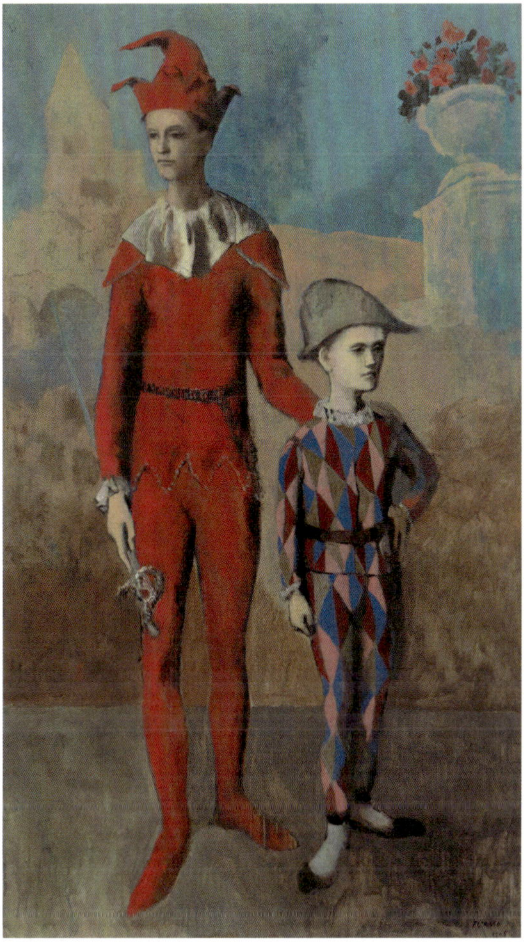

**PABLO PICASSO (SPANISH, 1881–1973)**
***ACROBAT AND YOUNG HARLEQUIN***
1905. Oil on canvas, 75 ¼ × 42 ¾ in. (191.1 × 108.6 cm). BF382

Saltimbanques, or traveling circus performers, were a favorite theme of Picasso's. These entertainers were a common spectacle in Paris, performing in the public squares of neighborhoods such as Montmartre, where Picasso lived from 1904 to 1909. The performers seen here seem to be gazing at the audience, as if a show has just ended. The taller boy, in a brilliant red costume and pointed hat, is dressed as an acrobat; the smaller boy wears the traditional diamond-patterned costume of the Italian theater character, Harlequin. The landscape behind them is probably a stage backdrop.

Because performers like this lived at the edges of conventional society, they became a symbol of artists as estranged bohemian outcasts. Indeed, Picasso used the harlequin figure as an alter ego in later works. This picture strikes a note of melancholy, as the vagabond figures display sad expressions, with drooping shoulders and downturned mouths at odds with the frivolity of their costumes.

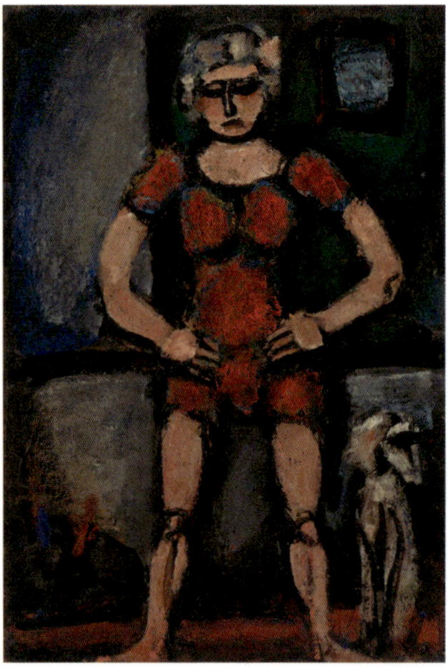

**GEORGES ROUAULT (FRENCH, 1871–1958)**
***ACROBAT WITH TWO DOGS (CLOWN)***
1924. Oil on canvas, 29½ × 20⅞ in. (75 × 53 cm). BF883

A circus performer stands with her arms akimbo, legs widely planted in a pose that would be confrontational if she were not looking down. Her sorrowful, pensive expression, however, suggests her lived experience offstage after the feats of her performance were over. A dog sits to her right like a guardian, also looking downward. Another dog is visible in the background at left, curled up on the floor.

Rouault was deeply religious, and his Catholic faith informed his work—in this case, seeing the humanity and spiritual light in people who lived on the fringes of society. The artist had worked in stained glass before turning to painting. This picture's jewel tones—ruby red surrounded by sapphire and emerald—and heavy black outlines evoke the lead-framed panes of stained glass windows in Gothic cathedrals.

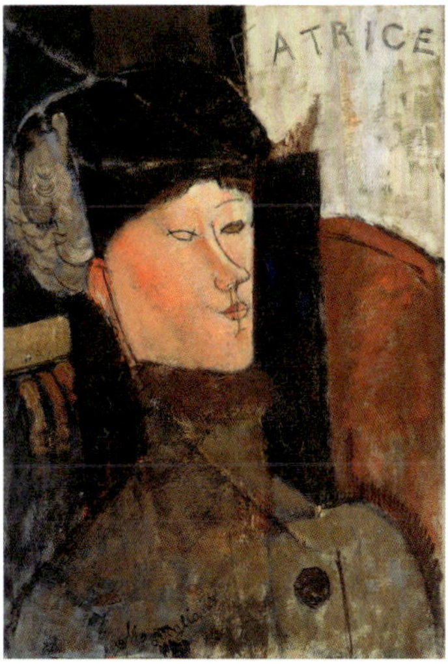


**AMEDEO MODIGLIANI (ITALIAN, 1884–1920)**
***BEATRICE***
1916. Oil on canvas with newsprint, 21¾ × 15 1/16 in. (55.2 × 38.2 cm). BF361

Modigliani painted this portrait of the British writer and journalist Beatrice Hastings when they were romantically involved in a tumultuous two-year affair. The lovers met after Hastings moved to Paris in 1914 and joined in the bohemian scene centered in the neighborhood of Montparnasse. Modigliani, himself an immigrant to Paris, may have found kinship with Hastings in their shared status as expatriates.

This is one of several portraits Modigliani did of Hastings, just as he made multiple portraits of his other lovers. The artist includes Hastings's first name above her head, a typical feature of his portraits of this period. The woman's masklike face and geometric presentation demonstrate Modigliani's experimentation with cubism, a twentieth-century art movement characterized by the breakdown of three-dimensional objects into flat planes. Hastings's portrait is unique in Modigliani's body of work as it once included a bit of newsprint on the surface of the canvas, perhaps in an allusion to her career as a writer and journalist. Traces of the newsprint ink remain visible below the name "Beatrice."

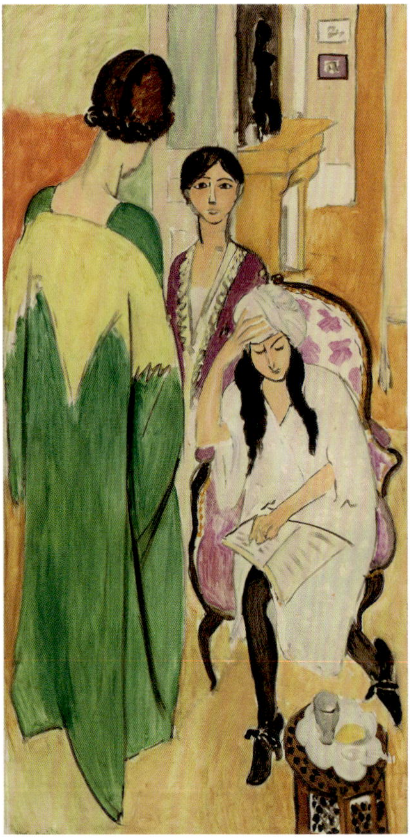 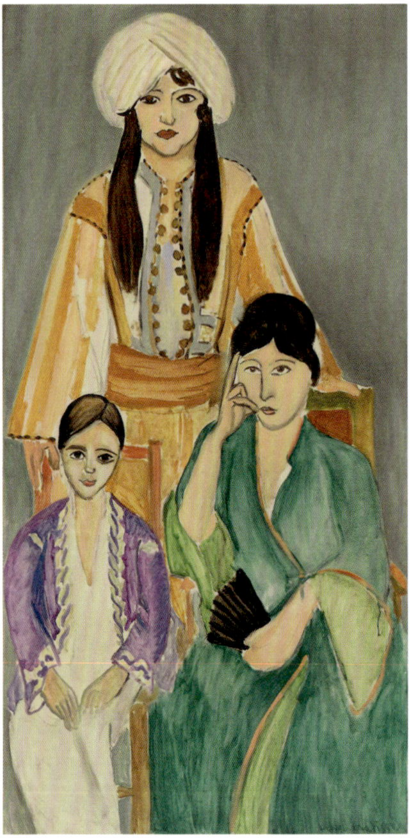

**HENRI MATISSE (FRENCH, 1869–1954)**

***THREE SISTERS WITH AN AFRICAN SCULPTURE***

1917. Oil on canvas, 77 ⅛ × 38 ¼ in. (195.9 × 97.2 cm). BF363

***THREE SISTERS WITH GREY BACKGROUND***

1917. Oil on canvas, 77 × 38 in. (195.6 × 96.5 cm). BF888

***THREE SISTERS AND "THE ROSE MARBLE TABLE"***

1917. Oil on canvas, 76 ½ × 37 ⅞ in. (194.3 × 96.2 cm). BF25

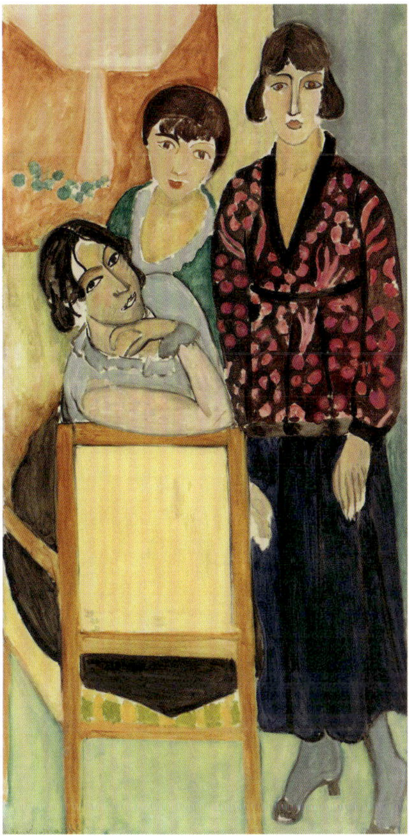

Although these three works are commonly called the "Three Sisters Triptych," it is likely that only two sisters served as models for all nine figures in the paintings—an Italian woman named Laurette and her sister Anna.

The three compositions respond to one another: the descending height arrangement of standing and seated figures in *Three Sisters with an African Sculpture* mirrors the ascending one of *Three Sisters and "The Rose Marble Table."* The two paintings, in turn, frame the balanced triangular composition of *Three Sisters with Grey Background*. Within these scenes, Matisse depicted works of art that provide clues to his inspiration and artistic process, including a Bambara female figure from Mali (likely in his personal collection) and his own painting in progress, *The Rose Marble Table*, now at the Museum of Modern Art, New York.

Dr. Barnes owned two of these paintings when Matisse visited the Barnes Foundation in December 1930. Matisse persuaded him to buy *Three Sisters with Grey Background* and reunite the trio. The artist specified the arrangement of the triptych, creating a lively rhythm of hand gestures and alternating greens, purples, and yellows.

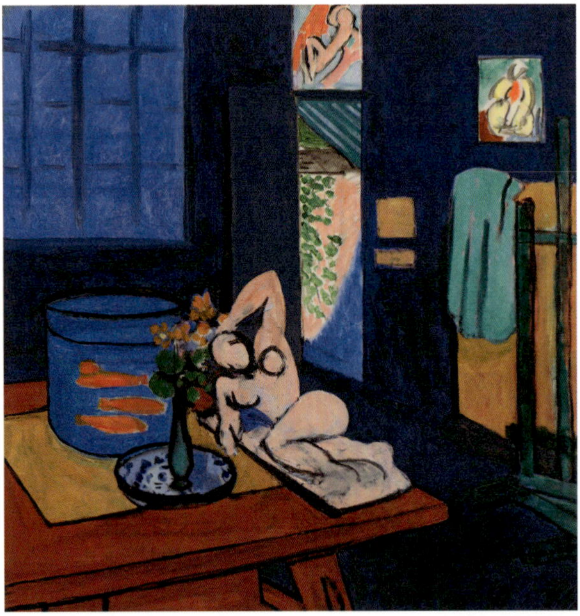

**HENRI MATISSE (FRENCH, 1869–1954)**
***STUDIO WITH GOLDFISH***
1912. Oil on canvas, 46 7/16 × 39 15/16 in. (118 × 101.5 cm). BF569

Matisse depicts the interior of his studio at Issy-les-Moulineaux, outside Paris. The table features a bowl of goldfish, flowers in a vase, and Matisse's own sculpture, *Reclining Nude I (Aurora)*. Two of his figure paintings appear on the wall at right. Beneath one canvas is a door open to a garden; beneath the other is an easel and a screen draped with a green robe, used by models when undressing.

Matisse painted this work in the spring or summer of 1912, after his first trip to Morocco. France had imposed colonial rule and created the French protectorate in Morocco earlier that year. As Matisse recounted, during his trip he saw local men in a café, contemplating a flower and a bowl of goldfish. Here, he evokes that meditative scene in his studio. The goldfish invite the viewer's absorption into the picture.

# ROOM 20

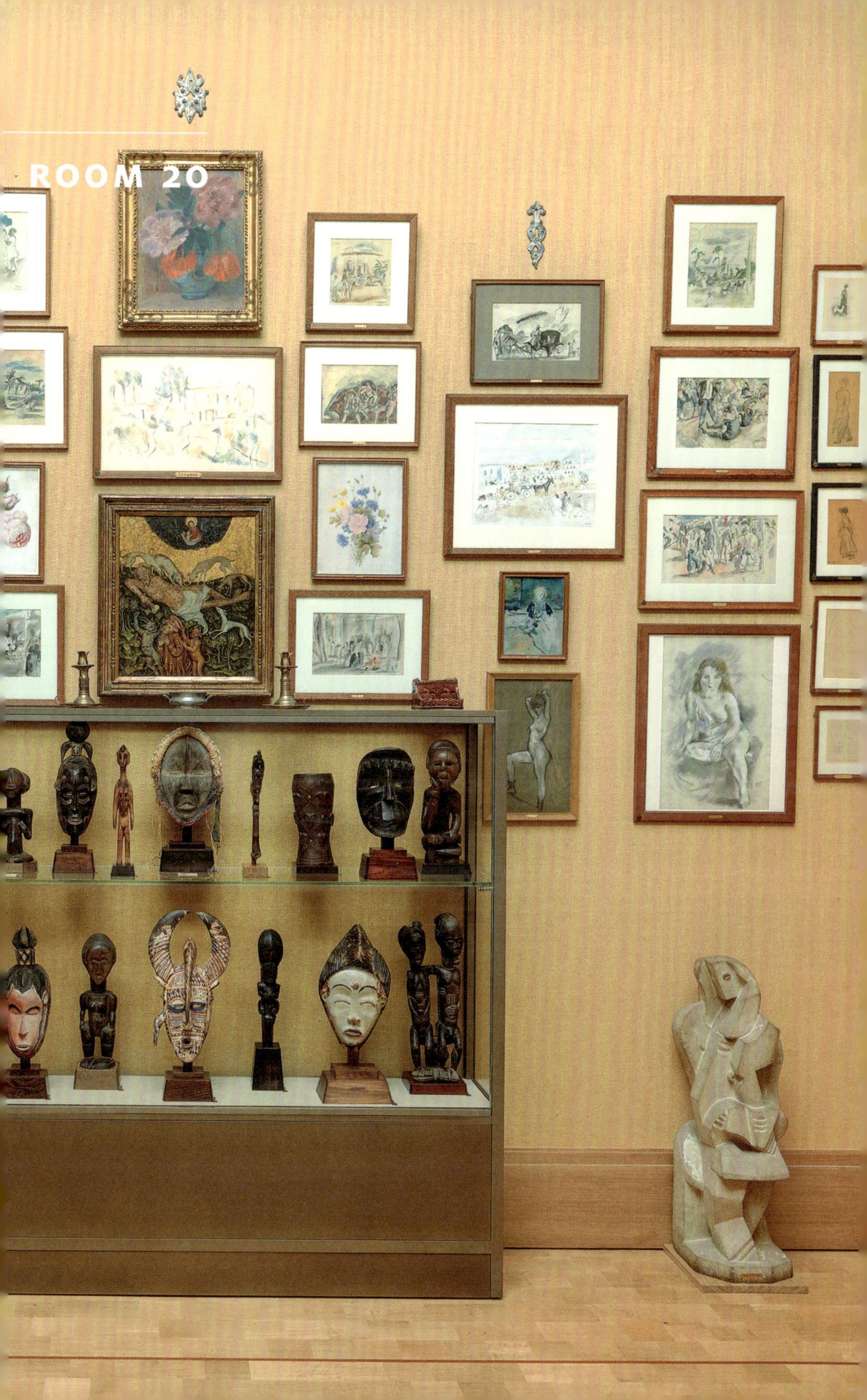

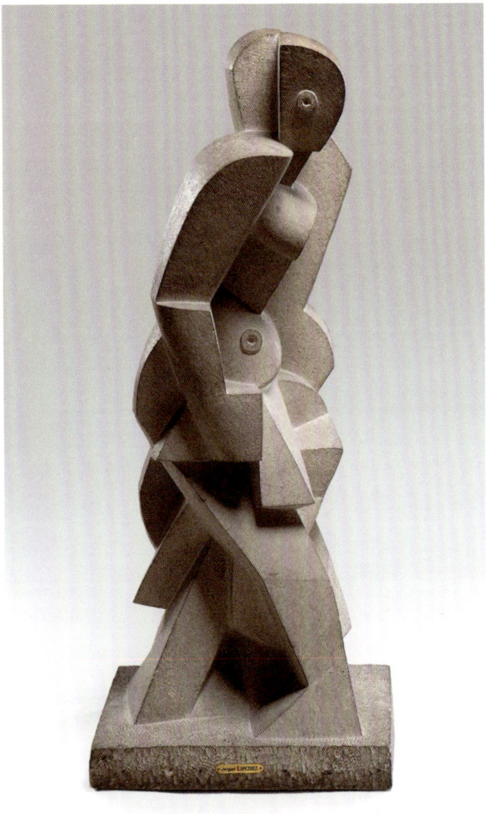

**JACQUES LIPCHITZ (FRENCH, ACTIVE IN THE UNITED STATES, 1891–1973)**
***BATHER***
1917. Limestone, 36½ × 14½ × 12 in. (92.7 × 36.8 × 30.5 cm). A201

Lipchitz here uses the traditional motif of the bather to investigate the strategies of cubism. He creates a bathing woman in motion, the geometric planes of her body torqueing around a central axis. Her right leg juts out, the inside of her right foot displayed to the viewer in an almost balletic gesture. She holds her hands at her waist, further emphasizing the twisting motion she makes with her body. The smooth planar limestone of the sculpture reflects light from each segment, enhancing the woman's turn and encouraging the viewer to move with the bather to view her.

Albert Barnes first met Lipchitz through Parisian art dealer Paul Guillaume and went on to be one of the sculptor's most enthusiastic American patrons. In 1922–23, Dr. Barnes commissioned Lipchitz to execute a group of stone bas-reliefs for Paul Philippe Cret's building for the Barnes Foundation in Merion, Pennsylvania. These bas-relief panels, like the *Bather*, distill the human body into planar geometric forms and are still present on the building's facade.

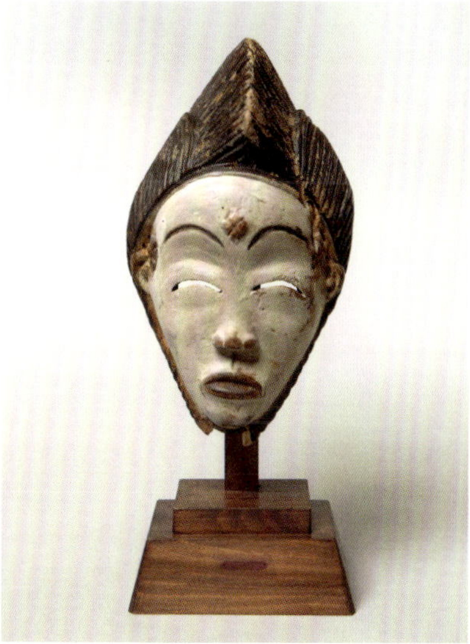

***MUKUDJ MASK* (PUNU)**
Unidentified artist. 19th–early 20th century. Wood and pigment, 12½ × 6½ × 7¼ in. (31.8 × 16.5 × 18.4 cm). A282

Masks of this type—with narrowly arched eyes, scarification patterns on the forehead and temples, and elaborate hairstyles—are known as *mukudj* and are common in the Ogowe River region of Gabon. This example was made by the Punu peoples and depicts an idealized image of womanhood. Likely the portrait of a local woman renowned for her beauty, the face of this mask is covered in kaolin, a white fine-grained clay that was locally sourced. The white appearance of the face connected the mask to religious ceremonies, and its wearer to the ancestral realm. When included in community celebrations of visiting dignitaries or funerals, these masks were worn by male dancers on stilts who performed elaborately choreographed acrobatics high above the audience.

*Mukudj* masks were among the earliest African sculptural forms to be acquired by Western collectors and to be admired by artists, including Man Ray, who photographed this mask in the early 1920s. For much of the twentieth century, however, these masks were considered exotic creations, entirely divorced from any of their original cultural associations.

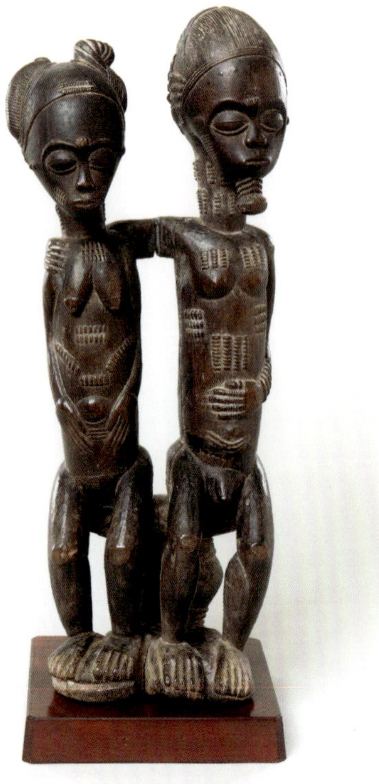

**MASTER OF THE BARNES BAULE COUPLE**

***SEATED COUPLE***

Late 19th century. Wood, 16 ⅞ × 5 ¼ × 5 in. (42.9 × 13.3 × 12.7 cm). A276

Carved from a single piece of wood, this couple is the finest work known by an unnamed artist with a recognizable style who worked in the late nineteenth century within the borders of modern-day Ivory Coast. Signatures of the artist's style include the blocks of scarification patterns that decorate the bodies of the man and woman and the appearance of rings carved onto the fingers of the male. The couple display a sense of unity through both the male's embrace and their shared upright forms and geometric facial features. Despite this, the two figures turn ever so slightly away from each other, perhaps a visual marker for their mutual but individualized roles within Baule society.

In their original context, such statues functioned as places where Baule nature spirits, known as *asye usu*, could rest when they were not inhabiting the minds and bodies of specific individuals. On occasion, such a sculpture would have been removed from its concealed shrine and displayed—most likely shielded by a cloth draped over it—in a public space where its owner, a professional diviner, would perform rituals to clarify a client's personal difficulties.

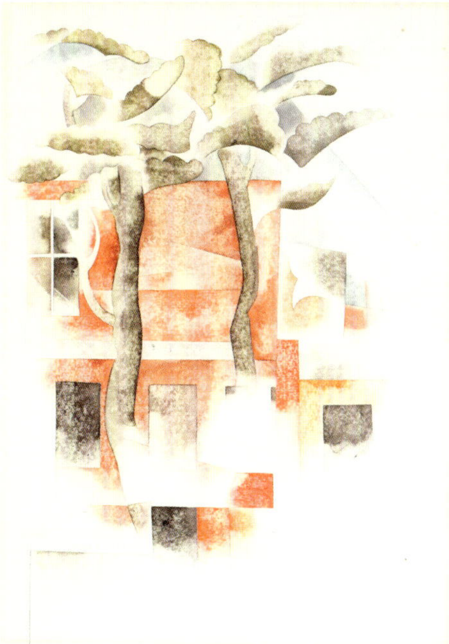

**CHARLES DEMUTH (AMERICAN, 1883–1935)**

***BERMUDA: HOUSES SEEN THROUGH TREES***

1918. Watercolor and graphite on wove paper, 14 ¼ × 10 in. (36.2 × 25.4 cm). BF647

Two tall trees with wavy trunks screen an indecipherable number of houses whose overall structures, windows, and doors are suggested by overlapping red and black rectangles. The setting—while compressed—reads as a series of receding registers, and probably depicts the view from a hotel on St. George's Island, Bermuda. Demuth stayed there with his friend Marsden Hartley after both had worked in Provincetown, Massachusetts, where they experimented with cubism (see page 156).

The elegant, atmospheric geometry of *Bermuda: Houses Seen through Trees*, interwoven with the trees' organic shapes, was inspired by cubism but free of any mechanistic approach. Dr. Barnes wrote of Demuth's landscapes that they "differ from typical cubistic pictures in that the color-planes are varied by tonal modulations similar to those in Cézanne's watercolors, and they interpenetrate much as the planes do in Cézanne's still-lifes. Frequently, Demuth varies his Cézanne-cubist form by injecting into its rhythm of interpenetrating angular planes an intertwining arabesque movement of various units, thereby giving a Chinese quality to the expression."

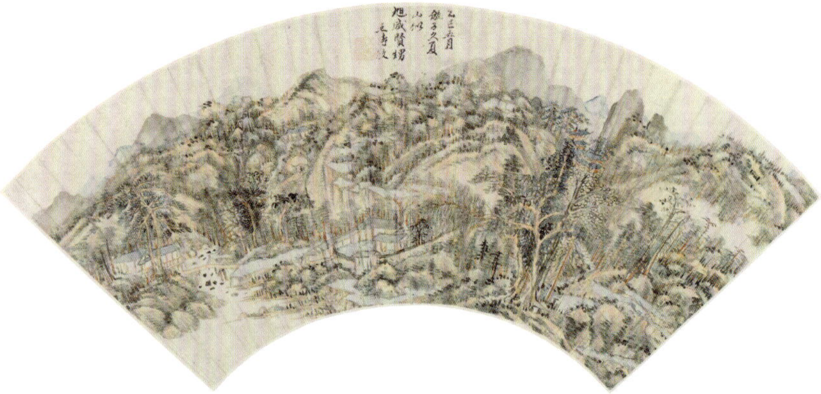

**WANG SHIMIN (CHINESE, 1592–1680)**
***FAN—MOUNTAINOUS LANDSCAPE***
1665. Ink on Japanese paper, 7 1/16 × 19 7/8 in. (18 × 50.5 cm). BF2508

In the small format of a fan, Wang Shimin provides a panoramic view of a mountain range with houses nestled in the cliffs and valleys and a stream running through the foreground. The inscription at the top indicates that the landscape was done in the style of the Yuan dynasty artist Huang Gongwang (1269–1354). Wang Shimin was a leader in a new school of landscape painting in the early Qing dynasty that sought to integrate the styles of masters of the Yuan and Song dynasties. The movement valued technique and brushwork over observation of the natural world, as art and nature were seen as distinct realms.

Here, modular forms denoting rocks and mountains build on each other across the composition. The horizontal movement of the mountains is carefully balanced by the verticality of the trees. Various brushstrokes create a highly textured surface, with fluid washes overlaid with dry brushwork and calligraphic strokes mixed with more descriptive outlines. Wang Shimin was the eldest of the Four Wangs of the Qing dynasty. The youngest was his grandson, Wang Yuanqi, whose own fan painting hangs nearby on this wall.

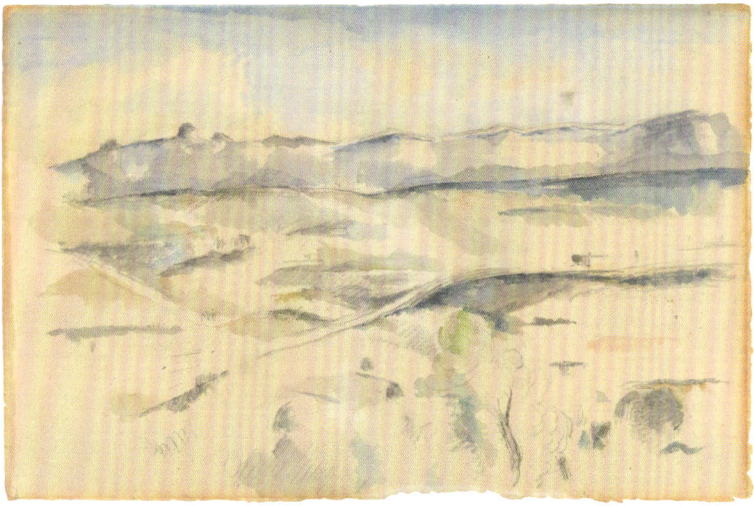

**PAUL CÉZANNE (FRENCH, 1839–1906)**
***THE CHAINE DE L'ÉTOILE MOUNTAINS***
1885–86. Watercolor and graphite on laid paper, 12 ⅜ × 19 in. (31.5 × 48.3 cm).
BF650 (recto)

With washes of subtle color, Cézanne constructs the forms of the Étoile mountain range in southern France and the surrounding landscape. The distinctive rock formation known as the Pilon du Roi is visible on the left. Cézanne regularly took long walks through the countryside of his native Provence, making numerous sketches along the way. He would often fill both sides of his paper, as was the case with this work. During a treatment in 2014, conservators discovered a previously unknown watercolor by the artist—an unfinished sketch of trees—on the back. Dr. Barnes was not aware of this second image when he acquired the work in 1921. It was one of six Cézanne watercolors that he bought from the writer and collector Leo Stein. Another of these watercolors, *Trees*, displayed nearby on this wall, also features a rediscovered sketch on the back—a detailed drawing of buildings in this same Étoile mountain landscape.

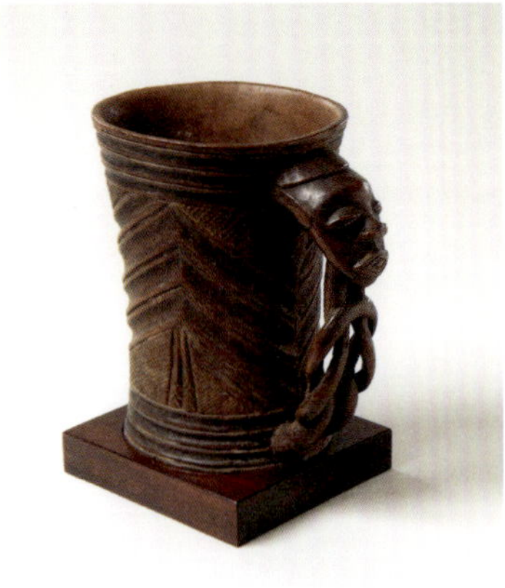

**_PALM-WINE CUP_ (KUBA OR NDENGESE)**
Unidentified artist. Late 19th–early 20th century. Wood and copper alloy, 6 × 5⅝ × 4⅞ in. (15.2 × 14.3 × 12.4 cm). A250

The elaborate handle and surface decoration of this cup add a symbolic layer to an otherwise ordinary object of daily use. Known as a *mbwoomngntey* within central African societies including the Kuba, a cup like this would have been used to consume palm wine, a popular drink made from the sap of palm trees. The geometric pattern that covers the outside of the cup is inspired by Kuba textiles woven from the long fronds of raffia palm trees. This woven aesthetic is also visible in the interlocking forms of the handle. The addition of a human head connects the cup to other examples that were made for elite members of Kuba society. Although the function of the object is prosaic, its decoration, with references to other artistic media, serves to express the status of its owner.

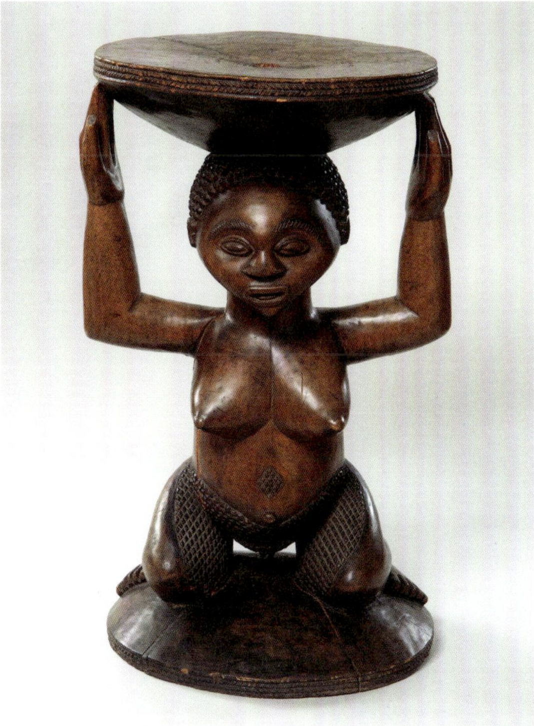

**CARYATID STOOL (KANYOK)**

Unidentified artist. Late 19th–early 20th century. Wood, 23¼ × 14¼ × 12 in. (59.1 × 36.2 × 30.5 cm). A185

Carved from a single piece of wood, this stool is remarkable for its simple form, which emphasizes the bilateral symmetry of the female human body. Better understood as thrones, seats like this were known by the central African Luba peoples as *lupona* and reserved for kings. The inclusion of the female supporting figure, known in other traditions as a caryatid, is not intended to imply the subservience of women to men, but rather to suggest a woman's role as the foundation of power. In addition to their role as mothers, Luba women played critical roles in political circles as advisers, counselors, and diplomats.

The polished surface of the woman's skin, along with her carefully arranged hairstyle and the scarification patterns on her inner thighs, derives from the beautification practices of Luba women. Such stools, while functional, are believed to serve as receptacles for a ruler's spirit. Guarded closely and covered when not in use, these objects hold great symbolic value as the repository and wellspring of Luba sacred authority.

# ROOM 21

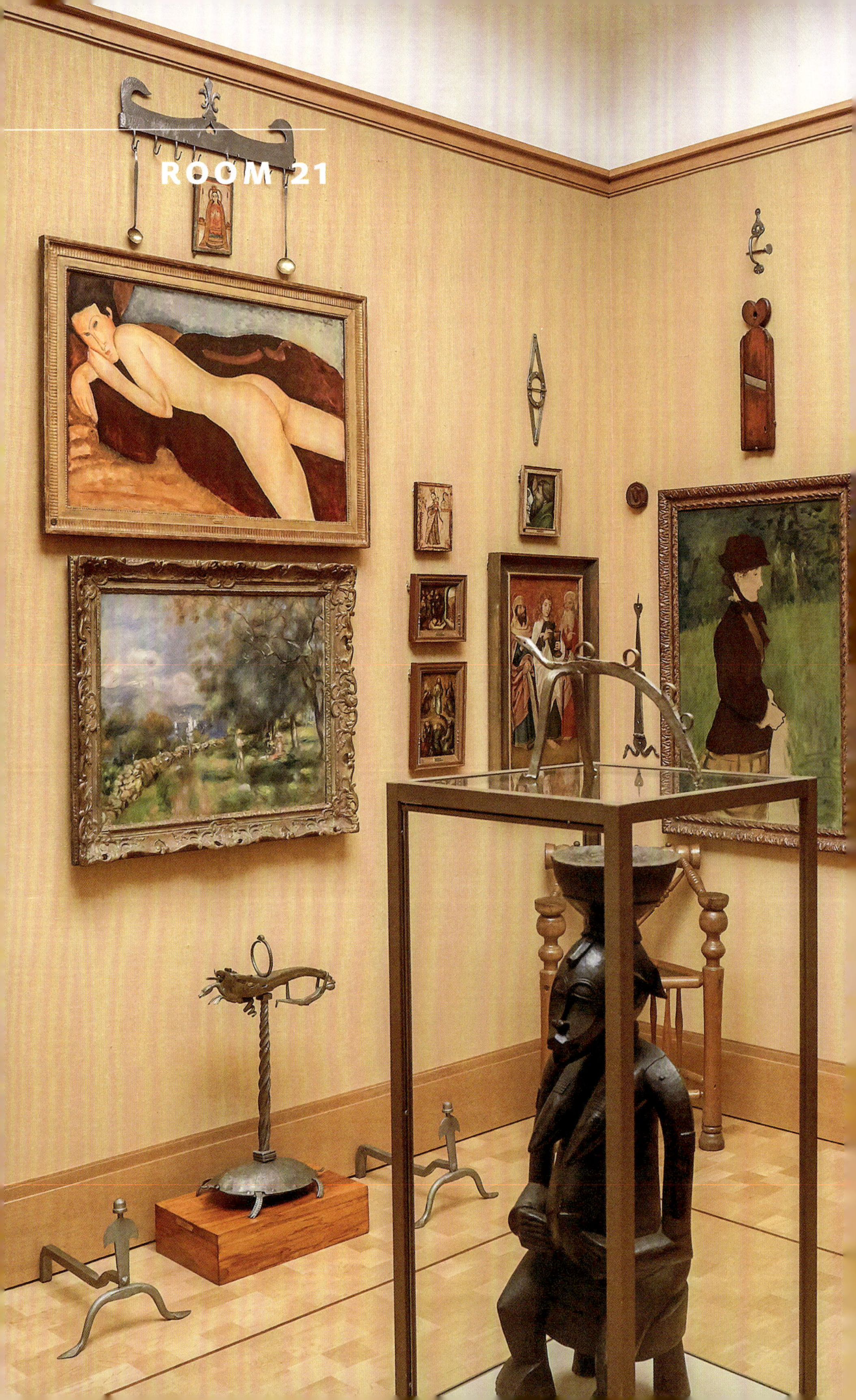

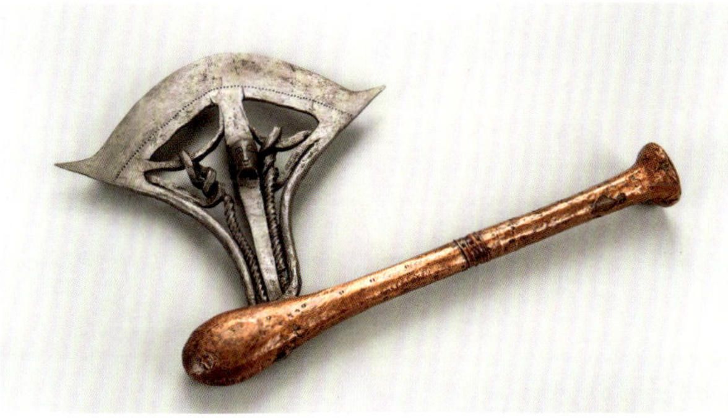

***CEREMONIAL AXE* (NSAPO)**
Unidentified maker. 19th century. Iron, wood, and copper alloy; 15¼ × 9⅞ × 1⅝ in. (38.7 × 25.1 × 4.1 cm). 01.21.07

Ceremonial axes like this one were not meant to be used but rather to be displayed. This example was made by artisans from the Nsapo, a subgroup of the Songye, located in the modern Democratic Republic of Congo. Renowned for their skills in working with iron and copper, these metalsmiths made objects that were owned and displayed by Songye rulers as emblems of power and prestige. The wooden handle of this axe is covered with sheets of copper, a luxury material obtained through trade. The forged blade, with its elegantly curved edge and twisted metal struts, demonstrates the smith's mastery of ironworking. The small face on either side of the central spoke may depict a *kifwebe* mask, linked to chiefly power.

The Songye idea of public presentation associated with the materials and design of ceremonial utilitarian objects, including this axe, resonated with Dr. Barnes's broader interest in metalwork. Similar to his celebration of the craftsmanship of utilitarian metalwork including keys, scissors, and andirons in his elaborate ensembles, Songye rulers from central Africa utilized the virtuoso creations of their society's metalsmiths as part of elaborate ritual displays.

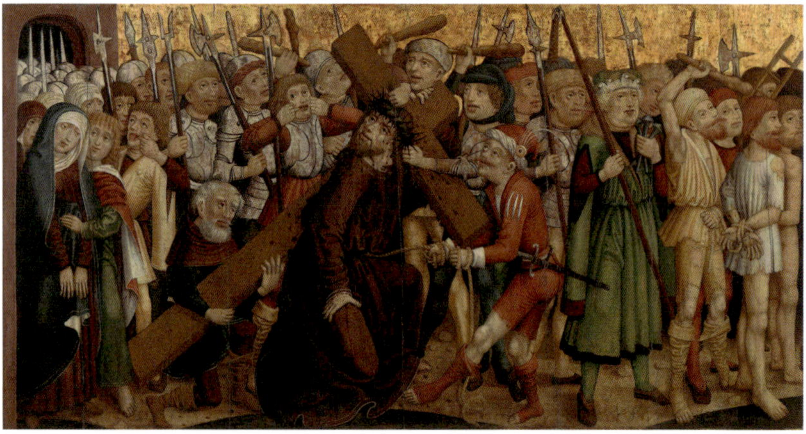

***CHRIST CARRYING THE CROSS*** **(AUSTRIAN)**
Unidentified artist. c. 1460. Tempera and oil with gold and silver leaf on panel, 29⅜ × 51½ in. (74.6 × 130.8 cm). BF396

This monumental, emotive devotional panel would have been made for public display within a church, installed perhaps on a nave wall or on a chancel or chapel screen. The condemned and bleeding Christ stumbles as he drags the Cross through the city of Jerusalem to the site of his Crucifixion. His mother and disciples—passing through the city gate at left—watch sadly and console each other. At center, an official in a green robe carries the enormous nails that will pierce Christ's hands and feet; at the far right are the two thieves, hands bound, next to whom he will be crucified. Crowds of soldiers and civilians taunt Christ and his followers. These antagonists' spears, halberds, and clubs mark the procession's progress against the gilt background. Their grimaces show physical evidence of their spiritual disorder, according to Christian belief. This harrowing scene provoked such a powerful reaction in its viewers that they scourged some of the faces—notice, for example, the scratches over the eyes and nose of the man pulling Christ with a rope.

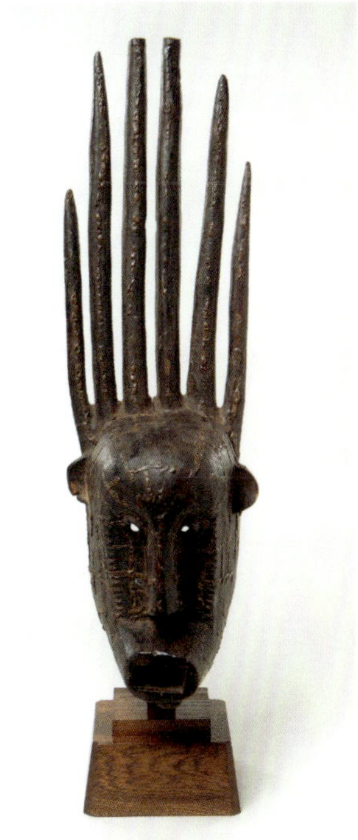

**_MASK_ (BAMANA OR MARKA)**

Unidentified artist. Late 19th–early 20th century. Wood, resin, and iron; 24 × 7⅝ × 6⅞ in. (61 × 19.4 × 17.5 cm). A224

Made in the late nineteenth or early twentieth century within the modern borders of Mali, this type of mask was worn by boys who belonged to the Bamana and Marka peoples. Known as *ndoma* masks, these objects played a central role in annual festivals associated with the harvest of millet, the main crop grown in this region of Mali. During these elaborate rituals, adolescent boys would cover their entire bodies, including their heads, hands, and feet, with cotton cloth, which placed a visual emphasis on the *ndoma* masks.

One of three examples of *ndoma* purchased by Dr. Barnes in the 1930s, this mask is notable for its rectangular mouth and the six large horns that extend upward from the top of the head. Within Bamana and Marka societies, six-horned masks were associated with knowledge and education because they recall the six senses of touch, taste, smell, sight, hearing, and orientation. This mask, like many of those on display in the galleries, was originally decorated with cowrie shells and red abrus seeds that created a strikingly colorful appearance during harvest celebrations.

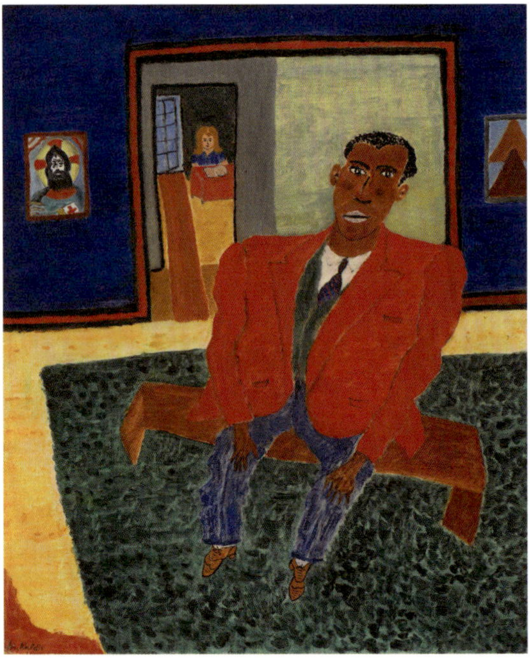

**ARISTODIMOS KALDIS (AMERICAN, 1899–1979)**
***ABSORBING ART***
1941. Oil on canvas, 30⅛ × 25⅛ in. (76.5 × 63.8 cm). BF988

An African American man sits on an art gallery bench and looks at a painting that is situated right where the viewer is standing. He engages the viewer in an intimate moment of human connection through the appreciation of art. Behind him, a religious icon and an abstract painting hang on the wall, signaling perhaps the connection between past and present art. A blonde-haired woman who seems to work in the gallery sits in a room in the back; she also looks out at the viewer as another visitor to the exhibition.

Kaldis, a Greek immigrant, was a painter, lecturer, and left-wing activist in New York. Dr. Barnes bought this work from the artist's first solo show in the city. Kaldis would later become known for richly colored abstract landscapes inspired by his Mediterranean childhood; this early work, however, attests to his artistic experiences in New York, where the Harlem Renaissance and the Great Migration placed Black people and culture at the heart of modern American art and urban life.

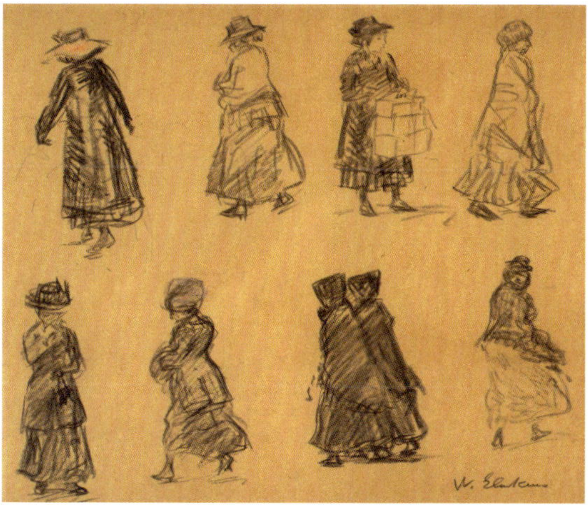

**WILLIAM JAMES GLACKENS (AMERICAN, 1870–1938)**

***EIGHT FIGURES***

c. 1910. Black crayon with gouache on brown wove paper, 12⅛ × 14⅜ in. (30.8 × 36.5 cm). BF641

In this series of small sketches, most likely on-the-spot impressions of New York sidewalk traffic, nine women dressed in overcoats walk with varying degrees of determination or leisure. One carries parcels; another's skirt billows in the wind. All are alone except for a pair in matching hoods and cloaks, who lean in toward each other as they proceed.

Glackens was, according to fellow artist and critic Guy Pène du Bois, "the father of the present school of illustrating," whose "notations on the life around him...fulfilled characters [even in] scenes but half drawn." Each figure is defined with crisp shorthand notations, a style he had developed while working as an artist-reporter for Philadelphia newspapers upon graduating from Central High School in 1890. Glackens relocated to New York in 1896 and soon developed these urban anecdotes into oil paintings, as well as illustrations for national magazines such as *Collier's*, *Scribner's*, and the *Saturday Evening Post*.

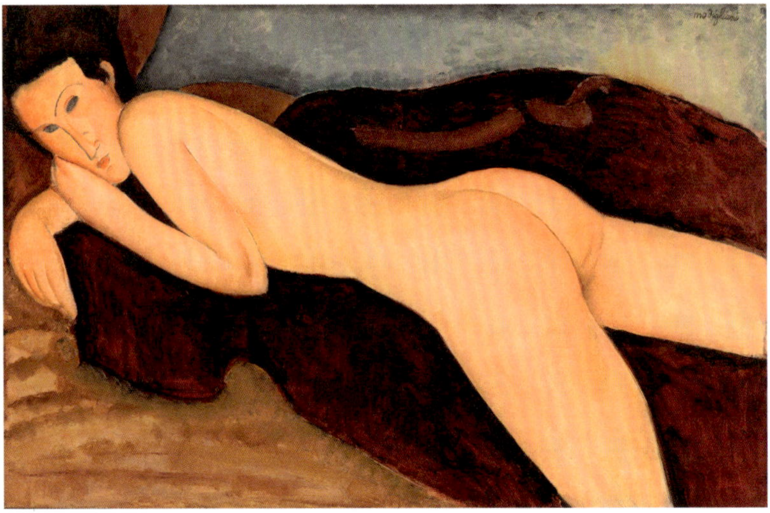

**AMEDEO MODIGLIANI (ITALIAN, 1884–1920)**
***RECLINING NUDE FROM THE BACK***
1917. Oil on canvas, 25½ × 39¼ in. (64.8 × 99.7 cm). BF576

From around 1916, Modigliani turned increasingly to the task of depicting the female nude, creating paintings that brought their traditional subject matter resolutely up to date. Here, the model's flat eyes form part of a mask-like face, reflecting the artist's engagement with African sculpture, while the languid body recalls iconic precedents from western European art.

Modigliani had only one solo exhibition in his lifetime; although it is unclear exactly which works were featured, the show included nudes that attracted censorship (a local chief of police complained that some had pubic hair). Perhaps the unapologetic sexuality of a figure like this also shocked contemporary viewers. Very few sales resulted from the show.

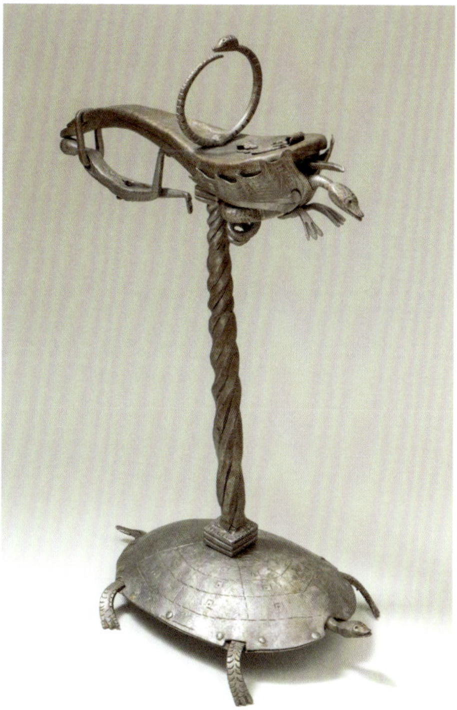

***PORTABLE OIL LAMP* (PROBABLY SPANISH OR FRENCH)**

Unidentified maker. Iron, 28½ × 11⅜ × 17½ in. (72.4 × 28.9 × 44.5 cm). 01.21.37

Assembled from unrelated fragments, this enigmatic object is a remarkable display of metalworking, even if its functionality as a portable lamp is questionable. A turtle forms the base, supporting a rod made of four twisted bars. Upon this sits the lamp itself. A nude human figure hangs from the nozzle; a winged dragon with a corkscrew tail is appended to the reservoir; and a round, serpent-shaped handle is affixed to the top. The serpent, which appears to eat its own tail, recalls the ouroboros, an ancient motif that originated in Egyptian iconography and was later associated with alchemy. The dragon could allude to the heat and light that the lamp would have produced. These allusions to alchemy, heat, and light would have appealed to Dr. Barnes, a chemist. So, too, would the assemblage of the lamp from fragments, as an analogy of his wall ensembles.

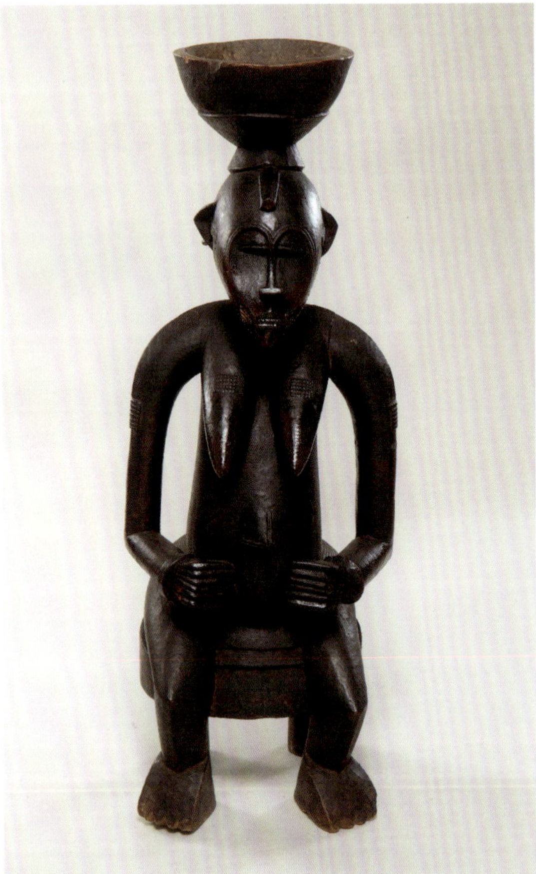

***SEATED FEMALE FIGURE OF THE SÃDO'O SOCIETY* (SENUFO)**

Unidentified artist. Late 19th–early 20th century. Wood, 34 ½ × 12 ¾ × 11 in. (87.6 × 32.4 × 27.9 cm). A209

Senufoland in northern modern-day Ivory Coast was, and to some extent remains, home to a wide variety of sculptural genres, many of which are linked to gender-based secret societies. The role of the Sãdo'o, a society strictly limited to women, was to control the ritual purity of the matrilineal Senufo lineages. The Sãdo'o also possessed wooden sculptures, the most important of them being seated female figures. In this example, a woman balances on her head a bowl that would have contained shea butter, a product associated with the work of women. Understood as a sign of womanhood, the production of shea butter lay entirely in the hands of Senufo women, and it was used both to smooth the skin and to create nutritious meals.

Once a year, usually shortly after the end of the vegetation cycle in November or December, the Sãdo'o organized a feast in which all members participated. It was during such celebrations that these seated statues would be taken out and used as intermediaries between the earthly and spiritual realms. Men were forbidden to attend these festivities and warned that they should not even come close to where the dancing would take place.

## ROOM 22

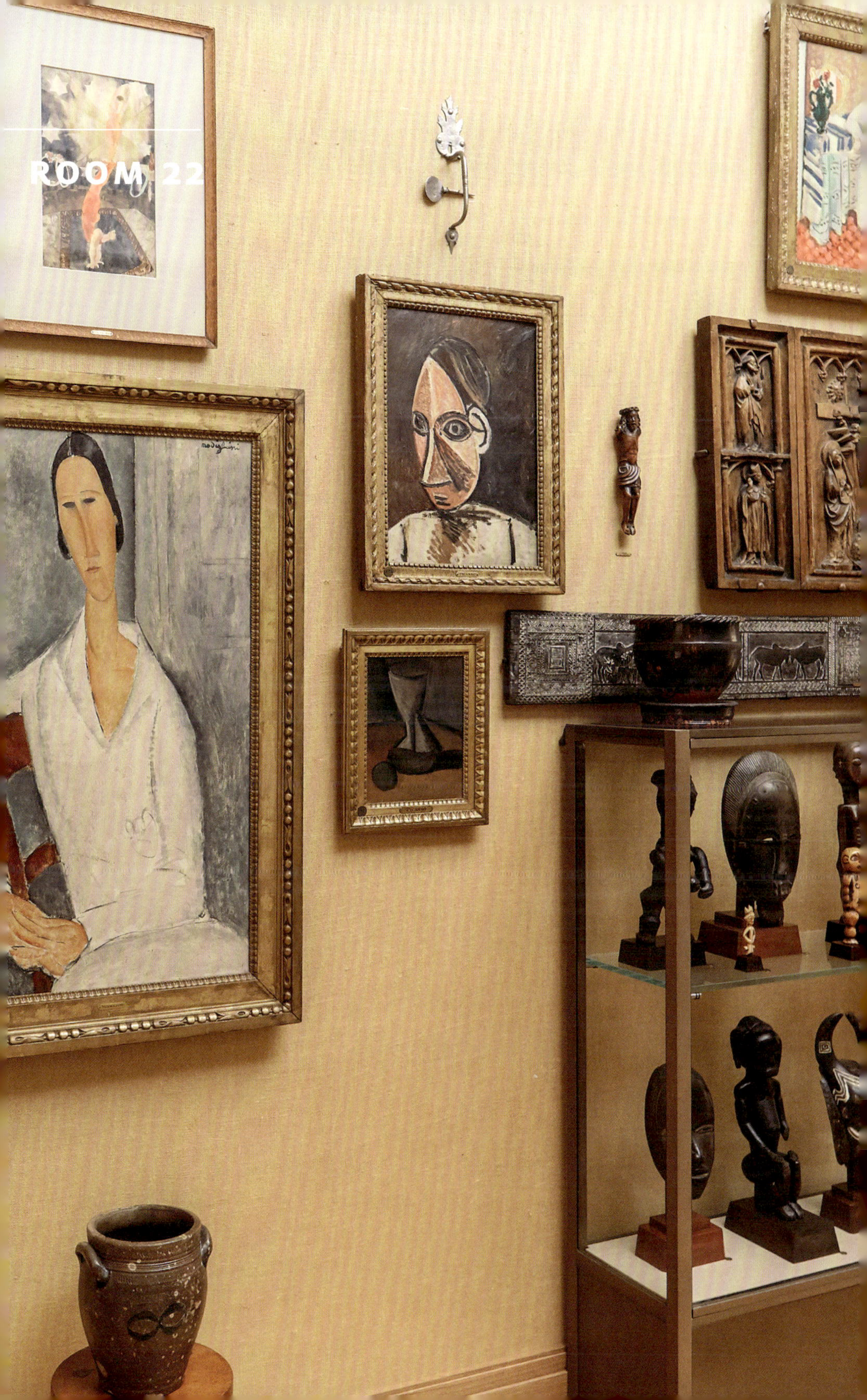

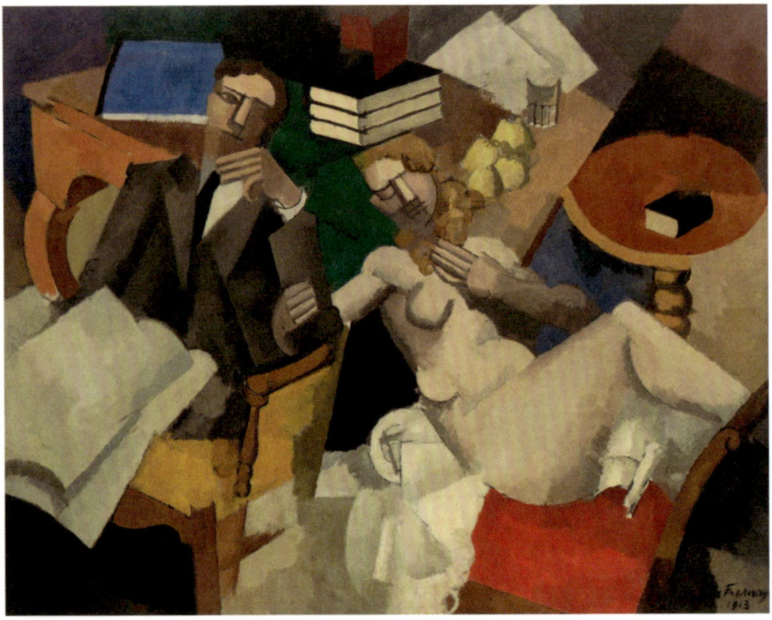

**ROGER DE LA FRESNAYE (FRENCH, 1885–1925)**
***MARRIED LIFE***
1913. Oil on canvas, 47 × 59½ in. (119.4 × 151.1 cm). BF971

La Fresnaye belonged to a collective of cubist artists and modern writers known as the Puteaux Group, after the Parisian suburb where several of the core members lived and gathered. He applied the geometric forms and fractured planes of cubism to this enigmatic depiction of a bourgeois couple at home. La Fresnaye was particularly interested in introducing color to cubism, as the bright planes of yellow, green, red, and blue in this canvas attest.

The man here remains clothed while the woman is nude, a juxtaposition that suggests previous infamous paintings in art history, including Édouard Manet's *Luncheon on the Grass* (1862–63, Musée d'Orsay, Paris); the domestic setting, however, produces a different narrative. These figures may represent an abstract concept such as culture versus nature: the man, an accumulation of sharp angles, has a newspaper on his lap; the woman is assembled from circular forms, echoed by the pears behind her. Their interaction might also be understood as an ironic depiction of the wife as muse in married life.

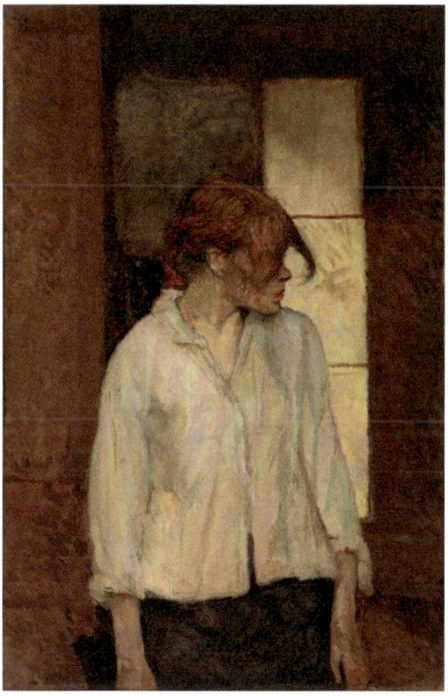

**HENRI DE TOULOUSE-LAUTREC (FRENCH, 1864–1901)**

***"A MONTROUGE"—ROSA LA ROUGE***

1886–87. Oil on canvas, 28 ⅜ × 19 ⅛ in. (72.1 × 48.6 cm). BF263

Carmen Gaudin, one of Toulouse-Lautrec's favorite models, poses as the prostitute Rosa La Rouge, a character popularized by the songs of the cabaret performer Aristide Bruant and named for her red hair and the blood of the clients murdered by her cutthroat pimp. Gaudin embodies Rosa La Rouge with her bangs hiding her eyes and her red lipstick enhancing rather than tempering her surly expression. The dirty brown palette and unwashed window set the stage for this grim scene.

The painting once hung in Bruant's nightclub, Le Mirliton, in the bohemian neighborhood of Montmartre in Paris. It was one of a set depicting working-class women representing various neighborhoods—in this case, Montrouge, on the southern outskirts of Paris. Toulouse-Lautrec was interested in the underbelly of Parisian culture, as he, too, inhabited the margins of society. Living with a rare disability, which restricted his growth and caused him physical pain, he also struggled with alcoholism. Cruelly, in his lifetime, some critics conflated his "ugly paintings" with his "ugly life."

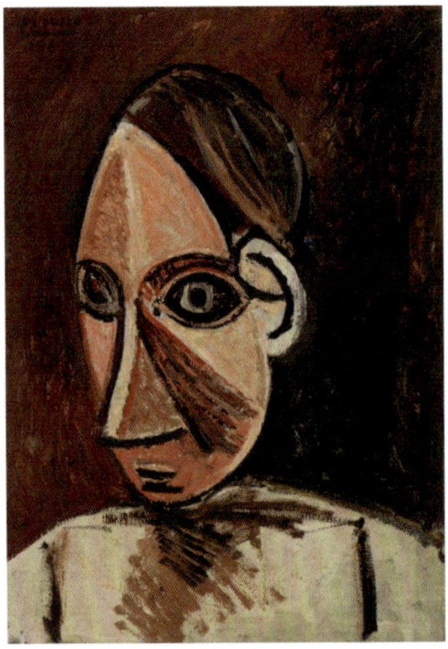

**PABLO PICASSO (SPANISH, 1881–1973)**
***HEAD OF A WOMAN***
1907. Oil on canvas, 18⅛ × 13 in. (46 × 33 cm). BF421

Around 1906, Picasso began to draw inspiration from the stylized geometric forms of ancient Iberian sculpture in the Louvre Museum as well as West and Central African sculpture at the Trocadero Museum in Paris. In this painting, the pointed oval head, oversize eyes, wedge nose, and folded ear have been synthesized from these various sources. The striations on the nose, cheek, and eyelid reference both the western European technique of crosshatching and the scarification patterns found on African objects like Kota reliquary figures (guardians of ancestral bones). The markings add volume to the flattened planes of the face, giving it the appearance of a carved mask. This picture is likely a study for one of the central figures in Picasso's major work *Les Demoiselles d'Avignon* (1907, Museum of Modern Art, New York), which occupied the artist for most of 1907.

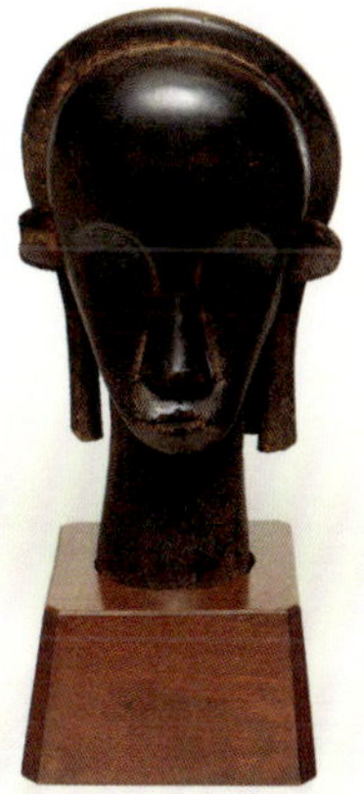

***RELIQUARY GUARDIAN HEAD*** **(FANG BETSI)**
Unidentified artist. 19th century. Wood, 15 3⁄16 × 6 7⁄16 × 6 3⁄4 in. (38.5 × 16.3 × 17.1 cm). A124

The Fang peoples of western equatorial Africa (modern-day Cameroon, Equatorial Guinea, and Gabon) practiced a type of ancestor worship known as *byeri*. Incorporated into this ritual practice were statuettes and sculptures of individual heads. This sculpture of a simplified head perched atop a tall cylindrical neck was known by the Fang as an *añgokh-nlô-byeri* ("whole head of the ancestor"). Sculptures of this type functioned in Fang society as guardians placed upon reliquary boxes that contained the skulls of important ancestors.

These ritual effigies were often adorned with jewelry and large osprey or touraco feathers, and initially the eyes were inlaid with circular brass pupils. The smooth appearance of the sculpture's surface was achieved through ritual anointments of palm oil, sacrificial blood, and *ba* powder (a mixture of oil and powdered padauk wood).

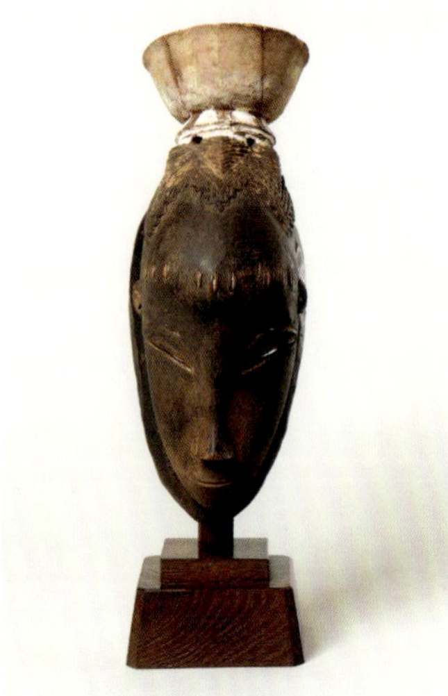

**THE BOUAFLÉ MASTER (GURO)**

***FACE MASK SURMOUNTED BY A BOWL***

Late 19th century. Wood, pigment; 12¾ × 5 × 5½ in. (32.4 × 12.7 × 14 cm). A106

Made by an artist referred to as the Bouaflé Master (named for the west African city where the object was found), this face mask (*gu*) is one of the best examples of its kind. The artist belonged to the Guro peoples and was based in the southern part of their territory in what is now Ivory Coast. Best known for the delicate style the artist used to represent the facial features of masks and sculptural heddle pulleys used for weaving, the Bouaflé Master has here represented a female face with elongated features, including an aquiline nose and long angled slits for eyes. Carved into relief on the woman's forehead are scarification patterns in groups of three, a number associated with women in Guro society. Her elaborately braided hair is organized into a chevron pattern that is partially obscured by a bowl balanced on her head. The series of holes carved into the edge of the mask along with the partial remnants of red and white pigment provide evidence of its original appearance as a colorful multimedia ensemble.

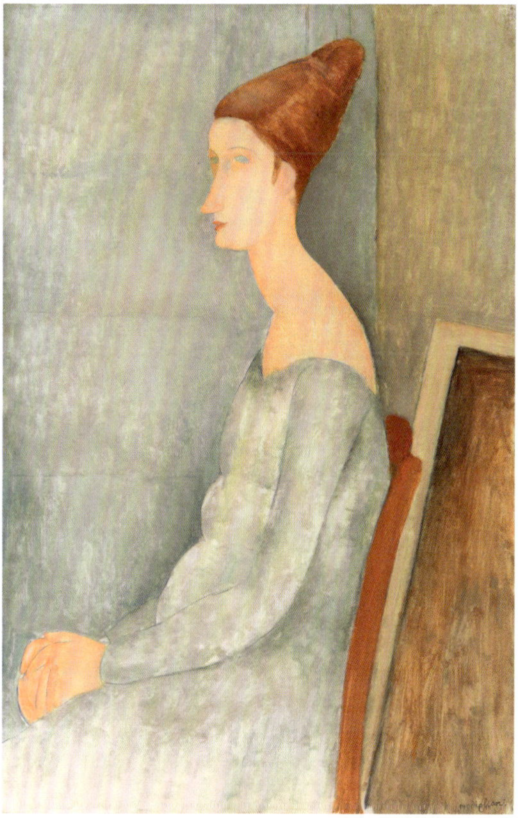

**AMEDEO MODIGLIANI (ITALIAN, 1884–1920)**

***PORTRAIT OF JEANNE HÉBUTERNE***

1918. Oil on canvas, 39¼ × 25½ in (99.7 × 64.8 cm). BF422

After Modigliani met Jeanne Hébuterne in 1917, while she was studying art at the Académie Colarossi in Paris, the two quickly became lovers. She also became his model of choice; Hébuterne appears in several paintings, in a range of different outfits, often in a state of pregnancy. Here, the artist portrayed his lover in profile, as if to emphasize her rounded stomach and dramatic choice of hairstyle.

Color also plays a key part in this work. The artist painted Hébuterne's dress and most of the background in gray and blue, using warmer tones to describe the remainder of the wall and an object that may be the back of a canvas. Her auburn hair and the wooden chair also share the same tonality.

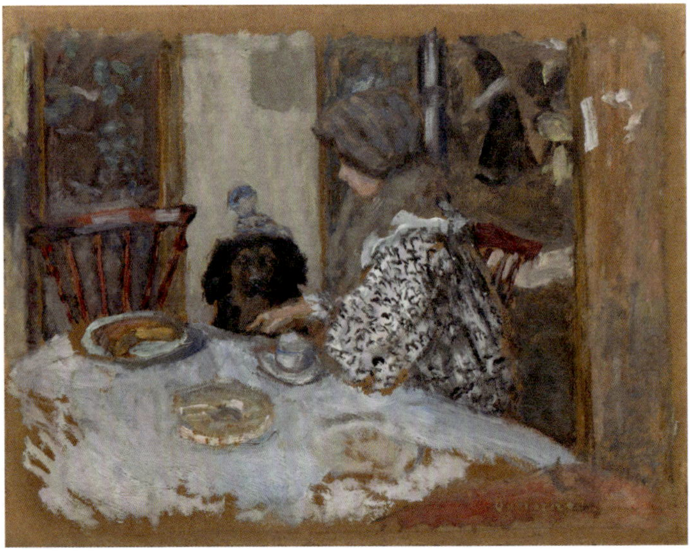

**PIERRE BONNARD (FRENCH, 1867–1947)**
***WOMAN WITH DOG, OR WOMAN AND DOG AT TABLE***
1908. Oil on cardboard (later mounted to cradled panel), 18 ⅝ × 23 ⅞ in. (47.3 × 60.6 cm). BF350

Bonnard's companion, Marthe de Méligny, is pictured at their dining room table in Paris. She seems to be telling their dog to sit—perhaps it smells the cake or soft cheese that rests on a light blue plate near Marthe's teacup. She is dressed for cool weather with a soft brown hat, a scarf, and a voluminous black-and-white dress or housecoat. Behind her are two folding screens of Bonnard's own design that seem to interact with the main scene and blur the boundary between foreground and background.

Bonnard painted these screens in the 1890s, when he was part of the Nabis, a group of artists known for working in multiple media and depicting intimate scenes of daily life. This work, made after the Nabis disbanded, continues these themes. By including his earlier work in this composition, Bonnard makes the continuity explicit while also investigating new artistic relationships of real versus painted space.

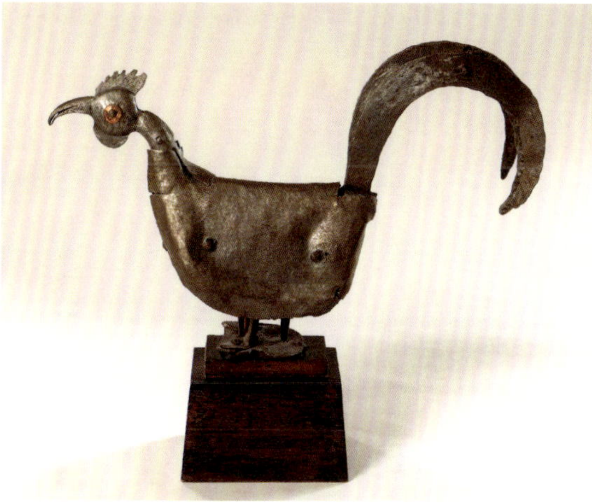

***STEEPLE-COCK* (FRENCH)**

Unidentified artist. 17th century. Iron with inlaid copper alloy eyes; overall (with mount): 17 13⁄16 × 5 1⁄4 × 21 in. (45.2 × 13.3 × 53.3 cm). 01.22.43

Designed to catch the wind in its tail feathers, this jaunty iron rooster originally perched atop a French church steeple. Here, it called parishioners to faith by heralding Christ's Resurrection, symbolized by the return of the morning sun. It also reminded them that Saint Peter—the eventual "rock" of the Roman Church—had thrice denied knowing Christ before the cock crowed following his arrest. In political contexts, this animal also functioned as an emblem of the French nation: the Latin word for rooster, *gallus*, recalls Gaul, the ancient Roman name for the territory of modern France.

Perhaps the steeple-cock carried this connotation for Dr. Barnes, who received it in 1937 as a gift from the Parisian dealer Étienne Bignou. Barnes believed that this object was medieval, and displayed it among others he attributed to the period—for example, a Dogon statue of a seated couple (see page 214) in the vitrine on which the steeple-cock stands, and a wooden triptych of Christ's Crucifixion on the south wall. All of these are actually modern, and participate with such works as Hugh Mesibov's *Byzantine Figure* (1945–46), Afro's *Saint Martin* (1948), and Alexis Gritchenko's scene of the Crusader city Mystras (1921) in a conversation about modern perceptions and adaptations of medieval forms.

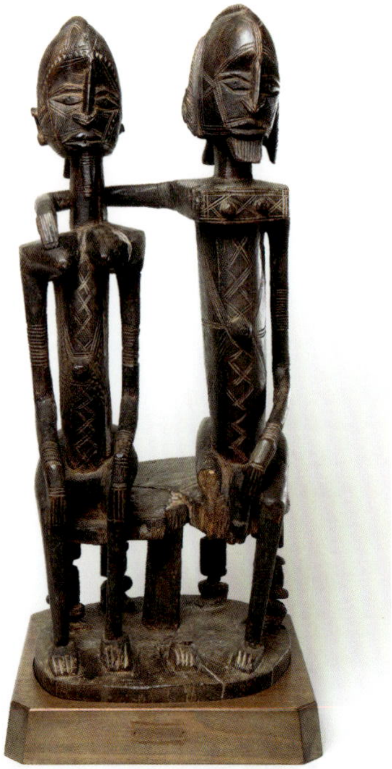

**BARNES FOUNDATION MASTER (DOGON)**

***SEATED COUPLE***

Late 19th–early 20th century. Wood, 27⅜ × 11 × 10½ in. (69.5 × 27.9 × 26.7 cm). A197

Sculptures of seated couples made by the Dogon peoples of Mali project an ideal vision of symmetry and balance in the roles of men and women. The two figures here are nearly identical in form and surface decoration, the latter an element that evokes scarification patterns. The overall composition is a balanced interplay of geometric form, the heightened angularity of each body echoing the other's. The man wraps his right arm around the woman's left shoulder and points to her breast, while his left hand points to his own genitals—gestures that underscore the couple's roles in creating and nurturing offspring. The woman carries a child on her back, reinforcing her identity as a mother, while the man carries a quiver on his back, suggesting his position as the family's protector or provider.

Little is known about the original context and function of this and similar sculptures. However, anthropological studies of the modern Dogon society reveal the inclusion of these objects in funerary processions. For Dr. Barnes, a sculpture such as this one reinforced his belief that artists from all over the world, from modern Europe to west Africa, use the creation of art objects as a form of material expression.

# ROOM 23

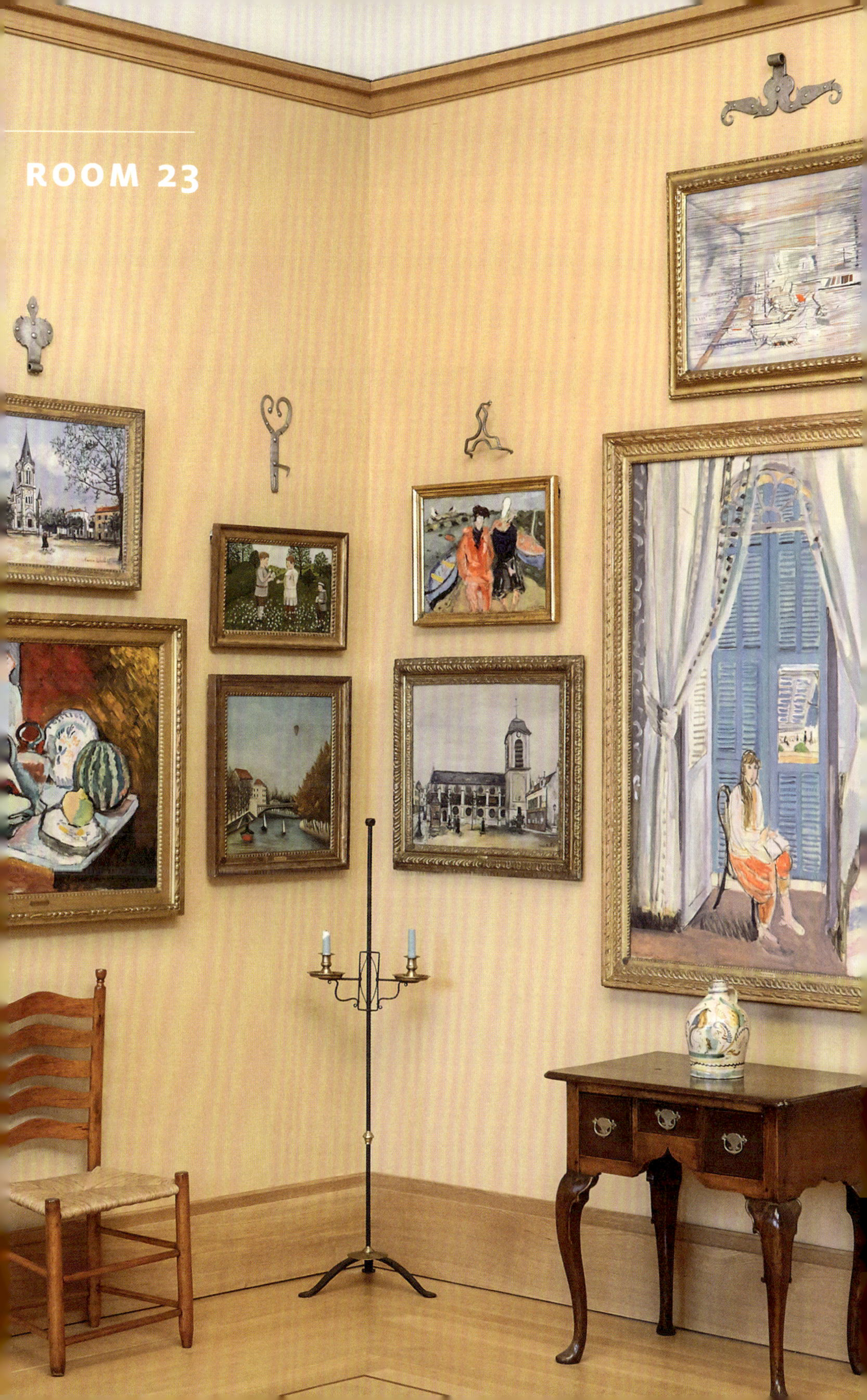

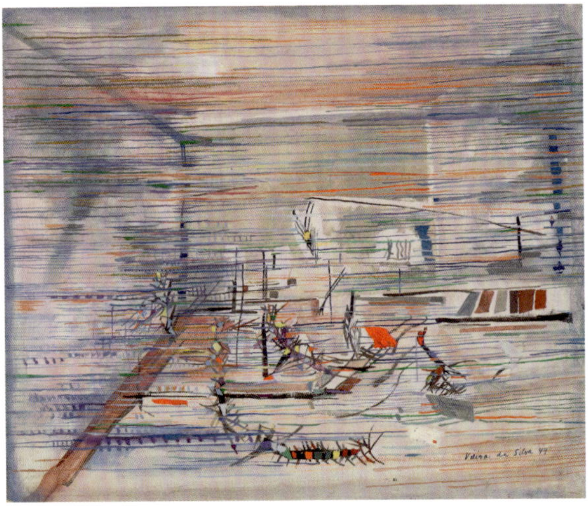

**MARIA HELENA VIEIRA DA SILVA (FRENCH, 1908–1992)**
***THE DOMESTIC SYMPHONY***
1947. Oil on canvas, 18 1/16 × 21 5/8 in. (45.9 × 54.9 cm). BF2521

Vieira da Silva liked to listen to music as she painted, and this abstract interior scene invites comparisons to the rhythmic nature of music. The painted perspectival walls enclose various colorful forms that could be read as furnishings—chairs, rugs, floor lamps—which are then overlaid with multicolor horizontal lines. These lines contradict the depiction of a three-dimensional room by flattening space, creating a densely woven composition that plays with mark making and perspective.

Vieira da Silva was born in Portugal but spent most of her career in Paris. She briefly left the city during World War II, when she fled to Portugal and then Brazil. She returned to Paris in 1947 and was regarded as a leading postwar abstract artist in Europe. In 1966, she was the first woman to be awarded the Grand Prix National des Arts by the French government.

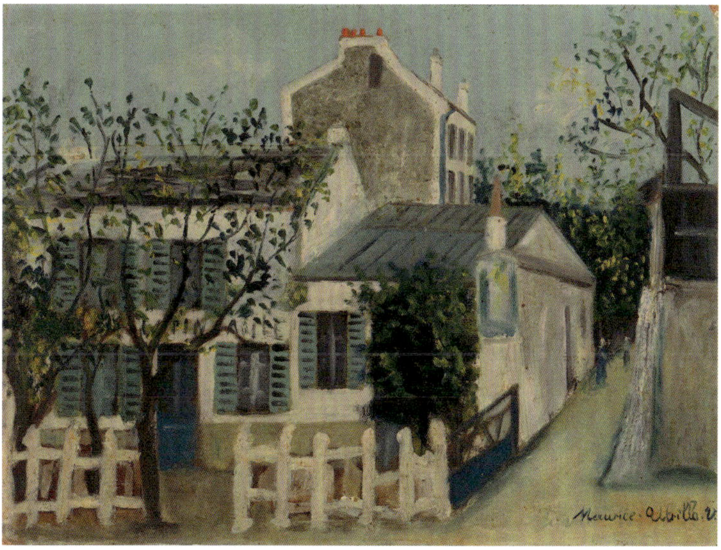

**MAURICE UTRILLO (FRENCH, 1883–1955)**
***LAPIN AGILE, MONTMARTRE***
c. 1911–14. Oil on cardboard (later mounted to plywood panel), 20 × 27 in. (50.8 × 68.6 cm). BF295

Utrillo spent much of his life in the hilly Parisian neighborhood of Montmartre, where he was born. The picturesque area was a haven for artists from the 1870s until around 1914, when its popularity drew more crowds and businesses, developing a bustling nightlife of cafés, dance venues, and cabarets such as the Lapin Agile (Nimble Rabbit).

What Utrillo shows, however, is a quiet street corner; the name of the nightclub is partially obscured by trees. Two small figures blend into the distant street, painted in the same blue color used throughout the composition. This peaceful nostalgia, which the artist became known for, reflected growing concerns about gentrification and urbanization.

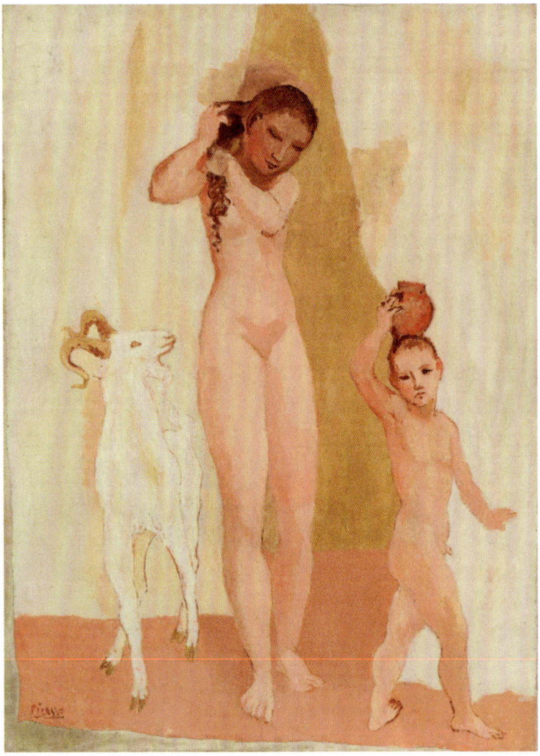

**PABLO PICASSO (SPANISH, 1881–1973)**
***GIRL WITH A GOAT***
1906. Oil on canvas, 54 ⅞ × 40 ¼ in. (139.4 × 102.2 cm). BF250

Picasso spent the summer of 1906 in Gósol, a remote mountain village in northeast Spain, where he began conceiving this enigmatic canvas. Over the previous year, he had been incorporating more roses and pinks into his palette and studying ancient art in the Louvre Museum in Paris. In this picture, his new tendencies and interests are apparent. The young girl evokes a classical Venus arranging her hair, while the boy with the water jug references a figure from Greek statuary. He is complemented by a goat on the girl's other side, a pairing that may allude to the ancient Roman figure of the satyr.

The palette is dominated by the fleshy pinks of Picasso's Rose Period. Steeped in the landscape of Gósol, however, the artist began to integrate ocher into his compositions. Here, a triangular swath of golden brown emphasizes the girl's elongated figure and hints at a mysterious space beyond the parted curtain.

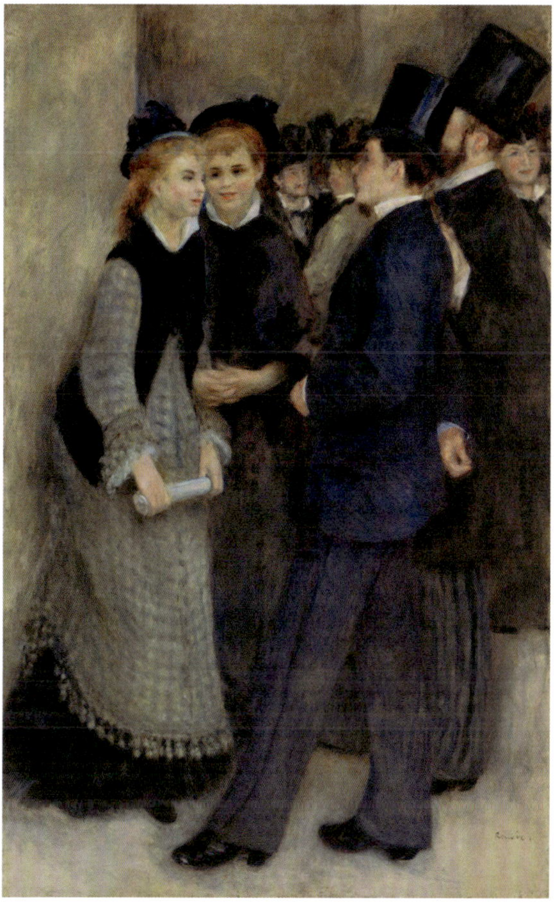

**PIERRE-AUGUSTE RENOIR (FRENCH, 1841–1919)**
***LEAVING THE CONSERVATORY***
1876–77. Oil on canvas, 73 13⁄16 × 46 1⁄4 in. (187.5 × 117.5 cm). BF862

Subtle body language conveys the flirtatious exchanges among a group of young Parisians gathered outside a music school. One man gently nudges his friend in a blue suit to talk to a woman holding a scroll of paper, likely a piece of sheet music. The would-be suitor extends his leg into her space as she leans in to hear what he has to say. Her friend, interlocking arms with her, seems to encourage her with a smile.

Although this painting appears to capture a transitory moment of urban life, Renoir carefully constructed the scene on the street outside his studio in Montmartre and not in front of the Paris Conservatory, which accounts for the vague architectural setting. He used friends and members of his bohemian circle as models. The painting is almost life size, inviting the viewer into the cacophonous scene. Its large scale suggests that it was made for exhibition, though it does not seem to have been displayed during Renoir's lifetime.

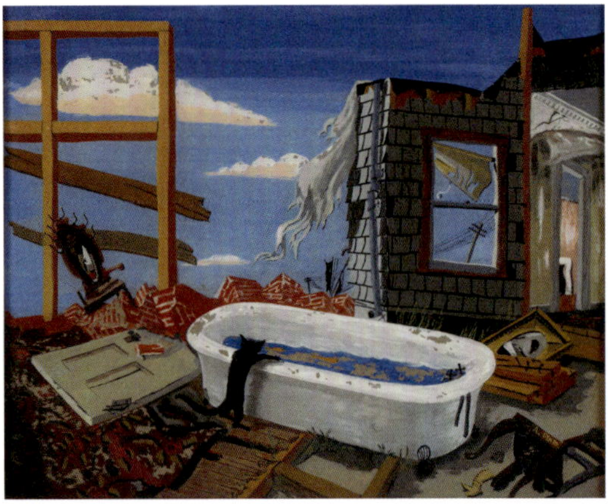

**ANGELO PINTO (AMERICAN, 1908–1994)**
***BATHTUB AND CAT***
c. 1944. Reverse painting on glass, 7¾ × 9¾ in. (19.7 × 24.8 cm). BF723

Angelo Pinto studied and taught at the Barnes Foundation and even served as its official photographer. His four brothers (Salvatore, Biagio, Joseph, and Dominic) also studied at the Barnes, and in the early 1930s, Angelo, along with Salvatore and Biagio, was awarded a traveling scholarship to study and paint in the museums of Europe. During this trip, Angelo met Henri Matisse and visited his studio in Nice, where the artist was painting his mural *The Dance* for the Barnes Foundation (see page 134). Dr. Barnes supported the brothers' art, writing introductions for exhibitions of their work in 1933 and 1934. In 1935, Pinto was appointed to the faculty of the Barnes Foundation, where he taught until 1992.

Pinto worked in different media but is best known for his reverse paintings on glass. Dr. Barnes purchased five of these works, including this scene of a partially collapsed home. Pinto has placed a bathtub at the center, with a cat peering over the edge at two small fish swimming in its water. The jumble of objects and debris, some with distorted angles, suggests an imagined landscape.

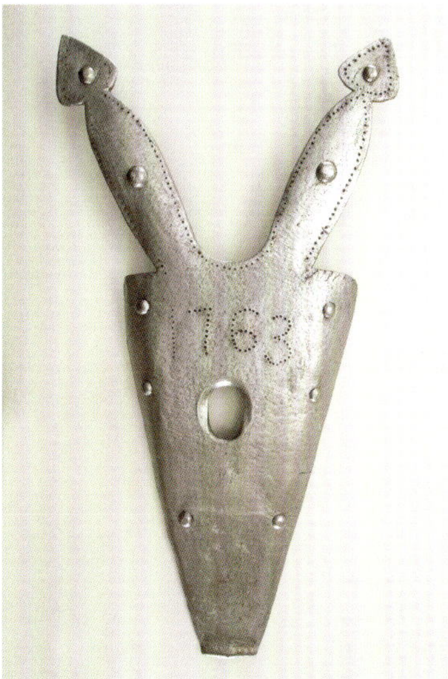


***REAR HOUND PLATE*** **(AMERICAN)**
Unidentified maker. 1763. Iron, 1⅝ × 8⅜ × 16 in. (4.1 × 21.3 × 40.6 cm). 01.23.42

Rear hound plates were part of the hardware of Conestoga wagons, a type of covered wagon named for the Conestoga River in Lancaster County, Pennsylvania. These wagons were used for trade and travel in what are now the eastern United States and Canada from the early 1700s—but were too heavy for pioneering toward western territories. Plates like this one were found in the undercarriage, connecting the long central reach to the two "rear hounds" that branched to the rear axle. This plate, shaped as a narrow trapezoid, has a center hole and two branching arms that resemble arrows. Punched dots decorate the upper edge and give the date "1763" at center.

Crowning the south ensemble of Room 23, the rear hound plate broadcasts Dr. Barnes's appreciation of the artistry of even the most utilitarian objects. It announces formal themes among the objects below: for example, sequences of trapezoids and V-shapes in Matisse's *Still Life with Gourds*, Israel Trask's coffeepot, Thomas G. Maling's crustacean creations (see page 222), the drawer-pulls on the chest, and the extended arms of Abraham Hankins's *Juggler*.

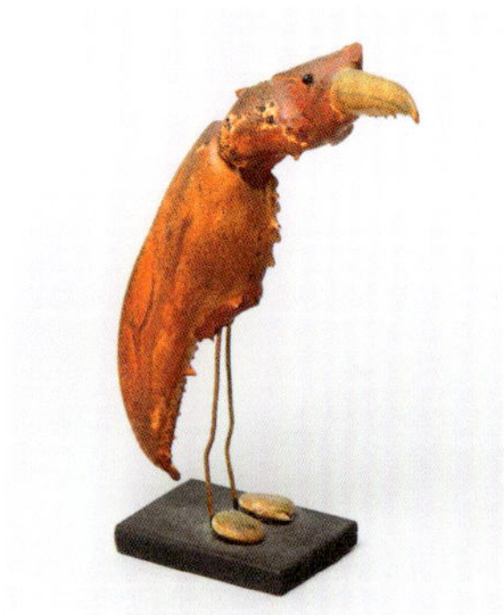 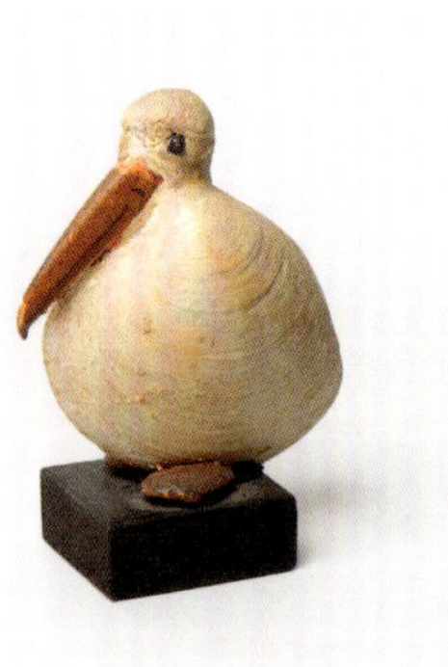

**THOMAS G. MALING (AMERICAN, DATES UNKNOWN)**

***BIRD***

c. 1940s. Lobster claw, iron wire, shells, paint, and wood; 6 × 2½ × 4⅛ in. (15.2 × 6.4 × 10.5 cm). 01.23.45

***PELICAN***

c. 1940s. Clam shell, stone, claw, shells, paint, iron, and wood; 4⅞ × 2 × 3⅞ in. (12.4 × 5.1 × 9.8 cm). 01.23.43

These charming objects are made from shells, lobster claws, and stones to create the forms of a tall orange-beaked bird and a squat white-bodied pelican. Perched on top of simple wooden bases, the birds are among several small-scale works of art made by Maling and given to Dr. Barnes in the 1940s. After meeting in Kennebunkport, Maine, where Maling was based, the two men exchanged a series of letters. In one, Maling described having come to the medium of crustaceans after seeing faces in the lobster claws hung in the shop windows of coastal Maine. Barnes so appreciated the unexpected charm of Maling's unusual sculptures that in one of his letters to the artist he promised that they would always be on view among some of the most important paintings in his collection, such as Matisse's *Still Life with Gourds*, which hangs above the birds in the gallery.

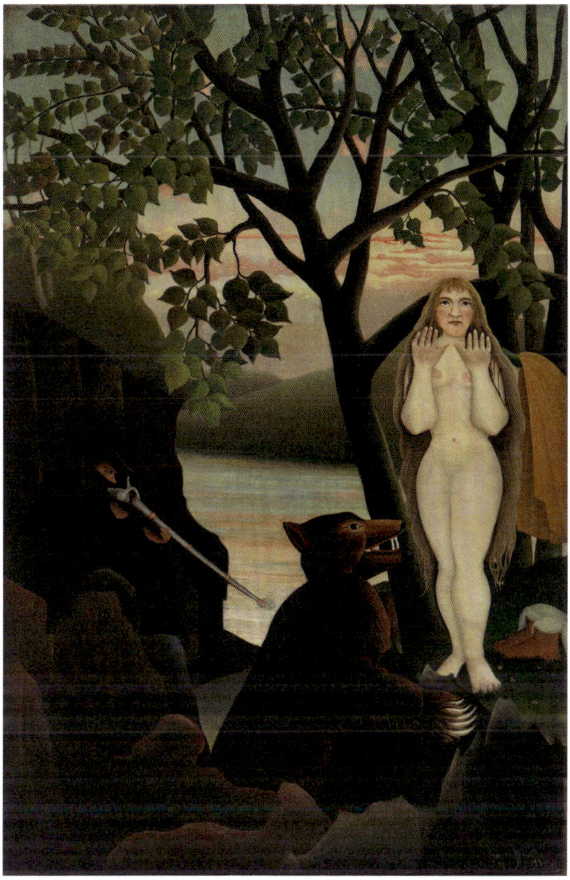

**HENRI ROUSSEAU (FRENCH, 1844–1910)**
***UNPLEASANT SURPRISE***
1901. Oil on canvas, 76⅝ × 51⅛ in. (194.6 × 129.9 cm). BF281

Smoke and fire emerge from the barrel of a hunter's rifle; it is aimed at a massive brown bear, who stands at the painting's center, ready to attack. Yet it is unclear which poses the greater threat to the naked woman, who looks to the skies, her hands raised in a gesture of fright or surrender. She is standing by a river, near her shoes and clothing, and this unpleasant surprise has likely disturbed her bathing.

At a time when anthropomorphism (animals adopting human behaviors) fascinated scientists and general audiences alike, Rousseau tapped into a contemporary trend with his image of a bear who almost seems to woo its prey. Sculptor Emmanuel Frémiet had won widespread acclaim in 1887 with his *Gorilla Carrying off a Woman*. Perhaps Rousseau hoped to create a similar stir with this deeply unsettling painting.

# FURTHER READING


Barnes, Dr. Albert C. *The Art in Painting*, 3rd ed. Merion, PA: Barnes Foundation Press, 2000. First published 1925 by Harcourt Brace & Co.

Barnes, Dr. Albert C., and Violette de Mazia. *The Art of Cézanne*. Merion, PA: Barnes Foundation Press, 1986. First published 1939.

———. *The Art of Henri Matisse*. Merion, PA: Barnes Foundation Press, 1978. First published 1933 by Charles Scribner's Sons.

———. *The Art of Renoir*. Merion, PA: Barnes Foundation Press, 1986. First published 1935 by Minton, Balch & Co.

———. *The French Primitives and Their Forms*. Merion, PA: Barnes Foundation Press, 1931.

Berman, Avis, ed. *William Glackens*. New York: Skira Rizzoli in association with the Barnes Foundation, 2014.

Bois, Yves-Alain, ed. *Matisse in the Barnes Foundation*. New York: Thames & Hudson, 2016.

Brownlee, David B. *The Barnes Foundation: Two Buildings, One Mission*. New York: Skira Rizzoli in association with the Barnes Foundation, 2012.

Buermeyer, Laurence. *The Aesthetic Experience*. Merion, PA: Barnes Foundation Press, 1924.

Clarke, Christa, ed. *African Art in the Barnes Foundation: The Triumph of L'Art nègre and the Harlem Renaissance*. New York: Skira Rizzoli in association with the Barnes Foundation, 2015.

Dewey, John. *Art as Experience*. New York: TarcherPerigee, 2000. First published 1934 by Minton, Balch & Co.

Dewey, John, Albert C. Barnes, Laurence Buermeyer, Mary Mullen, and Violette de Mazia. *Art and Education: A Collection of Essays*, 3rd ed. Merion, PA: Barnes Foundation Press, 1954. First published 1925.

Dolkart, Judith F., Martha Lucy, and Derek Gillman. *The Barnes Foundation: Masterworks*. New York: Skira Rizzoli in association with the Barnes Foundation, 2012.

House, John, and Martha Lucy. *Renoir in the Barnes Foundation*. New Haven: Yale University Press in association with the Barnes Foundation, 2012.

Mullen, Mary. *An Approach to Art*. Merion, PA: Barnes Foundation Press, 1923.

Rudenstine, Neil L. *The House of Barnes: The Man, the Collection, the Controversy*. Philadelphia: American Philosophical Society, 2012.

Wattenmaker, Richard J. *American Paintings and Works on Paper in the Barnes Foundation*. Philadelphia: The Barnes Foundation in association with Yale University Press, 2010.

Wattenmaker, Richard J., and Anne Distel, eds. *Great French Paintings from the Barnes Foundation: Impressionist, Post-Impressionist, and Early Modern*. New York: Alfred A. Knopf in association with Lincoln University Press, 1995.

Williams, Tod, and Billie Tsien. *The Architecture of the Barnes Foundation: Gallery in a Garden, Garden in a Gallery*. New York: Skira Rizzoli in association with the Barnes Foundation, 2012.

# INDEX

# ACKNOWLEDGMENTS

This handbook builds on the Barnes Foundation's collection catalogues and the collaboration of colleagues from all areas of the institution. In particular, the project has been shaped from the outset by the advice of the docents and members of our Guest and Protection Services team who serve in the galleries on a daily basis. We are especially grateful to the following people, without whom the book would not have been possible:

Kerry Annos, Visual Resources Manager

Lynda Black, Public Programs Coordinator

Kelly Borgeson, Lead Editor

Barbara Buckley, Senior Director of Conservation and Chief Conservator of Paintings

Andrea Čakars, Collections Registrar and Manager

Tenara Calem, Senior Programs Coordinator for Community Engagement and Family Programs

Thom Collins, Neubauer Family Executive Director and President

Robin Craren, Collections Research Coordinator

Valerie Gay, Deputy Director of Audience Engagement and Chief Experience Officer

Timothy Gierschick, Preparator

Amy Gillette, Collections Research Associate

Kathleen Greene, Curator of Public Programs

Daniel Huppman, Assistant Editor

Nancy Ireson, Deputy Director for Collections and Exhibitions & Gund Family Chief Curator

Kaelin Jewell, Senior Instructor, Adult Education

Cindy Kang, Associate Curator

Margaret A. Little, Senior Conservator of Objects

Martha Lucy, Deputy Director for Research, Interpretation and Education

Amanda McKnight, Manager of Archives, Library, and Special Collections

Pauline Nyren, Graphic Designer

William Perthes, Bernard C. Watson Director of Adult Education

Matthew Pruden, Preparator

Anya Shutova, Conservator of Paintings

Erica Simonitis, Senior Director of Guest and Protection Services

Julie Steiner, Senior Director of Admissions and Retail Operations

David Updike, Director of Publications

Olivia Verdugo, Art Director

Carl Walsh, Postdoctoral Research Fellow

Amalia Wojciechowski, Collections and Exhibitions Research Assistant

Barbara Wong, Director of Community Engagement

Margaret B. Zminda, Executive Vice President, Chief Financial Officer, and Chief Operating Officer

# ARTIST COPYRIGHTS